THE LIES WE TELL OURSELVES

DR. CHRIS THURMAN

A JANET THOMA BOOK

THOMAS NELSON PUBLISHERS ®
Nashville

AUTHOR'S NOTE: Clients' names and details of their stories have been changed to protect their identities.

Published in Nashville, Tennessee, by Thomas Nelson, Inc.

Library of Congress Cataloging–in–Publication Data
Thurman, Chris
    The lies we tell ourselves / Chris Thurman.
      p. cm.
    Includes bibliographical references.
    ISBN 0-7852-7343-3 (pbk.)
    1. Christian life. 2. Conduct of life. I. Title.
VA4501.2.T5234 1999
248.4—dc21

                                      98–53699
                                        CIP

This book is dedicated to my wife,
Holly,
and my three children,
Matthew, Ashley, and Kelly.
I am a rich man because of you.

CONTENTS

The Battle for Our Minds The Truth Workout—Week One: Identifying the Lies You Tell Yourself Week Two: Knowing Your A-B-C's Week Three: Challenging Your Lies with the Truth Week Four: Dealing with Past Events Week Five: Overcoming Perfectionism Week Six: Defeating the Need for Approval Week Seven: Facing Problems Week Eight: Discovering Your Identity and Worth Week Nine: Rejecting Your "Have To's" Week Ten: Facing Your Own Death Week Eleven: Being Needy, Meeting Needs Week Twelve: Developing the Mind of Christ

■
ACKNOWLEDGMENTS

My thanks to the staff at Thomas Nelson Publishers for allowing me to take my first three books (*The Lies We Believe, The Truths We Must Believe,* and *The Lies We Believe Workbook*) and put them into this one volume. It has been a pleasure to work with such a great group of people. Special thanks to Janet Thoma, who has been with me from the very start of my writing endeavors and has been especially supportive over the years. Janet, your efforts on my behalf mean more to me than you will ever know.

Lynda Stephenson, Dr. Dennis Hensley, and Bill Butterworth served as editors on my original books. Each did a great job of taking my unpolished drafts and turning them into books that expressed what I wanted to say better than I could. Thank you for making me look as though I know how to write.

Dr. Frank Minirth and Dr. Paul Meier were very encouraging to me about taking my interest in cognitive therapy and turning it into a book. Without their support it wouldn't have happened. Thank you for championing my desire to write and to conduct seminars on this topic.

I owe a debt of gratitude to colleagues in the field of cognitive therapy: Dr. Albert Ellis (whose A-B-C model of emotional health and writings on irrational beliefs play a significant part in this book), Dr. David Burns (whose writings on cognitive distortions form the basis of Chapter 5), Dr. William Backus, Dr. Larry Crabb, and Dr. David Stoop. Each has made a significant contribution to helping us understand the destructive role that faulty thinking plays in our lives, and my efforts truly stand on their shoulders.

I am deeply indebted to my clients over the years for allowing me to take an intimate look inside their lives. They have shown me what courage is all about as they attempted to face the truth and grow into mature human beings. I owe them more than they know, and I will never be the same for having been allowed the privilege of working with them.

My family is the greatest earthly blessing of my life. Holly, thank you for twenty years of love and support. You, more than anyone else, graciously sacrificed so that what I felt called to write about could be put into print. Thank you for being there for me in so many ways. Matthew, Ashley, and Kelly, you have given me more to smile about and be thankful for than you will ever know. I thank God for blessing me with you.

My utmost thanks are to God for loving me and patiently walking along with me as my journey through life has unfolded. If there is anything of value in this book, God was gracious enough to use me as His mouthpiece to say it. I will never fully understand why God called someone like me to be His. The fact that He did is the most significant event of my life and always will be.

Finally, to you, the reader, I want to say "Thanks" for choosing this book. My prayer is that God will bless your efforts to read it and that the truth you learn from this book will help set you free.

Chris Thurman, Ph.D.
Austin, Texas
October 1998

PROLOGUE

He enlisted in the navy at age sixteen. Early in his career he was chosen for a program aimed at turning promising seamen like himself into officers. Not only did he become an officer, but he rose up through the ranks to become an admiral. As if that were not enough, he was the first enlisted man in the history of the navy to become chief of naval operations, the highest ranking officer in the navy. He was a dedicated and loving family man, admired by the people who served under him, and a living testimony to how far hard work and perseverance can take a person.

On May 23, 1996, he took a .38-caliber handgun, pointed it at his chest, pulled the trigger, and killed himself.

Why? Why would someone who had achieved so much, who was respected by so many, and who had such an important position do such a thing?

If you believe the newspaper and magazine accounts, it was because the man made a mistake he simply couldn't live with. He supposedly made the mistake of wearing commendation ribbons on his uniform that he was not entitled to wear. In the navy, that is an offense punishable by court-martial and expulsion from the service.

But was that what led this man, Admiral Mike Boorda, to commit suicide? Was it wearing medals he had not earned the right to wear? Was it the fact that the press had found out and was closing in on him? Was it that he felt he had dishonored the very organization that had been his whole life since he was a teenager?

No, in the final analysis, I don't believe that any of these factors were the true cause of Admiral Boorda's death. What really killed Admiral Boorda was neither painful circumstances nor a self-inflicted gunshot to the chest.

Lies killed Admiral Boorda.

Not lies he may have told others. Not lies others may have told him. Admiral Boorda's death was caused by the lies he told himself. And the lies you tell yourself every day are killing you as well. Every lie that goes through your mind is slow, self-inflicted psychological and spiritual death. Every lie you think costs you your life. The lies we believe are the mental bullets that kill our souls, and they inflict significant damage often without our even realizing it until it is too late.

Sometimes it takes a personal crisis such as the one Admiral Boorda faced for the lies we believe to surface. It may be getting laid off from a job, being in a troubled marriage, finding out you have a terminal illness, struggling with an addiction, or having something tragic happen to one of your children. Even minor events, such as getting stuck in traffic, having someone cut in front of you in line, or waiting for a person who is a few minutes late, can do the trick. But whatever the circumstance may be, we often realize we were not mentally armed with the right thoughts and thus unable to handle life effectively.

If you think that you might be slowly committing emotional, relational, and spiritual suicide by telling yourself lies, you need this book. Read it carefully. Take it seriously. Uncovering the lies you tell yourself—and defeating them with the truth—is the only real hope you have for a healthy life here and eternal life in the hereafter.

PART I

THE LIES WE TELL OURSELVES

1

THE TRUTH ABOUT THE LIES
WE TELL OURSELVES

The mind is its own place, and in itself can make
a heaven of hell, a hell of heaven.
—John Milton

Cheryl sat nervously on the edge of my office couch, unsure where to begin. It was her first session with me. She'd never seen a psychologist before, and I could see that she was feeling embarrassed. The depression she'd struggled with for several months was getting worse, or she'd probably never have decided to come at all.

She finally said, "Dr. Thurman, I don't really know where to begin. It's just that I've felt so unhappy lately. Nothing seems to be going right in my life."

"Why don't you start with what is bothering you the most?" I suggested.

She shook her head, nervously straightening her skirt. "I guess the biggest thing is that my husband and I aren't getting along very well. The smallest issue can turn into a huge fight. For instance, I stayed up late the other night finishing a project that was due at work the next day. He knew I had to get up that next morning as early as he did, that I had to feed the kids and get them off to school, but he didn't lift a finger to help. He never offers to help. So I asked him to do something for me, and he blew up! That's how it is all the time with him. I do everything, and he does nothing."

"The two of you are fighting a lot then," I said.

"Yes," she said with a sigh, "and if our relationship keeps going in the same direction, I'm afraid we will either be miserable the rest of our lives or end up divorcing."

"You said that everything is going wrong. What else is bothering you?"

"I'm upset about my weight and how it affects my mood," she said. "The other morning I weighed myself and was thirty pounds over what I should be. I really hate myself for putting on all the extra weight I have. While I was making breakfast, totally preoccupied with how fat I'd gotten, I ended up dropping

3

a pitcher of orange juice on the floor. Then what did I do? Yelled at the kids when they ran right through it and tracked it into the den. I actually made them get down on the floor and clean it up." She glanced down "The only happy family member that morning was the dog," she added, glancing back up. "He loves orange juice."

I smiled uneasily, knowing full well that her story wasn't funny. "You sound pretty down on yourself for being overweight and also for how you let it affect you."

She nervously began picking lint from her skirt. "I hate myself over it. And I shouldn't have taken it out on the kids. I'm turning into an awful mother."

"It hurts to admit that you are taking out your frustrations on your children," I replied.

"Yes, I can't stand it that I'm making my kids pay for things that are bothering me. That isn't fair to them, and it kills me inside when I realize I'm doing it," she answered with tears streaming down her face.

"What else is bothering you?"

"Work is okay, but I'm constantly worried that I'm going to make a mistake that will get me in trouble. And the people I work with, they're all right, but I'm just not close to any of them. I feel like I'm going nowhere in all my relationships, not just at work but at church too. I just can't make myself get close to anyone anymore. I've been hurt and disappointed so many times before. The bottom line is, I don't have many close friends."

"You feel lonely but afraid to get close to others because you might get hurt. You mentioned church. Is it much help or comfort to you?" I asked.

She caught herself compulsively picking lint, folded her hands into her lap, and sighed. Then she said, "Church isn't a great place, either. Everybody acts happy, but it seems so superficial, you know? And besides, I always feel guilty because I know all the things I should be doing—things a good Christian should do—and I don't do any of them. I just know God's disgusted with me. I can feel it. I'm definitely disgusted with myself."

❑ ❑ ❑

Cheryl was obviously miserable. If you asked her what was causing her misery, she'd probably tell you that her marriage, her weight problem, her flaws as a mother, her loneliness, and many other things were the problems.

Would you be surprised, though, if I said Cheryl was missing the real cause of her emotional problems?

The real cause was the *lies* she was telling herself. She believed a number of destructive lies, and they were the true cause of her misery.

What are some of those lies? Unless you are experienced at looking for them, you may not have even noticed she was telling herself any lies at all. But she was. Let's look closely at some of the many lies she unknowingly revealed to me, and let's compare them to the truth. She was telling herself that

- making mistakes is awful, when the truth is that people make mistakes all the time and they are rarely catastrophic. To be human is to make mistakes. This is the "I must be perfect" lie I'll discuss in the "Self-Lies" chapter.

- her husband was causing all the marriage problems, when the truth is that she was responsible for them to some degree as well. This is the "it's all your fault" lie you will learn about in the "Marital Lies" chapter.

- being overweight makes her a worthless person, when the truth is that being overweight has nothing to do with worth as a human being. This is the "my worth is determined by my performance" lie I'll explore in the "Worldly Lies" chapter.

- God is disgusted with her because she isn't acting like a "good" Christian, when the truth is that God loves her regardless of how she behaves. This is the "God's love must be earned" lie, which I'll explain in the "Religious Lies" chapter.

Lest you think that Cheryl is uniquely plagued by lies, she isn't. She is really no different from you and me. Most of us, like Cheryl, have bought into a whole bunch of lies and are paying just as high a price as she is. The more lies we believe, the more troubled we are.

Most of our emotional struggles, relationship difficulties, and spiritual set-backs are caused by the lies we tell ourselves.

That is a critically important truth—and the major premise of this book. And unless we identify our lies and replace them with the truth, a truly abundant life is impossible.

Your Mental Tape Deck

Your brain is like a tape deck. It can both record and play back, and it has access to a personal library of thousands of tapes ready to play at a moment's notice. These tapes hold all the beliefs, attitudes, and expectations that you have "recorded" during your life.

Some of the tapes inside your brain are truthful, such as, "You can't please everybody," or "You reap what you sow." Some of these tapes are lies, such as, "Things have to go my way for me to be happy," or "It is easier to avoid problems than to face them."

Many of the lies you tell yourself have been around for a long time, some even since early childhood. You've listened to these lies play in your mind for so long, they may actually seem to be true even though they are really lies. The longer and more frequently a lie is played, the more deeply you believe it to be true.

Many lie tapes play in your mind without your even knowing it. They play unconsciously when life presses the "Play" button through some kind of circumstance. Unconscious or not, these tapes dramatically affect your feelings and actions each day. James Allen, in his book *As a Man Thinketh*, puts it this way: "A man is literally what he thinks, his character being the complete sum of his thoughts."[1] (See Appendix A for secular and biblical statements on the importance of our thoughts in determining our psychological and spiritual health.)

One of the main challenges in living our lives well, then, is not to alter the unpleasant circumstances surrounding us, although there is nothing wrong with improving them when we can. The challenge here is to make our mental tapes as truthful as possible so that we can live life the way it was meant to be lived—experiencing emotional health, intimate relationships, and a deep sense of purpose.

Thoughts produce after their own kind: lies produce death; truth produces life.

This psychological and spiritual "law," gives even the most miserable and desperate person real hope. Why? Because truth is accessible to all of us, making real life available to anyone who is willing to dedicate himself to knowing, believing, and doing the truth.

I want to add one important caveat about truth before I go any farther. I strongly believe that certain truths, ultimate truths, can be learned only with supernatural help. Truth is like an iceberg. The truth we learn on our own from our day-to-day experiences is just the tip of truth. To know the deeper truths that are the most powerful and life-sustaining of all, we have to look beyond our intellect and skills of observation and depend on God to reveal them to us.

Cheryl and Her Lies—A Closer Look

Let's go back to Cheryl. She was totally unaware of the lies causing her misery. Remember that she was much more focused on the external circumstances of her life, convinced that those circumstances had to change before she could ever be happy again. Let me show you how, with truth as the guide, I helped Cheryl to see her situation.

"Cheryl, you mentioned that you worry a lot about making mistakes. Do you always get down on yourself when you mess up?" I asked.

"Well, yes. I shouldn't make mistakes, especially the ones I've made before," she said.

"Why not?"

"Because mistakes are stupid; because smart people don't make mistakes," she said, stiffening.

"Do you mean you don't think you're smart if you ever make a mistake?" I asked.

"Well, I don't *feel* too smart, that's for sure."

"So you don't feel too smart or like yourself when you yell at the kids or spill orange juice on the floor or put on some extra weight?" I asked.

"Not too many people like fat, clumsy, angry mothers," she said with a smirk.

"They don't?"

She eyed me. "You know what I mean . . ."

"No, I don't think I do. What do you mean?"

"Do you like *yourself* when *you* make mistakes?" she said, trying to turn the tables.

"I don't like that I made a mistake, but I try not to make it the end of the world or a matter of personal worth." I calmly gazed at Cheryl. "Is that what you're doing?"

"Worth!" She frowned in thought a moment. "Well, maybe. But . . . I *want* to do the best I can at everything!"

"And if you fail to live up to that standard, what does that say about you? That you're worthless?"

"Well . . . I have to admit that I feel worthless, but yes, I know, in my head, it doesn't really mean I am," she finally confessed.

"Cheryl, play psychologist for a minute. Do you see any lies you are telling yourself in all this?"

"Lies?"

"Yes, lies."

"No, not really," she answered.

"How does this one sound? 'I can't accept myself unless I'm perfect.'"

"Why is that a lie?"

"Because it doesn't fit reality. Nobody is perfect, and if you wait until you're perfect before you accept yourself, you'll wait the rest of your life."

She arched an eyebrow. "What are you saying?"

I leaned forward, looked her straight in the eyes, and said with every ounce of authority I could muster: "You are telling yourself one lie after another and believing them all. That is why you're so depressed. That is why, to a certain degree, your relationships with your husband and children are not going the way you want them to. And that is why your faith in God isn't a source of comfort or help. But you can get rid of these lies—and all the suffering that goes with them—if you are willing to put some serious time and effort into the matter."

I paused and let all that I had said bang around in her soul for a moment or two. She stared back, looking somewhat surprised, giving me that "deer in the headlights" look of a person too shocked to run but too afraid to stand still. I decided to press the point a little farther just to see what might come of it.

"For instance, what one lie might you be telling yourself about your weight?"

"Lie? Well . . . ," she mumbled, thinking.

"How did you feel fixing breakfast this morning?" I said.

"That's easy. I felt ugly. I felt stupid and worthless because I have gained thirty pounds."

"And what lie or lies might be underneath feeling that way?"

"I suppose something like I've got to be slim to be worth anything?" She paused, sat back on the couch, crossed her arms, and added, "Or that if I am overweight, everything in my life is horrible. I guess those are lies, really. I guess I've always known that, even though it doesn't make me feel any different."

"Still, that's a good start," I told her, and it was. Cheryl would come to see many more of her lies during our work together. She would come to see how they controlled her life and damaged her emotional health, her relationships, and her spiritual life. She would courageously replace many of her lies with the truth, and she would begin to experience freedom from the misery that originally brought her into my office for counseling.

Seeing through your lies to the truth is hard work. Trying to do it by yourself is even harder. Consider this book a way—a potentially life-changing way—to see your lies for what they are and get back to living your life based on the truth. In the following pages, we are going to unmask the lies that we tell ourselves, the lies that masquerade as the truth, the lies that are making us miserable in marriage, in daily living, in faith. And then we are going to learn what we can do to get rid of these lies and replace them with truth that can set us free.

As you read, you'll often feel that you are reading about yourself, but you'll see your coworkers, friends, family, even your minister in these chapters too. We believe a lot of the same lies that the people we know and love believe. We also have another thing in common—the ability to change. The truth about change, though, is that you must *want* to change. Like Cheryl, you make your life miserable, but also like Cheryl, you can take steps to do something about it. Are you willing to do what it takes? Think that over before you read any farther. If you can't honestly answer yes, I suggest that you put this book down and not pick it back up again until you can.

To be healthy and whole emotionally, relationally, and spiritually, dealing with reality as it is—that's the goal of this book. If you are ready to begin the journey, set your inner tape recorder on "Pause," and read on.

Growthwork

At the end of each chapter, I'm going to give you homework, which I've labeled *growthwork*. It is aimed at getting you to do things that will help you overcome the lies you tell yourself. The first assignment is to ask you to complete the questionnaire in this section. Read each statement, and indicate your degree of agreement/disagreement with it using the scale provided.

Two ground rules I would like you to follow are (1) avoid using 4 as your answer if at all possible (try not to sit on the fence in reacting to these statements); and (2) answer from your gut, not from your head. (Don't answer in terms of how you think you should think. Answer in terms of how you really think!)

1	2	3	4	5	6	7
Strongly Disagree			Neutral			Strongly Agree

_____ 1. I must be perfect.

_____ 2. I must have everyone's love and approval.

_____ 3. It is easier to avoid problems than to face them.

_____ 4. I can't be happy unless things go my way.

_____ 5. My unhappiness is somebody else's fault.

_____ 6. You can have it all.

_____ 7. My worth is determined by my performance.

_____ 8. Life should be easy.

_____ 9. Life should be fair.

_____ 10. You shouldn't have to wait for what you want.

_____ 11. People are basically good.

_____ 12. All my marital problems are my spouse's fault.

_____ 13. If my marriage takes hard work, my spouse and I must not be right for each other.

_____ 14. My spouse can and should meet all of my emotional needs.

_____ 15. My spouse owes me for what I have done for him/her.

_____ 16. I shouldn't have to change who I am to make my marriage better.

_____ 17. My spouse should be like me.

_____ 18. I often make mountains out of molehills.

_____ 19. I often take things personally.

_____ 20. Things are black or white to me.

_____ 21. I often miss the forest for the trees.

_____ 22. The past predicts the future.

_____ 23. I often reason things out with my feelings rather than the facts.

_____ 24. God's love must be earned.

_____ 25. God hates the sin and the sinner.

_____ 26. Because I'm a Christian, God will protect me from pain and suffering.

_____ 27. All of my problems are caused by my sins.

_____ 28. It is my Christian duty to meet all the needs of others.

_____ 29. A good Christian doesn't feel angry, anxious, or depressed.

_____ 30. God can't use me unless I'm spiritually strong.

I believe each of the statements in this questionnaire is a lie, a way that we mentally distort reality into something it isn't. (See Appendix B for secular and biblical truths that dispute these lies.) Thus, the more you agreed with each statement, the more you were actually agreeing with a lie. Go back through your responses, and put a check mark next to any statement that you gave a 5, 6, or 7. Those are the lies that you tend to believe the most strongly and the ones you may want to pay attention to as you read this book.

Now, go one step farther. For the lies that you agreed with, write on a piece of paper why they are lies. What evidence is there that the statements you agreed with are, in fact, erroneous ways to think? For example, why is the statement "I must have everyone's love and approval" untrue? What evidence is there in the real world that this is a faulty way to think? Unless you can make the case that it is untrue, you will keep thinking that way, and it will continue to damage you and your relationships.

Once you have completed the questionnaire and written down why the lies you agreed with are lies, I want you to do one more thing—take a deep breath and pat yourself on the back! You have already made some progress on the road to defeating the lies you tell yourself and are on the way to a better life.

2
■
SELF-LIES

Julie had begun counseling with me over an industrial-sized case of bitterness. "Everything seems to go wrong for me," she complained. "Like driving over here today. I got stuck behind this gravel truck. Suddenly, gravel was everywhere. Some hit my windshield and cracked it! So I tried to move over to miss the rest, and this jerk in the other lane wouldn't let me in—honked at me loud enough to wake the dead! Why do things like that always happen to me?"

"One of those kinds of days. Yet you sound as if you think it's better for other people."

"Looks to me like it is. Other people's lives seem to be a lot easier than mine. I just feel that I'm always getting the short end of the stick. My ex left me for another woman. I can barely make ends meet on what I make. My son has a learning disability, struggles every day in school, and comes home in tears. I just found out last week that my dad is going to need to be put in a nursing home, and there is no one else but me to take care of all the arrangements."

"And on top of it all, gravel breaks your windshield," I added.

"Yes, gravel breaks my windshield. If things keep going like they have been . . ."

A lot of us feel like Julie. We think that most people have it easier than we do. We believe that we are somehow uniquely afflicted with life's ills. We tell ourselves that unless things start going our way, we can't ever be happy again. We start to drown in bitterness and self-pity. We may even start to think that the future is inescapably bleak and that life is not really worth living. It didn't take long for Julie to find herself struggling to keep her head above water emotionally, all because she believed a pack of lies—a pack of self-lies.

The lies that we deceive ourselves with, as Demosthenes suggested in his statement at the beginning of this chapter, often reflect what we *wish* were true. Wouldn't it be wonderful if everything did go our way? What a great thing that would be! Spouses are faithful, children don't need braces, and no waiting at checkout lines. Sounds good to me! Yet it is one thing to wish life were this way and quite another to deceive ourselves into expecting it to be.

The five lies we'll discuss in this chapter are perhaps the most destructive self-deceptions of all to the human soul. They destroy any chance we have for life, liberty, and personal happiness. Let's start with what I believe is the single most destructive lie of all—one that's rampant in our success-oriented world.

"I Must Be Perfect."

Jim, a highly successful executive of a communication systems company, came to see me several years ago. He told me how he'd spent most of his life struggling with feelings of inferiority and how he'd tried to overcome those feelings by being a hard-driving superachiever. Nothing he accomplished, though, made him feel any better about himself or his life. In fact, he was chronically depressed and felt little joy and satisfaction at all.

"I think the bottom line is that I hate myself," he told me one day.

"Why do you think you hate yourself?" I asked.

"I don't know, really. I never feel that I do anything as well as it should be done."

"Never?"

"Never!" Jim said, his arms folded, back as stiff as a yardstick. I could tell it was an answer he had practiced many times.

Jim was saying something extraordinary. Most of us feel good about *something* we do. His answer shed some light on just how perfectionistic he was. "Jim, you know you're talented. I find it surprising to hear you say you never do anything well enough."

"Yeah, well, it's true."

"Maybe your standards are too high."

Jim flinched, visibly not liking what I had said. "I don't think my standards are too high. If anything, they have gotten me where I am in life."

"And where is that?"

He looked at me quietly, deflated. He knew the answer to that one.

Most perfectionists think the way Jim does. They have unrealistically high standards that they have never met and can't possibly meet, yet they hang on to them as if their whole lives depended on it. They unmercifully beat themselves up when they fail to attain these standards. Even though they feel depressed, even suicidal at times, the idea of lowering their expectations is blasphemous. Much to their own destruction, they hold on to their perfectionism as if it is the only way to ensure being a happy, successful person when it ensures just the opposite.

Each of us feels inferior to one degree or another, just as Jim does. That is human nature. As psychologist Alfred Adler once put it, "To be human is to feel inferior." Some of us cope with inferiority feelings by accepting our imperfections and trying to do the best we can to improve. Unfortunately, some of us struggle with these feelings by overcompensating and trying to be perfect. It's as if we say to ourselves, "If I can just be perfect, then I can finally put these feelings of inferiority to rest and accept myself." Any drive for perfection, though, is doomed from the start.

What exactly is perfectionism? What are the characteristics of a perfectionist? Dr. David Burns, a psychiatrist who is a leading expert on the subject, offers a good answer:

> I do *not* mean the healthy pursuit of excellence by men and women who take genuine pleasure in striving to meet high standards. Without concern for quality, life would seem shallow; true accomplishment would be rare. The perfectionists I am talking about are those whose standards are high beyond reach or reason, people who strain compulsively and unremittingly toward impossible goals and who measure their self-worth entirely in terms of productivity and accomplishment.[1]

Sound like you? If so, you know all too well the emotional price one pays for being perfectionistic. The need to be perfect creates a no-win scenario. When you achieve something, all you can say to yourself is, "That's what I should have done. No big deal." If you fall short, though, even just a little, you no doubt think, *What is wrong with me? What a stupid idiot I am! I can't do anything right.* Either way, you lose.

If I sound especially outspoken on this lie, it's because I have battled it ever since I was knee-high to a grasshopper. I remember as a youngster being upset after hitting a home run during a Little League game because it hit the top of the outfield wall before it went over (a "perfect" home run, of course, clears the fence by at least fifty feet!). I remember being bothered that I made a 100 on a quiz in elementary school one time because there were 5 bonus points, and

I didn't get any of them. As a tennis player in high school and college, I'd hurl tennis rackets across the court when I didn't play "perfectly." I broke so many rackets in anger, I kept the local sporting goods store in business. I made a fool of myself on more occasions than I care to admit. Why? Because I believed it wasn't good enough unless I played perfectly.

Jim began to face his struggle with perfectionism during our work together. A couple of things I challenged him on were accepting that he was a human being, not a machine, and learning to take small steps rather than always "swinging for the fence" in everything he did. One of our exchanges went like this:

"Look, if I don't strive to be perfect, I'll just be mediocre," Jim said, admitting his biggest fear.

"So, you want to be a robot?" I asked.

Jim had been tapping his fingers on the chair's arm. He stopped his tapping. "What?"

"Only a robot, a machine, can be that perfect."

Jim laughed. It was the first time I'd seen him laugh in several sessions. "Funny you should put it that way; I often feel like a robot or that I'm trying to be like one."

"And how does that feel?"

"Awful." Jim sighed. "I feel stuck. Clogged up. Like I can't be a normal person."

"That's it," I said. "Your perfectionism isn't really allowing you to be a human being, is it? Jim, as paradoxical as it seems, I think you will find that the more human you allow yourself to be and the more realistic your standards become, the happier you will be and the better you will actually do. You can have your cake and eat it too—achieve your best but get to be a healthy human being in the process."

Jim thought a minute. Then he said, "That sounds good in theory, but how do I know when I'm being realistic and not perfectionistic?"

"That's a good question. You're a golfer, right? What's your average score over eighteen holes?"

"I usually shoot around 90," he said.

"Could you leave this office today and shoot a 72?" I asked.

"No, that wouldn't be possible," he admitted.

"Why not?" I pressed.

"It's just not realistic. Nobody can shave that many strokes off his score in one try. At least I couldn't."

"Wouldn't it be realistic, then, to try to make small improvements in your golf game? What about realistic goals such as keeping your head down more often or keeping your left arm stiffer so you can drop a stroke or two off your score in the months to come rather than perfectionistically stepping out on the golf course thinking you should play like Tiger Woods right now? In its extreme form, your perfectionism is the equivalent of thinking you should hit a hole in one every time you step up to the tee. Nobody, not even Tiger Woods, can do that, and it is just downright self-defeating to try."

Jim tapped his fingers on the chair's arm for a long moment until finally he said, "I'm beginning to see what you're getting at I suppose I could work on making small improvements, a little at a time."

Jim was starting to get it. He first accepted that perfectionism is self-defeating He began to see that beating it demanded that he allow himself to make the same mistakes that other mortals make. He had to focus on doing *his* best and not worrying about how he compared to others. It meant letting "good enough" be good enough. It meant being willing to see mistakes as an opportunity to learn and grow rather than as a launching pad for self-hate and condemnation. It meant focusing on making progress toward a goal rather than demanding to be there right now.

Jim is working hard to defeat his perfectionistic approach to life. Oh, he is still a "driver" by nature and probably always will be to some degree, but he is slowly learning to accept his limitations as a human as he holds himself up to more realistic standards. For the first time in years he is beginning to feel some satisfaction and contentment in his life. He is beginning to experience positive feelings as the lie of expecting himself to be perfect is gradually done away with. Jim, in a sense, has joined the army in that he now focuses on being "all that *he* can be" rather than trying to be somebody perfect that he never could be. And, oh, yeah, his golf game has gotten better.

"I Must Have Everyone's Love and Approval."

People who believe this lie are basically saying to themselves, "It is essential that everyone I come into contact with like me/accept me/approve of me/love me/think I'm the greatest thing since sliced bread, or my life as I know it isn't worth living." Such people become social chameleons in that they often change "color" to fit the interpersonal "terrain" they are in so that everyone will approve of them. But after people do this long enough, they lose all sense of who they really are, their true "color" as persons. "Who am I? What do I really think? What do I really feel?" These are the questions I hear from clients burdened by this lie.

Denise grew up being a "pleaser," and she derived most of her identity and sense of security from keeping people happy with her. Her grades were always good. She rarely caused her parents any trouble, and she went along with her friends on most everything. Now at age twenty-three, she was beginning to see that all the years of pleasing others had come with a big price tag. One of her first statements to me told the whole story: "I can't stand it when someone is upset with me. I feel that I have to do something to make him feel better toward me." Then she glanced down. She was not one for a lot of eye contact.

"Something happen recently?" I ventured.

"I started going to a church that's a different denomination from my parents'. They don't like it and are putting pressure on me to switch back," she mumbled.

"How would you feel if you did?"

Denise looked me straight in the eye. "I'd hate it. This new church is what I have been looking for, and I feel closer to God there. But Mom and Dad, they're making me crazy. I feel as if I'm about to explode! I don't know what to do!"

"I get the impression you know what to do."

"I do? What? You mean, I need to go to this new church?"

"Isn't that what you're telling me? Don't let me put words in your mouth," I said, knowing full well she might try to please me too.

"Yes," she said quietly, "it is. I really want to stay there."

"What about your parents' approval?" I asked.

"I sure hate not having it. Maybe I can explain it to them and they'll understand?"

"And if they don't?"

"I would feel horrible," she said. "I know I need to be more independent of what they think, but I really struggle with it."

Denise's need for approval was a no-win scenario in the same way that perfectionism is. If you get someone's approval, you can't really enjoy it because you changed "colors" to get it and weren't really being yourself. Yet if you let yourself be who you are and someone doesn't like you, you become anxious and knotted up inside. Each day is a lose-lose proposition and presents the same life-draining task: Can I gain and keep people's approval?

This lie puts our emotional well-being into the hands of others. It gives people a sizable amount of power over us, and some people will gladly take advantage of it. Manipulation, especially from those nearest to us, is made far too easy. We pleasers end up being victims who take better care of others than of ourselves, often hiding our ever-growing resentment and bitterness in the process.

The truth is that some people aren't going to like us no matter who we are or what we do. In an attempt to gain everyone's love and approval through chronic pleasing, though, we lose any sense of who we really are. We can never really enjoy it when others like us because we feel that we "faked them out" in getting their approval. The bottom line is that we must be courageous enough to be who we are and stand up for what we know is right, whatever the cost may be, and let it be the other person's problem if he doesn't like us for it.

As a person who struggles with wanting to please others, I know all this is easier said than done. It is hard to make the shift from seeking everyone's approval to authentically being who you are and living your life by proper values and ethics. Steps in that direction are very painful. Not taking those steps, though, makes our lives even more painful. In the end, having a lot of people's approval won't be meaningful if it came at the expense of living life with integrity. What *does* it profit us if we gain the whole world's approval and lose our own souls in the process? Absolutely nothing.

"It Is Easier to Avoid Problems Than to Face Them."

When I was a college professor, I noticed an extremely interesting phenomenon among my students. I'd give them a reading assignment, but most of them wouldn't do it! Can you imagine? I found that fact out by giving pop quizzes (you should have heard the moans!). The students who didn't do the assignments must have believed that the best way to deal with a problem in life is to avoid it. Oh, the "avoiders" wasted a lot of time worrying, made Fs on the quizzes, ended up doing poorly in my class, and often crammed four years of college into seven, but they still thought avoiding painful things was the easiest route to go.

Other students, fewer in number, took the approach of doing the assignments whether they wanted to or not. The "facers" went back to their dorm rooms, apartments, or the campus library and cracked the books, however little desire they might have had to do so. When they were quizzed, they were ready. When final grades were given out, they did well. When four years of college had passed, they walked across the stage and received their degrees.

In life "avoiders" ignore problems, hoping they will either go away or be solved by others for them. Of course, we all know that problems just don't go away and that our lives get much worse when we are unwilling to face them. Psychiatrist Scott Peck noted in *The Road Less Traveled*:

> Fearing the pain involved, almost all of us, to a greater or lesser degree, attempt to avoid problems. We procrastinate, hoping that they will go away. We ignore them, forget them, pretend they do not exist. . . . We attempt to get out of them rather than suffer through them.
>
> This tendency to avoid problems and the emotional suffering inherent in them is the primary basis of all human mental illness.[2]

I am concerned that far too many of us as parents damage our children by rescuing them from facing their problems in the misguided "love" empowered by this lie. I, unfortunately, do this with my kids every so often.

A number of years ago, we began attending a new church. My young (at the time) son, Matt, wasn't thrilled with the Sunday school class. And at a very high decibel level, he expressed his feelings each time we dropped him off. It was unpleasant, to say the least, to walk away from him crying and frightened as he was. For six Sundays in a row, I wanted to say the heck with it, turn around, pick him up, and take him into "big" church with us. That short-term solution would have made his problem go away and all of us feel better. The long-term result, though, would have been disastrous. He'd begin to expect me to rescue him whenever he cried loudly enough about other things, and I'd be stuck in a pattern of being the rescuing Dad with a spoiled brat of a kid. So I stuck it out, faced the problem, and made Matt face his— being in a Sunday school class he initially didn't like. And as often is the case, Matt grew to enjoy Sunday school to the point that he'd become upset if he couldn't go. Go figure.

Yet I still mess up. One night during the last school year *I* was up until *two in the morning* putting the finishing touches on *my son's* science project while *he* had a grand old time *sleeping*. I was facing his problem for him, not making him face it himself. Ugh! I hate it when I do that!

When parents make a habit of rescuing a child from her problems, the child is deprived of the chance to develop the appropriate coping skills she'll need for handling life later on. The child often turns into an adult who is incompetent, lacks confidence, and constantly looks to other people to solve her problems. We must, absolutely must, show our kids how much we truly love them by making them face their own problems even if they think we are "the most horrible, awful parents on the planet" for a while. It may take them twenty years or so, but they will thank us later.

We, as adults, must model all this for our children by facing our own problems for them to see. We can't afford to be like my college students who run from doing their homework just because it is unpleasant. Each day has enough problems of its own, and these problems become like a huge snowball rolling downhill and crushing us at the bottom if we don't have the courage to face them every day.

Those who avoid their problems usually end up with more problems in the long run. Those who face their problems each day save themselves a great deal of unnecessary suffering down the road. It's as simple as that.

"I Can't Be Happy Unless Things Go My Way."

I once had a teenage client who was quite obsessive about things having to go a certain way for him to have a good day, so I asked him to write a list of what would have to happen for a day to be a good one. His incredibly detailed list included the following:

- Wake up to my favorite music playing on the clock radio.
- Wear certain clothes and tennis shoes.
- Don't have to eat anything I don't like for breakfast.
- Get to sit in the back of the school bus.
- All my friends are nice to me all day long.
- Get to go skateboarding at the end of the day.
- No homework.
- Get to watch my favorite TV shows all evening.
- Get to go to bed when I want to.
- Parents don't bug me about doing chores or keeping my room clean.

The list was so long and detailed that it was literally impossible for things to go just as he wanted. Consequently, he'd never had a happy day. Something always spoiled it.

Be honest: Are you the type who can enjoy life only if things go the way you want them to? Can you be happy if your car breaks down, someone talks too loudly in a movie theater, service is slow in a restaurant, a friend is five to ten minutes late all the time, and the cleaners ruin your favorite outfit? Yes, you say?

In reality, things sometimes (oftentimes?) don't go the way we want them to. That is an inescapable reality of life. Traffic lights turn red right as we get to them, people interrupt us when we are busy, kids spill grape juice on the brand-new carpet, and companies lay us off when they downsize. Welcome to the real world. But how many of us have come to truly accept that about life without allowing it to turn into a huge source of resentment? How many of us have really come to grips with life being difficult? From my observations, not very many.

Some years ago, I put a videotape in our VCR, and the tape came straight back out! Since our VCR doesn't have an automatic eject feature, I lifted the little plastic door to see what the problem was and guess what—inside our expensive VCR were two toy cars, a stick, and a couple of Band-Aids! My young son had stored his most prized possessions there. At that moment, with a costly repair bill dancing through my brain, I was more than a little angry that life wasn't going my way. And at that same moment, I told myself the lie that I couldn't be happy (or content or peaceful or thankful or anything else emotionally "good") given what had just happened. What a horrible price we pay for thinking things have to go our way in order for us to be happy.

I see the "my way" lie at its worst in marriage. The "I" in many marriages is so strong that the "we" is never allowed to develop. These marriages often become nothing more than two "I's" pulling in separate directions and fighting all the time, sometimes over the silliest matters.

Jon and Debbie, a young couple I've been counseling, come to mind. They had been college sweethearts, inseparable. But during the first half-dozen or so sessions they had with me, they sat at opposite ends of the couch. For five years they'd been married, and except for the first few months, their whole marriage had been a battle of wills.

"I feel Debbie always has to get her way," Jon bitterly remarked in one session.

"I feel the same way about you," Debbie chimed in. "You're always so focused on what *you* want that what *I* want never gets noticed."

"That isn't true. I do things for you all the time," Jon answered.

"Only things you don't mind doing," Debbie muttered, inching even farther into the corner of the couch.

"Okay," I said, "let's stop a minute. How do both of you feel about the word *we*?"

They both looked at me as if I'd lost my mind.

"I'm not sure what you mean," Debbie finally said.

"The *I* in your marriage is stronger than the *we*, and both of you are resentful about that. Do you think in *I* or *we* terms?"

"Well, I guess mostly *I*," Jon said, leaning closer, his eyebrows cocked in the suspicious position.

"Yes, me too. I think more about making sure I get what I want than making sure Jon gets what he wants," Debbie added.

"It's obvious that both of you are hurting a great deal," I said. "Even when one of you gets your way, you usually do it at the expense of the other person, which, again, makes the marriage suffer."

"I don't like to admit it," Jon said, admitting it, "but I do get so intent on fighting Debbie for what I want that I don't even think about the fact that we both end up worse off."

Then Jon explained how the night before they had wanted to see a movie. Of course, they didn't want to see the same movie, and neither wanted to sacrifice and see the other's choice. They had a big fight over which movie to see and ended up driving home in anger, not having seen a movie at all. Their "my way or the highway" mentality was the kiss of death to intimacy and harmony that evening and had cost them a total of five years of marital unhappiness.

Jon, Debbie, and I talked about how to negotiate with each other so they could avoid fights like that one. We talked about the importance of serving each other (try to sell that idea in this day and age!), developing a strong "we" mentality in the marriage, compromising when possible, and not allowing selfishness to ruin their marriage. We talked about standing firm on your convictions (Debbie felt strongly about not going to see R-rated movies) but being willing to flex when possible. As the "we" in their marriage began to replace the "I," they got along better and intimacy grew.

Life has a nasty habit of reminding us that it will not always go the way we want it to. Each and every day is proof of that. In light of that fact, we have a choice to make. Either we can throw a little hissy fit every time life dares to not treat us like royalty, or we can get off our high horses and accept that life is going to "dump" on us every so often just as it does every other human being on the planet.

The next time things don't go the way you want them to, make a decision to accept it (not necessarily like it, but accept it), do what you can to face it, and allow yourself to feel content, even peaceful, in spite of what happened. Is it idealistic of me to challenge you this way? Maybe, but the alternative isn't much of a challenge, is it?

"My Unhappiness Is Somebody Else's Fault."

"You make me furious when you do that!"

"What you said yesterday really hurt my feelings."

"I wouldn't have yelled back at you if you hadn't yelled at me first."

"I wouldn't be the mess I am today if my parents had raised me right!"

The main theme of this book is that our way of thinking about the circumstances of our lives is what makes or breaks us. The lie we just looked at said that things have to go the way we want them to before we can be happy. The lie I want to focus on now takes that notion one unhealthy step farther. It says that my external circumstances cause me to feel and act in certain ways. This mind-set allows me to pass the buck for all my emotional upsets and wrong actions onto anybody and anything nearby. It points a finger outward. No responsibility is taken here.

Let me give you an example of what I am talking about. Picture yourself in a long movie theater line, and it is five minutes until show time. The line is moving slowly, and you are getting more frustrated by the minute. You notice out of the corner of your eye two people who walk up and ease their way into the line ahead of you. Your blood boils, steam comes out of your ears, and you feel angry enough to shoot the two people dead on the spot.

Now, let me ask you a question. What made you mad? If you are honest, you will have to admit that you believe what made you mad was the fact that the two people had the nerve to cut in front of you, right? It is all their fault that you are angry, right? Well, you're dead wrong. What they did didn't *make* you mad. Nothing, I repeat, nothing, can *make* you mad (or happy or sad or anything else). External events don't have the power to make us feel what we feel or act the way we act, period. Coming to grips with that fact, I believe, is a key issue that separates the psychologically healthy person from the psychologically disturbed person. Psychologically healthy people take responsibility for their feelings and actions, and psychologically disturbed people blame theirs.

You might say, "Okay, but what about certain events that do cause everyone to react the same way, such as the death of a loved one? Isn't that an example of an event that *makes* us feel sad?" First of all, there are no events to which everyone reacts in the same way. Even in the case of the death of a loved one, we can think of a variety of reactions.

Grandpa, for instance, a devout man of faith, has been suffering painfully for months with a terminal illness and passes away. The religious people in the family might react to his death with relief *and* joy, believing that his suffering is over (relief) and that he is now with God (joy), while the nonreligious family members might react with the same relief but none of the joy. It is the same event for both groups, but each filters the reactions through different "tapes" about death. Thus, they end up with different reactions.

But even if *everyone* on the planet only felt sad about death, that would just mean that everyone views death as a bad thing. Same view, same reaction. It still would remain true that the death of a loved one did not cause everyone to be sad. Cause-and-effect applies to inanimate objects, but it does not apply to human beings.

So, the long-winded bottom line here is that everything you feel and everything you do comes from within you and is not caused by someone or something else outside you. As Stephen Covey, author of *The Seven Habits of Highly Effective People*, put it, "In between stimulus and response is choice." You feel and act the way you do because you think the way you do. No one and nothing is to blame for your emotions or your behavior while you live on this planet!

Of course, the "somebody else's fault" lie pervades every aspect of life, every relationship, every action. Thirty-year-old Beth based much of her life on it without a hint of what was happening to her. One day, she told me how her sister would call and literally waste hours of her time "droning on about her problems." Beth blamed these calls and many other things for her constant misery. When she finished telling me about all this, I suggested she call her sister and tell her (kindly, of course) how she felt. Beth looked surprised. "I couldn't do that. It would hurt her feelings," she said.

"If you were honest with your sister, she would feel hurt, and that would be your fault?"

"Yes, I would have hurt her feelings," she replied, refusing to budge.

"What if I told you that your sister isn't the problem here? But you are," I said—and waited.

She looked even more surprised, even a little bit angry. "*I'm* not the problem. She is. If she wouldn't call and waste my time, I wouldn't be so mad!"

"So it's her fault that you are angry at her?"

"Exactly," she answered, sitting back in her chair. "How could I possibly be the problem when it's her calling me that makes me angry?"

"Are you the only one she calls?"

"No," she said, wondering what I was up to.

"Any of the others get as angry as you do?"

Beth frowned. "I don't know. I guess it's possible they don't. I'm not sure where you're heading," she said, turning a little away from me.

"Well, let's say you call ten people and ask for donations to your favorite charity," I said. "Four of them hang up on you, three politely tell you they don't want to contribute, and three gladly give. All ten of them got the exact same phone call from you, but you got three different reactions. Are you to blame for the different reactions?"

"No," she said. "I don't guess I could be, could I? The way they reacted had more to do with who they are." She stopped and looked at me out of the corner of her eye. "I think I get what you're saying. It's my problem, not hers—is that it? I'm choosing to react to my sister a certain way, yet blaming her for it."

Yes, that was exactly what I was getting at. Beth was *choosing* to listen to her sister drone on and on about her problems and was *choosing* to get really angry about it. In realizing that truth, Beth was finally giving herself the chance to move from the victim role of "Look what she does to me!" to the healthier role of seeing what she was doing to herself. She could now move from passively waiting for her sister to stop calling as the solution to assertively talking with her sister to get the problem solved. Even if it means her sister *chooses* to have hurt feelings.

We mold our emotional lives by the way we choose to think about what happens to us. We choose our emotions and actions whether we realize it or not. No one can force a feeling on us or force us to act in a certain way. To think otherwise is to be irresponsible, to place responsibility for our lives in the hands of every person and event life throws at us. This blame game is one of the deadliest games we can play. If we want our lives back, this game must stop.

Growthwork

When I was in graduate school preparing to become a psychologist, I was exposed to a counseling approach developed by psychologist Albert Ellis that made a lot of sense to me.[3] Dr. Ellis developed an A-B-C model of emotional health that is quite helpful in enabling people to change destructive beliefs. I want to teach it to you and get you to use this tool throughout this book. It requires a pencil and a legal pad to be your journal and some on-the-spot self-awareness.

For this assignment, I want you to focus on just the first letter of this model. The "A" represents the events that happen to us as we go through life. Some events are what I would call "5¢" (nickel) events in that they are small and insignificant, such as a friend being one minute late for lunch. Other events, though, are at the other end of the spectrum, what I would call "$500" events, such as losing a loved one in death, being fired from a job, experiencing the birth of a child, and getting married.

Some of the events that happen to us are not our fault in that we are not responsible for their happening. For example, I had a client who had exited off an interstate highway and was waiting at the red light on the access road when another motorist came off the interstate going sixty-five miles an hour and hit her from behind. My client had multiple fractures, a punctured lung, and other serious injuries from the crash. I certainly would not go up to her and say, "This was all your fault." The event was the other motorist's fault, not hers.

On the other hand, some events that happen to us are our fault. I was running errands around Austin one day a few years ago. I wasn't paying attention and went through a school zone at thirty-five miles an hour. One of Austin's finest stepped out into the street, waved me over, and gave me a ticket for speeding. Now, the event called "getting a ticket" was my fault, not anybody else's. By not paying attention, I brought the event on myself and got to hand over $118 of my hard-earned money to the fine city I live in.

With all that said and done, here's what I want you to do. I want you to keep a journal for one week on the various events that happen to you. First, write down the event ("boss chewed me out in front of some coworkers"). Second, assess the value of the event using my scale from 5¢ (someone is a minute late) to $500 (death of a loved one). Third, decide whether the event was your fault ("locked my keys in my car"), somebody else's fault ("close friend gossiped about me"), or no one's fault ("tornado destroyed my home"). Create three columns on your sheet, and enter the information as I have done here:

Event ("A")	Value	Fault
Misplaced car keys, found them a minute later	$1.00	Mine
House broken into, stereo/television stolen	$250.00	Theirs
Late for an important meeting at work	$50.00	Mine
Tree knocked over by high winds in front yard	$25.00	Nobody's
Ran (literally) into coworker rounding corner	$5.00	Both

Do the best you can to keep a detailed account of the events. Don't worry about assessing the value perfectly. (Remember, you are no longer a perfectionist, right?) Just make the best guess you can. Pay special attention to the events you feel upset (depressed, angry, sad, hurt) about.

The purpose of this assignment is to help you become more aware of the events that trigger you in life, their relative value, and who is responsible for them, all important issues in maintaining good mental health. We will build on this assignment in later chapters, so make sure you do this before reading further.

3

■

WORLDLY LIES

The truth must essentially be regarded as in conflict with this world; the world has never been so good, and will never become so good that the majority will desire the truth.
—Søren Kierkegaard

Grab for All the Gusto!
Look Out for Number One!
Do Your Own Thing!
If It Feels Good, Do It!
Your Feelings Are Your Best Guide!
You Deserve to Be Happy!

Advertisements, television shows, movies, magazines, music, and self-help books shout messages like these at us every day. And in childlike naiveté, we listen and believe. Often without even realizing it, we buy into what the "world" tells us, as if it knows how we should think and how we should live our lives. We look for truth in a jingle.

How trustworthy are the messages we get from our world each day? I want to suggest to you that many, if not most, are extremely dangerous and will destroy our lives if we live by them. Unfortunately, we are so brainwashed into believing these lies, minute by minute, day by day, that they not only appear harmless, but also true.

I'm sure you have heard a speaker at one time or another use the "frog and water" metaphor. You know the one. If you drop a frog into boiling water, it will immediately jump out because it can tell quite clearly the danger it is in. Yet if you put a frog in room temperature water and slowly heat the water until it is boiling, the frog will remain in the water and boil to death. A frog adjusts to the small changes in the water's temperature over time until it loses its life for having done so.

Now, I tell you all this to make an important point: you are the frog, the world you live in is the water, and the philosophies that the world teaches provide the heat that is boiling you ever so slowly to death. Millions of us are being boiled to death every day by some of the most incredibly stupid and destructive lies to ever hit the planet, and the cost in terms of emotional health, intimacy with others, and spiritual maturity is incalculable.

What are these "worldly" lies that destroy us? There are so many of them that writing about each one would fill volumes. In the following pages, I want to focus on what I believe to be six of the most toxic to our souls. These lies are taught to us from the time we draw our first breath until we draw our last. These lies put us in our graves at an earlier age because of how deadly they are.

"You Can Have It All."

Who says you can't have it all? A popular beer commercial once shouted that question. The underlying aim of that question, I believe, was to get us to believe that in drinking beer and in living life itself we can and should have it all (and ought to be really hacked off if we don't). The company's beer, we were told, had it all so that it "tastes great" but is somehow "less filling" at the same time. I'm not a beer-drinking kind of guy, mind you, but I'm a little skeptical about the idea that *anything* in life can "taste great" and still pull off the "less filling" part. Seems to be wishful thinking to me.

I believe that one of the deadliest lies we are told by our world each day is that we can have it all. However commercials, self-help books, songs, or movies choose to phrase it, the notion that we can have everything in life we have ever dreamed of is baloney. Absolute baloney. There is not one single person who has ever had it all. And there is a simple reason why.

Every yes is a no, and every no is a yes.

Confused? Allow me to explain.

In life, we are constantly having to make decisions between things. For example, when you go to a restaurant, the waiter doesn't come to your table and ask, "Are you having the whole menu tonight?" He says, "May I take your order?" He wants to know which entrée out of all the ones listed you have decided to say yes to. If you say yes to chicken fried steak, you are saying no to grilled fish, steak, and everything else on the menu. You can't have everything on the menu.

Life is like that. Life is a menu of things you can choose from, but saying yes to being a huge success at work usually means saying no to getting home by six and being able to live a balanced life. Not always, but usually. The point is that no one has ever had it all because whatever a person says yes to inescapably means he had to say no to something else.

Maybe, though, you're like a lot of people who look around and see others who appear to have it all. We look at them and think they got the whole enchilada and all we got was rice and beans. So, we start salivating for more. Scratch below the life that looks like it is the whole enchilada, though, and you will invariably find a life with painful gaps in it.

Tim is one of those "whole enchilada" kind of guys, at least on the surface. He is a highly successful business contractor, and from every appearance, he lives the American Dream. He drives a Mercedes, wears a Rolex watch, and is a member of three country clubs. His wife is beautiful and intelligent, and has personality plus. They have three healthy kids, live in a home the size of Rhode Island, and go on fantastic vacations to places such as Bora Bora. Tim, though, is one of the most unhappy people I've ever known.

"I always thought when I reached this level of life I'd be happy," he said the first day he visited my office. He slouched low in the chair in front of me. "I know this sounds crazy, but all the things I have don't make me happy. They've actually become a burden."

"A burden?" I asked. "How?"

"We have more debt than ever. All that we own is just that much more to take care of. I don't know. It just seems the more we get, the more we want, you know?" he said, fiddling with his diamond pinky ring.

"Like what?"

"Right now we live in a really nice home, but we've got our eyes on an even more expensive one. It's in an even nicer neighborhood and all. My wife really wants to move. But the mortgage, I have to admit, will put a lot of pressure on me."

"And that pressure is something you wouldn't like?"

"Well, keeping up financially with all that we currently have is enough pressure by itself, but this would cause even more." He ran his hand through his head of distinguished gray hair. "If we don't move, my wife will be very disappointed."

"She's pressuring you?" I asked.

"Yes . . . but I want to move too."

"In spite of all that you have, it isn't making you very happy," I added.

"I'm embarrassed to admit it, but it's true," he said, glancing down at the floor, then back up at me. "Sounds bad, doesn't it? I mean, having all that we do never seems to stop our desire for more. We never seem to say no to ourselves anymore. The more we have of what we thought would make us happy, the more miserable we get."

Tim was living proof that no one has it all even when he looks as if he does. He had said yes to a number of things in life (a big home, lots of expensive stuff, exciting trips), but without even seeing it, he was simultaneously saying no to a number of more important things in life (peace of mind, a reasonable work life, time with his family). No one has it all, even the people who seem to have it all.

The best case study for the ultimate futility of the "you can have it all" lie can be found in the Bible. If anyone had it all, the great King Solomon did. Our man Solomon was the John D. Rockefeller, Albert Einstein, and Hugh Hefner of his day all rolled into one very special person. He was the wealthiest and most intelligent man on earth, had hundreds of wives and concubines, and denied himself no worldly pleasure. Listen to him describe his life:

> I made my works great, I built myself houses, and planted myself vineyards. . . . I made myself water pools. . . . I had greater possessions of herds and flocks than all who were in Jerusalem before me. I also gathered for myself silver and gold and the special treasures of kings and of the provinces. I acquired male and female singers, the delights of the sons of men, and musical instruments of all kinds. So I became great and excelled more than all who were before me in Jerusalem. Also my wisdom remained with me. Whatever my eyes desired I did not keep from them.[1]

I don't know about you, but I'd consider that having it all. I would love to have the life King Solomon had, wouldn't you? Man, would that be something! With all that going for him, you'd think Solomon would have been one happy and content fellow, right? Well, listen to some of the conclusions he reached:

- "The abundance of the rich will not permit him to sleep."[2]

- "He who loves silver will not be satisfied with silver."[3]

- "I have seen all the works that are done under the sun; and indeed, all is vanity and grasping for the wind."[4]

In Solomon's efforts to have it all, he had everything but the one thing that completes it—contentment. The end result of the "you can have it all" lie is tremendous dissatisfaction, even ungratefulness, with what you do have and a

vain "grasping for the wind" in trying to find greater happiness through having more. Like Solomon, many of us live our lives around the adage that "the
grass is always greener on the other side of the fence," and we work hard to get
on that other side. The only problem is, when we get to the other side of the
fence, we find out that we can't have it all there, either.

The apostle Paul had the right attitude when he penned these very wise
words: "For we brought nothing into this world, and it is certain we can carry
nothing out. And having food and clothing, with these we shall be content."[5]
Isaac Bickerstaffe, a man from a later century, put it this way: "If I am content
with little, enough is as good as a feast." Those are great truths to live by.

I wish I could say we are a country "content with little," but the truth of
the matter is, we are a country that *demands* and *expects* a feast. We are rarely,
if ever, satisfied with what we have and seem to always be looking around for
more. Keeping up with the Joneses is not so much an attitude as it seems to be
a birthright.

The "have it all" lie is a destructive delusion that cheapens life, making us
anxiously live for the future rather than appreciate and enjoy the present. Very
few of us are immune to it, but all of us have a choice whether to live by it. We
can fight always having to have more to be happy. We can fight the part of us
that believes we are entitled to everything we lay our eyes on. We can realize
that to say yes to one thing in life is actually a choice to simultaneously say no
to something else. We can learn to be content with little so that we gratefully
receive enough as a feast

"My Worth Is Determined by My Performance."

"I haven't closed a deal in months," said Ted, who is a real estate salesman.
Things were rolling along fine in his life until the real estate market went belly-
up. Because he was depressed and couldn't shake it, he came to see me.

"We keep dipping into savings to get by. That can't last forever," he
moaned. He sat hunched over his knees, his hands massaging his temples.

"How does doing that feel?"

He stopped, sitting straight up. "I can't stand it. I've never been so depressed.
I'm normally an 'up' kind of guy! This has never happened to me before."

"Before the real estate market went bad, how did you feel?" I asked.

He sat back in his chair. "Oh, I felt great."

"Your happiness and self-worth seem to have gone up and down with the
market," I observed.

"Well . . . I guess you could put it that way."

"Okay, let's stay with that thought. You feel good about yourself when things are going well. So does that mean you're only as worthwhile as your performance?"

"Well, I don't like looking at it *that* way." He paused.

"Is it true?"

"Yeah, I guess," he mumbled. "I mean, I know I feel a lot more worthwhile when things are going good."

Our culture has an obsession with performance. We want to know how many units a salesman sold, how many home runs a baseball player hit, how many As a student made, how many degrees an applicant has, and on and on These are somehow the signs of being not just successful but worthwhile in our culture. Somehow we've gotten achievement mixed up with worth—if a sales-man, for instance, sells a million widgets, he must be a great, worthwhile person. This attitude may be an inescapable part of competitive living in the modern world, but it has created a feeling in many of us that we have about as much personal worth as we can earn.

You may remember the story of Kathy Ormsby. It was 1986 in Indianapolis, Indiana, the site of the NCAA track-and-field championships. Kathy was a premed honor student and track star at North Carolina State University. She also happened to be the collegiate record holder in the women's ten-thousand-meter run. Something quite unexpected happened during the championship race. Kathy fell behind and couldn't seem to catch the front-runner. In a startling move, she ran off the track and out of the stadium to a nearby bridge, where she jumped off. The forty-foot fall permanently paralyzed her from the waist down.

Not knowing Kathy personally, I can only guess that the pressure she put on herself to be perfect coupled with a tendency to equate her worth with performance created a level of misery she couldn't handle. Many of us who struggle with those two issues—having to be perfect and having personal worth dictated by achievement—reach a point of total despair, even suicide, when we experience failure.

The "worth equals performance" lie is a tough one to crack. Many things around us reinforce it every day. Yet with some effort we can challenge and overcome it. Let's get back to Ted and his struggle with this lie.

"That sounds a little stupid, I know," said Ted, shrugging, "the fact that I feel I am more worthwhile when I'm doing well at work. But I put so much of myself into it. And when I was on top, everybody else told me how great I was. It's just natural to value yourself more when things are going well."

"Maybe in that light the slowdown in the real estate market is a good thing for you," I suggested.

"Whoa," he said, raising his hands. "Back up. How could that be?"

"Well, it is giving you a chance to face the fact that you have based your worth on what you do—not who you are."

"Yeah, well, what worth do I have apart from what I do?" he asked in a low voice out of the side of his mouth.

"That's a good question, but I think *you've* got to answer that," I said, and I waited.

Ted stared at me a moment, shuffled his feet, then said, "I guess we need to keep talking then."

And we did. Ted grappled with the fact that he had spent his whole life equating his worth as a human being with how he did on the field of competition. Growing up as a kid, he allowed sports to determine his worth. In college, grades decided his worth. As an adult, the amount of money he made dictated the matter. Ted saw the destructiveness of living his life this way, and he made a concerted effort to separate how well he performed each day from his personal worth.

The real estate market slowdown and his depression about it did prompt Ted to face a very important question: What is the basis of human worth? That's the $64,000 question here, isn't it? I believe that you can choose from three answers, two of which don't work. Let me walk you through them.

One way to answer the question, "What is the basis of human worth?" is to use Ted's approach. You can try to earn worth through performance. You can compete with others and hope that you do well enough to earn the sense of worth you seek. But as we have already discussed, this approach leaves you with an unstable sense of worth that fluctuates with each performance you give. That roller coaster isn't worth riding.

A second approach to solving the worth issue is the humanistic approach. The idea is that we humans have worth because we exist and are the highest of all living things. We are living beings and the apex of everything that draws breath—that gives us worth. Yet the idea "I exist, therefore I have worth" seems a shallow way to solve the problem to me. Ants exist. Do they have the same worth I do? And the fact that I may be higher on the food chain than a monkey hits me as a basis for *not* having much of a sense of worth.

The third option is to get theological. This approach says that one thing and one thing only gives human beings worth—we are made by God in His image. In other words, worth doesn't come from the fact that you perform at a certain level, that you exist, or that you are higher than monkeys in the chain of being. It comes from being "fearfully and wonderfully made" by the Creator of the universe. To use a car analogy, worth doesn't come from the fact that your engine is running, that you are faster or prettier than other cars, or that you function at a higher level than a bicycle. Worth comes from who made your car. Period.

This vertical point of view provides at least two significant clarifications. First, it means that you have permanent worth. God never unmakes us in His image, so you always have worth. Second, it means that you have the same worth as everyone else, even if others outperform you. This truth ought to be comforting to those of us who are inexpensive little economy cars in a world that worships high-dollar luxury cars. The theological answer to the worth issue is the only true solution. Everything else falls short.

Living this truth, though, is harder than believing it. How can we find a stable sense of worth in a world that focuses on what we do instead of who we are? Many of us have gone the route of Solomon, striving for achievement, power, success, material possessions, and sexual prowess in an effort to feel worthwhile. What we find, however, is usually the same feeling of futility that Solomon did.

Earlier in this chapter, Ted posed a very important question: "Who am I apart from what I do?" Let me ask you that. Who are you apart from what you do? Do you have to "do" to have worth, or are you clear yet that you "are" a person of innate worth because of whose image you bear? We all need to make sure we have an answer to that question.

"Life Should Be Easy."

Automatic dishwashers, microwave ovens, garage door openers, central air-conditioning. Let's face it. Of all the people on earth, we Americans have the most gadgets designed to make our lives easier. The moment we have them, we all but decide we can't live without them.

Granted, there is probably nothing wrong with making life as difficulty free as possible. Finding ways to make our existence easier makes good sense. What causes trouble is that this attitude often shifts into one that *demands* that life, in all its complexity, be easy. We often give ourselves over to the pleasure principle— a basic tendency in each of us to minimize pain and maximize pleasure. This bent toward pleasure and away from pain, though, leads us to run from problems that need to be faced.

Life is *not* easy, no matter how many gold cards and garage door openers and microwave ovens we have. The very first words of the best-selling book *The Road Less Traveled* are golden on this matter: "Life is difficult."[6] That is one of life's all-time great truths. But most of us can't stand the fact that this happens to be true, so we keep looking for a life free from difficulty and bitterly resenting it when one doesn't come.

Remember Julie at the beginning of Chapter 2? She was convinced that life was easy for everyone but her. Why did she get the husband who left for another woman? Why did she have a son with a learning disorder? Why did she have to put her father in a nursing home? Why did her windshield get cracked? She was certain she was the only one in the world who had it tough. What was the result of her attitude? Bitterness. Resentment. Depression. I see these three emotions most often in my patients who live this lie.

Life is not easy. Never has been, never will be. Whether we like it or not, the fact of the matter is that life is tough. The willingness to accept this, truly accept it, helps us to have a life free from bitterness and resentment. Julie was right about one thing. Some people do have it better than she does. But some people, many people, have it a whole lot worse. And all of us have crosses to bear.

The other day, Julie came to a session smiling. She sat down with a *plop* and said, "Dr. Thurman, I had a wreck yesterday."

"Really?" I said. "Are you all right?"

She said, "Oh, yes, I'm okay. It was a fender bender, but you know, the woman in the other car jumped out screaming, 'Why does this always happen to me! I can't take anymore of this!' She went on and on, and as I stood there watching her . . ."

"What went through your mind?"

"I forgot all about my bent fender for a moment. All I could see was that woman. She was 'me' all over! I felt ashamed of myself."

"Really? Why?" I asked.

"I realized that the woman really believed that somehow life singled her out for all the bad stuff, and I saw how bitter she was. I saw her emotionally come apart at the seams right in front of me, and it wasn't pretty," Julie admitted.

"And you saw yourself in her?"

"Yes, I realized that I have done that so many times, I can't even count them. I guess I saw how childish and immature that is in people—to think that things should always go great and that when they don't, it is unique to me. I don't even like admitting it to you," she confessed.

"Julie, I appreciate your telling me all this. I know how painful it can be when you see something about yourself you don't like. The wreck, I guess, turned out to have a silver lining in it for you, didn't it?"

"Yes, I guess so. It forced me to see what I think you have been trying to help me see all along. It sure is painful, though."

Julie began to experience less bitterness as she exchanged her "life should be easy" lie for the truth that life is difficult. She came to grips with the fact that while people's difficulties may differ to some degree, everyone has problems in one form or another. Thus, she saw that life is difficult for everybody and that she needed to move from whining about that to accepting it and facing whatever her problem was. She quit thinking she was uniquely singled out for a difficult life and came to understand that we are all in this together. Her anger, depression, and resentment subsided over the months that followed, and she began to experience greater calm in the face of life's storms.

"Life Should Be Fair."

"Hey, that's not fair! Your piece is bigger than mine! Mom!"

"Chris, share with your brother. Be fair."

Most of us were taught from day one about the importance of fairness. Parents, teachers, coaches, and clergy repeatedly told us to make sure that we acted as fairly as possible in dealing with other people. If one child gets three cookies, then the other one should get three as well. If one child gets to watch his favorite television program for half an hour, then the other child gets to do the same. If one child gets to go first this time, then the other child gets to go first the next time. Life should be fair. At least we are told that is the way it should be.

I'm all for things being fair, but I wonder if a lot of us don't come out of childhood and adolescence with a misguided belief that life will always be fair, which it most definitely is not. I'm only half joking when I say I wish my mom and dad had, on occasion, given my brothers and me unequal pieces of pie and said, "Hey, we love you guys all the same, but life isn't fair sometimes, and we want you to learn to deal with that early on."

This "fair life" offshoot of the "easy life" lie is just as pervasive and just as destructive. It's wishful thinking, and it's damaging. Day-to-day reality provides frequent, painful reminders that life isn't always going to be fair. A young man is killed by a drunk driver who walks away without a scratch. Drug dealers and pornography peddlers make millions and live in mansions. A less qualified applicant gets the job. The best runner is tripped from behind by another and loses the race. Our response is, "It isn't fair," as if labeling it that way somehow changes things. King Solomon, thousands of years ago, understood life's unfairness when he noted that the wicked sometimes get what the righteous deserve and the righteous sometimes get what the wicked deserve.[7]

Beth, a client of mine a number of years ago, got a very bitter taste of life's unfairness. She grew up in a family where her older brother was favored, subtly and not so subtly, by her parents. They bought him a car in high school, paid his way through an expensive Eastern college, and then helped him get through law school. For Beth, the family car and a nearby state college were good enough, and there was no money for graduate education. "My father said they had only so much money and I'd just get married anyway," she commented.

"I went along with all that until my midtwenties," she explained. "Then suddenly it all hit me like a lightning bolt, and I was livid. It wasn't fair. I needed my own car just as badly as he did. I was just as smart, even smarter probably, and could have done graduate work. Yet just because he was firstborn and a son to boot, he got preferential treatment. That stinks!"

Unfairness is a hard thing to accept. We have an internal code of right and wrong imprinted on our souls, and unfairness violates that code. The issue here isn't, "Is life going to be unfair?" Of course, it is. The real issue is, "How are you going to handle unfairness when it comes your way?" Allow me to offer a few suggestions.

First, you need to call things what they are, so the starting point in dealing with unfairness is to call it unfairness. That may seem obvious, but far too often we make excuses for others, we act as though what they did wasn't unfair, or we call unfairness by some other name just to smooth things over or keep the peace.

Second, you must allow yourself to feel hurt and angry when something unfair happens. Notice I said hurt and angry. I didn't say bitter, resentful, and enraged. There is a big difference. It is appropriate to feel hurt and angry when something unfair happens, so let yourself feel these emotions.

Third, you need to decide whether you want to assert yourself and try to correct the unfairness. Some things are worth speaking up about (they overcharge you for repairing your car just because you are a woman), whereas other things are not (someone gets a few more french fries in an order than you did). There is a time to stand up and say, "I am not going to take this!" and a time to say, "No big deal, I'm gonna let this one slide."

Fourth, you need to work on not taking what happened personally (something we will discuss in a future chapter). Whether someone intentionally or unintentionally acted unfairly, what happened wasn't a personal statement about you. Some of us are so personally insulted when something unfair comes our way, we grossly overreact. Though easier said than done, we must realize that unfairness toward us is about the other person who acted unfairly, not about us.

Finally, and most difficult of all, you need to forgive. Forgiving others for being unfair doesn't mean forgetting what they did, nor does it mean saying that what they did was okay. It also doesn't mean that you let them keep doing it to you. Forgiveness is an act of your will where you decide to wipe the slate clean and make a conscious commitment not to hold what the people did to you against them. It means letting go of the past so that you can live more fully in the here and now. It means letting something truly be "water under the bridge."

Beth had to work on every one of these issues in counseling except the first one. She clearly had come to see that the preferential treatment her parents showed her brother was unfair. Here is how one of our sessions went when we worked on the issue of forgiving her parents and letting what they did be "water under the bridge":

"Beth, what happened to you was certainly unfair. And I can understand why you feel hurt and angry about it," I offered. "What concerns me about all this is how you are allowing the past to ruin your life today."

"What do you mean?" she said.

"You're allowing something that happened twenty years ago to wreck your life right now, aren't you?"

"Well, I guess . . . ," she hesitated. "Should I just sweep it under the carpet as if it didn't happen?"

"I think you know that doesn't work," I said, "but it's how you keep it alive that is ruining you."

Beth thought about that for a second, gazing out the window, then responded, "You're saying that I keep reliving what happened in a way that only makes me more resentful, right?"

"Right," I said. "It seems to me that you think something like this shouldn't have happened to you, so you are going to make your parents pay by staying miserable over it. You keep playing the role of the victimized daughter who can't move on with her life because of what was done to you years ago. The family martyr, maybe."

Tears filled her eyes, and I wondered if they were from realizing the truth of what I was saying or if I had been too rough. After what seemed like an hour, Beth landed on the right side of the fence.

"It isn't easy to admit this, but I have been feeling this way for a long, long time. I haven't moved one inch in the direction of accepting what happened and forgiving my parents for it. Every time I hear about how well my brother is doing, I become even more resentful. I have been mired in this for a long time," she sobbed.

"It sounds like you are in quicksand—the more you struggle against what your parents did, the more you sink into bitterness," I observed.

"That's sure how it feels. I guess if I am ever going to get out alive, I have to let go and forgive."

Beth worked hard to step out of the victim's role over what her parents had done to her. She came to see more deeply that it was unfair, that it had nothing to do with her, that she was just as deserving of the help that her brother got, and that it was time to forgive her parents for what they did. All of this was hard work, but Beth saw that it was even harder to play the role of the bitter, shortchanged daughter. Much to her credit, she moved out from under the shadow cast by the unfair way she was raised and broke free from the resentment she had harbored for years. She got her life back.

None of us will escape life's unfairness. It is delusional to think that we will. We can make some choices, though. We can choose to victimize ourselves over what others do to us that isn't fair. We can return evil for evil and do something unfair to them. Or we can accept what happened, hurt over it, and forgive it. It's up to us to handle unfairness so as not to pay twice for it—once when it happened and once again when we allow it to wreck our lives.

"You Shouldn't Have to Wait for What You Want."

Elaine loves clothes. She always looks as if she stepped off the cover of *Vogue* when she comes to see me. But that love is the very reason she seeks counseling. Elaine, a spendaholic, is deeply in debt. She seems unable to stop herself from buying everything she sees.

"I did it again," she said. "I bought a dress I didn't need. I just couldn't resist. It was the most beautiful thing I'd ever seen."

"You felt you couldn't live without it," I ventured.

"Right. Even though it cost four hundred dollars, I had to have it."

"Didn't you tell me last session that you had charged your credit cards to the limit?" I asked.

"Yes, but one bank increased my limit," she said sheepishly.

"How do you feel about what you've done?" I asked.

"Guilty. I know I shouldn't have bought the dress. At the same time, getting the dress sure felt good."

Earlier, we talked about the "you can have it all" lie. The "don't wait" lie is a variation on the same theme; its falsehood stems from the same impulse. You can have it all, so why wait? Why not have as much of it as you can *right this very second?* Whip out that credit card; shortcut that degree; don't hold back on the impulse to tell off that person who offended you.

Most of us know the lure of instant gratification in small daily ways. We really shouldn't have those greasy, calorie-laden french fries with the hamburger, but what the heck? We only live once. We'll start that diet tomorrow. Why wait?

I find out pretty quickly which of my patients live by this "don't wait" lie. Many come for help thinking that psychologists have magic words that will instantly make their lives free from pain. Once they see that therapy is going to be laborious, difficult work, some don't come back. These patients come to therapy to be immediately changed by the psychologist, not to change themselves over time with hard work.

Waiting is a lost art in our country today. Far too many consumers aren't waiting until they actually have the money before they buy something, far too many couples aren't waiting to give their relationship time to grow, far too many teenagers aren't waiting until marriage to have sex, far too many people don't wait until someone is finished speaking before they start saying their piece, and far too many drivers don't wait to merge. It is an "I shouldn't have to wait" culture, and credit card debt, divorce, unwanted pregnancies, rudeness, and highway deaths are just part of the price tag.

What about you? Are you willing to wait?

"People Are Basically Good."

Amy, an attractive twenty-five-year-old computer programmer, has been seeing me lately to try to sort out the reasons for her series of bad relationships with men. She is a bright, articulate, and responsible woman whose life is mostly in good shape, except for one area. Every relationship she has had with a man since she was a teenager has been chaotic and painful.

"I just don't know what keeps causing my relationships to go bad," she said one day. "I end up feeling used and hurt every time."

"When you date a man, what assumptions do you make about his intentions?" I asked her.

She looked a bit startled. "Assumptions? Well, I don't know. I guess I assume he's like me."

"What do you mean?" I asked.

"I assume his intentions are that he wants to get to know me for me and see if a relationship can develop."

"Honorable intentions, then?" I said.

"Yes, honorable, I guess."

"Specifically, how do you see them being honorable?" I asked.

She smiled, a bit chagrined. "You know what I mean. That the guy is moral. That sex isn't the only thing on his mind. That he likes my company."

"And what have you discovered?" I asked.

She grimaced. "That a lot of men are out for themselves. They don't care who they hurt."

While Amy's troubles with men are caused by a number of factors, one of the more important is her underlying assumption that men, and people in general, are basically good. She entered dating relationships thinking that each guy was well-intentioned, really cared about her, and wanted only her best. She found out that just the opposite was more likely to be true.

Now, this may be the point where you are tempted to put this book down permanently. One of our more treasured notions is that people are basically good (loving, kind, decent, fair, caring, honest). Well, at the risk of triggering a fit, I want to tell you in no uncertain terms that *people are not basically good! People are basically selfish, self-centered, dishonest, and deceitful.*

I may be one of the few psychologists in the world who thinks this way, but that is how I think. In an age when *human potential* and *self-actualization* are buzzwords and when best-selling books include *Personal Power* and *Awaken the Giant Within*, the idea that our nature is seriously flawed tends to bother us because it forces us to give up cherished notions about our goodness. Many of us prefer to accept more "positive" views of human nature. For example, here is the view held by noted humanistic psychologist Abraham Maslow:

> This inner nature, as much as we know of it so far, seems not to be intrinsically or primarily or necessarily evil [but rather] neutral . . . or positively "good." . . . Since this inner nature is good or neutral rather than bad, it is best to bring it out and to encourage it rather than to suppress it. If it is permitted to guide our life, we grow healthy, fruitful, and happy.[8]

This view of human nature certainly makes us feel better, but is it true? I don't think so, and I can point to two main pieces of evidence.

First, the history of mankind is characterized by man treating his fellow-man badly. Human history is marked by war, greed, jealousy, envy, hatred, and murder, not helping out one another, not getting along peacefully, and not loving one another. How we humans have treated one another throughout recorded history is irrefutable evidence that people are not basically good. If people were basically good, we would have seen much more peaceful, loving coexistence among us than there has been.

Second, people in their personal lives are more selfish than selfless, more shallow than deep, more self-destructive than growthful, and more discontented than contented. Look at almost anyone's life and ask yourself if that person is physically, emotionally, and spiritually *healthy*. Most people struggle in all three areas of life—physically out of shape, emotionally troubled, and spiritually immature if not dead. If people were basically good, the average person would be physically fit, emotionally stable, and living a moral life. That is not the average person, not by a long shot.

Now that I have depressed you, I want to make it clear, though, that I don't agree with those who say that people are *worthless scum* and *are no darn good*. That is also a lie. However bent toward selfishness and self-destruction we may be, human history and each individual's personal life provide ample evidence that the spark of the Divine does exist in us and that we are capable of being loving and kind and noble. I am just saying that acting "divinely" is not our nature and that anyone who tells you so is grossly misleading you.

Too many of my patients are casualties of the "people are good" lie. Like Amy's expectations, their expectations of people are the highest and purest when a healthy skepticism would serve them better.

"Is it wrong to think the best of people?" Amy exclaimed after I suggested that people are not as good as she might think.

"It's not proving to be true, is it?"

She stopped, a bit startled, then shook her head. "That's for sure." She sighed. "But what's the alternative? Should I assume all guys are pigs and not trust any of them?"

It was my turn to shake my head. "That sounds like going to the other extreme."

"Yes, I guess so."

"What would be an honest middle ground?" I asked.

"Well, let me think," she said, shuffling her feet and looking down at the carpet. "Maybe I should hold off on assuming anything." She looked back up at me. "I mean, I can't really know about a guy's intentions until I check them out."

"So you wouldn't think *either* way?" I said.

She nodded. "I wouldn't assume they are good or bad. In fact, I wouldn't assume, period. Maybe I wouldn't give so much of myself emotionally so quickly, either. Maybe I need to study the guys I date a little more before giving them any of my heart."

"Well, I agree that you need to study guys more carefully and take time to let them reveal their true intentions. How would that affect your dating life?" I asked.

"I'd pace my relationships slower. I wouldn't be so totally naive." She paused for a second. "I trust too quickly, don't I," she said, more of a statement than a question. "They can't use me unless I let them; I know that. So I should work on patience, on letting the relationship go slowly. Then I will be able to see what a guy is really like and whether I want to be around him."

Amy did just that. She realized that the evidence didn't back up her assumptions about men (and people) being basically good. She realized that all people have some good in them that needs to be affirmed but not blindly trusted. She realized that slowing things down in her dating relationships gave her more time to see what was "under the hood" before she made any decisions about becoming involved with anyone. She opened herself up to a lot less emotional pain without making the mistake of shutting herself off from relationships unnecessarily. She quit looking at people through rose-colored glasses and moved toward a more realistic view of who people are.

You may not buy the idea I am suggesting here—that people are not basically good. It may be a notion you just can't (won't?) accept. I would ask you to examine this from one final angle before you move on: Are *you* basically good? Is *your* natural bent toward kindness, integrity, loyalty, honesty, service, self-sacrifice, growth, maturity, and the like? Or do you find these qualities to be ones that you have to work at triple-time to exhibit on a regular basis? I think if you are honest with yourself, the simple truth of the matter is that these traits don't come naturally, and we have to work on them if we ever hope to have them. Just raise children and I think you will know what I mean.

In a world that often attributes wrong actions in people to low self-esteem, I wonder if the real problem isn't that we think too highly of ourselves. We think we are basically good when we are not, and we walk around arrogant and puffed up rather than humble and broken. Pride of this kind goes before our own destruction. We must come to grips with the fact that our inner nature must be killed off, not encouraged as Abraham Maslow suggested earlier. Encouraging our inner nature leads to thorns, not flowers.

Growthwork

Your last assignment involved tracking and assessing the event ("A") level of the A-B-C model. Now, I want you to jump past "B" and track the "C" level. The "C" level represents our reactions to the events that happen to us. These reactions can take three forms.

First, we often react physiologically to certain events with increased heart rate, muscle tension, and rapid and shallow breathing. This is the fight-or-flight reaction to certain events, such as almost being hit by someone running a red light or being criticized by a boss. Our bodies react with alarm in a way that prepares us physiologically to run away or face the event.

Second, we react emotionally to events. We feel angry, hurt, sad, peaceful, content, anxious, joyful, and so on. The event could be something like getting a promotion at work. We might feel happy about it, joyful maybe, possibly even anxious about the extra responsibilities that go with the promotion. Whatever our feelings may be, we are wired to respond emotionally to life.

Third, we often react behaviorally to the things that happen to us. We may yell, pace, cry, hit, hide, or whatever, but we humans often show what we are feeling by our behavior. Someone feeling anxious might bite his fingernails; someone feeling angry might slam a door; someone feeling sad might cry. The exception to this is that some people "stuff" what they are feeling and won't show you through their actions that they are feeling anything. Someone could be very angry about something but put a smile on his face to throw you off the trail.

Here is what I want you to do. For one week, I want you to keep a journal of how you react to things. Make two columns. The left column has "A" at the top, and that is where you need to describe the event. The right column is the "C" column, and that is where you write down how you reacted physiologically, emotionally, and behaviorally. To help you along, I have presented some examples for you:

"A" (Event)	"C" (Response)
1. Got stuck in traffic	1. *Physiological*: muscles got tight, sweated some *Emotional*: felt angry, anxious *Behavioral*: honked my horn, rode people's bumpers, cut in and out of traffic
2. Was told I did a good job on a report at work	2. *Physiological*: breathing got shallow *Emotional*: felt happy, proud *Behavioral*: called a friend and told him what happened
3. Received an overdue bill notice	3. *Physiological*: heartbeat got faster, breathing became more rapid, muscles tightened *Emotional*: felt worried *Behavioral*: bit my fingernails, ate a bowl of ice cream

These entries ought to give you a good idea of what to put into your journal for a week. The purpose of this growthwork is to make you more aware of how you are reacting to the events that happen to you. Pay special attention to any reactions that show up frequently and/or were way out of proportion to the event.

In keeping this journal, you will learn important things about yourself. You may realize that physiologically, you tend to respond to a lot of events with rapid and shallow breathing or muscle tension. You may come to see that emotionally, you worry quite a bit or get angry often. You may realize that you behaviorally respond to stressful events by overeating or working too much or watching television. Be careful not to use this information for self-condemnation—that only makes matters worse. Use this information for the sake of better understanding yourself so that you can make positive changes.

4

■

MARITAL LIES

To understand the realities of the marital relationship
it is essential first to recognize the unrealities.
—William Lederer and Don Jackson[1]

Joe and Carol had a storybook romance. He was handsome and attentive. She was stylish and smart. They became engaged and expected to live happily ever after. Then they got married. And instead of happily ever after, they were living unhappily all too soon. Where Joe once seemed handsome to Carol, he now seemed vain; where he once seemed attentive, he now seemed controlling. As for Carol, she no longer seemed stylish and smart to Joe, but materialistic and a know-it-all. Soon they were fighting more often than not and have been ever since. Two nice people who were very much in love turned into two unhappy people wondering if they had made the biggest mistake of their lives.

What happened? Nothing that couldn't happen to any couple. Reality moved in. When Joe and Carol married, both had very unrealistic notions of what life together would be like that came straight from fantasyland. When real life didn't live up to their dreams, troubles ensued.

Marriage is hard work. Yet blinding romantic notions keep us from seeing that. Many couples experience a great deal of heartache and misery *after* they walk down the aisle because they never understood how faulty their beliefs about marriage were *before* they walked down the aisle.

In this chapter, I want to explore six lies that wreak havoc on most marriages. Many couples would not admit to believing these lies because they are so clearly unrealistic ways to think. Yet if you look at the destructive way spouses actually act toward each other, it is clear that these lies are the underlying cause.

An old joke says there are three rings in marriage: the engagement ring, the wedding ring, and suffering. The lies we are about to examine are the primary cause of the suffering that many couples experience. They are also the reason why so many people divorce. If we want to save our marriages, we have to overcome these lies.

"All My Marital Problems Are My Spouse's Fault."

Have you ever heard the expression, "It takes two to tango"? Well, there are far too many married people who simply don't believe that. They believe that it takes one to tango. They believe that the marriage they are in is in horrible shape solely because of the other spouse—that he or she is *the* reason that things are going badly.

It was clear from the very first minute of my initial session with Joe and Carol that they believed this lie. Joe sat with his body turned away from Carol, Carol with her legs crossed away from Joe. And each started into the "all your fault" tirade.

"Dr. Thurman, Carol never has a kind word to say to me. *I* want our marriage to be a good one, but how can it be if she stays on me like she does all the time? She always finds something to be upset with me about," said Joe.

"That's because you come home from work and complain about how little you think I do and how awful you think I am," Carol answered.

Joe shot back, "If you did more around the house and treated me better, I wouldn't complain so much."

Carol sat up indignantly. "Yeah, well, if you didn't complain so much, I'd feel more like straightening the place up and being nicer to you," she countered.

They had played this game of verbal volleyball all their married life. Both admitted they had argued like this for twenty years, and neither seemed willing to call a time-out and look at his or her contribution to why the marriage had been so bumpy. When I tried to open their eyes to what each was doing to create an unhappy marriage, you would have thought I had spit on the American flag. They were in no mood to look into their own backyard. Each clearly felt that the marriage was troubled solely because of the other.

The truth about marriage is that it is a *relationship* between *two* people who pool all of their strengths and weaknesses together to *cocreate* what happens. *All of a marriage's problems are never one person's fault.* Yes, a specific problem may surface between a husband and a wife that is caused by one person, but even then, how the offended spouse reacts plays a huge role in making things better or worse. It takes two to tango in marriage, even when one spouse may be stepping on the partner's toes the most.

Think of marriage as playing mixed doubles in tennis. Individually, both players have some shots they hit well, some they hit okay, and some they are not very good at. Their respective strengths and weaknesses may differ—he may be good at volleys but bad at backhands, whereas she may be good at serving but not so good at lobs. One player may actually be better overall than the other (although, in general, people marry at the same "skill" level), but they are still playing as a team. We have heard something said many times in the sports world that is true in the marital world—you win as a team; you lose as a team.

The "all your fault" lie is basically the message that "I have my act totally together and you are a complete mess. If it weren't for you, we would be getting along fantastically." People, listen up: no one has his act totally together. All of us have flaws, and the flaws make our marriages less than fantastic.

Try telling all this to Patty, who found out two months ago that her husband had an affair. She feels crushed by this revelation, as anyone would, but she unfortunately takes this a deadly step farther. Patty is convinced that her husband's affair is *the* reason their marriage is on the rocks and that *he* is to blame for *all* the misery they are now going through.

"What he did destroyed our marriage," she spewed during our most recent session.

"How so?" I asked, knowing full well what she was saying.

"I will never be able to trust him again! I can't even bear to look at him! I could just kill him!" she exploded.

"I know you are in a lot of pain over this, Patty, and understandably so. At the risk of sounding insensitive, though, I want to explore something with you, okay?"

"Okay," she said with hesitation in her voice.

"We have been talking about what your husband did for a while now, and we have spent a lot of time focusing on how much you hurt and how much this has damaged your ability to trust and respect him. It is what I *haven't* heard you say that concerns me," I offered.

"What do you mean?"

"Well, I haven't heard you say anything about yourself yet."

"About me?"

"Yes, about you."

"What is there to say about me in all this? I didn't have an affair. I didn't break our vows. I didn't betray him. What have I got to do with any of this?" she said defensively.

"Don't you think it takes two to make a marriage what it is?" I asked.

"Yes, but are you saying it is my fault he had an affair?" She was almost yelling.

"No, not at all. That was his choice, and it was a very selfish, destructive one. What I'm saying is that I'm concerned about the fact that you haven't said anything about the part you have played in the marriage not being a good one. From what you have said, his affair is the only reason the marriage is in trouble. From that, I would take it that you don't think you have done anything wrong," I stated, knowing full well I was on pretty thin ice.

"Sure, I have done some things wrong," she begrudgingly admitted, "but nothing like this. He has wrecked everything, and I don't know if I can ever love him again."

"Let me ask you this. Before you found out about the affair, would you say that you were more loving toward your husband than he was toward you?"

"What do you mean?"

"Do you believe that you were more caring, supportive, attentive, affectionate, understanding, and so on?"

"Yes, I was," she said without missing a beat.

"Were you all of those things all of the time?"

"No, but who is? I met a lot more of his needs than he ever met of mine," she bragged.

"But there were ways you didn't meet his needs when you could have, right?"

"Of course. I didn't have an affair, though. He did. Should I just act like that is no big deal and sweep everything under the rug?"

"No, what he did was a big deal, and sweeping it under the rug only allows it to fester. I just wonder how your marriage is ever going to heal if you aren't willing to do what he has already done."

"What, have an affair?"

"No, come clean about what you have done in the marriage that has contributed to its being so troubled. You seem to have a pretty bad case of the 'all our problems are his fault' syndrome, and you are looking right past the part you have played."

"What part have I played?" she asked incredulously.

"Let's talk about that in the next session."

Patty was in a lot of pain, and my effort to get her to examine her behavior in the marriage was risky, to say the least. Her pain was keeping her from being willing to look at herself. All she could see was what her husband did. Since she had been told about his affair, all she had done was hammer away at him for what he had done, spending little, if any, time looking honestly at herself.

Intense emotional pain triggered by something such as a spouse having an affair has a way of interfering with our willingness to do any honest self-examination. Yet I knew Patty had to do that to save her marriage. I pushed her for weeks to find the courage not only to honestly face what her husband did and what it said about him but also to x-ray herself to see what was cancerous in her own soul. I challenged her to examine all the ways she had wounded him over the years by not being loving. Patty responded to this by continuing to blame her husband for all of their marital woes, and a little more than a year from the time her husband told her about his affair, they ended up divorcing.

For a marriage to work, each spouse must take to heart the biblical teaching to look at the plank in his or her own eye before pointing out the speck (or plank) in the spouse's eye.[2] This does not mean stuffing your feelings about what your spouse did, downplaying things, or taking any responsibility for your spouse's destructive actions. It just means that until you honestly look at who you are, you will be unable to respond to your spouse properly when he or she messes up.

Can you imagine a marriage in which each spouse puts this one teaching into practice? Can you picture a relationship in which each spouse looks honestly at personal flaws and takes responsibility for his or her actions each day? Can you imagine a relationship that involves two people who stay in their own "backyard" rather than peering over the fence into the spouse's? It would be something!

The next time you are tempted to blame your spouse for all the problems in your marriage, I want you to think about Patty. She is at great risk of spending the rest of her life bitter and alone, a pretty high price to pay for seeing herself as a problem-free person. If pride does go before destruction, she would be a classic example of that truth.

It takes two to tango. Say that to yourself a dozen times a day. Etch it in your brain. The next time your spouse does something you feel hurt and upset about, you will need to play that tape as loudly as possible in your soul. If you don't, your chances of a good marriage are zero.

"If Our Marriage Takes Hard Work, We Must Not Be Right for Each Other."

Back at the beginning of this chapter, I said marriage is hard work. Make that marriage is *very* hard work. *Tremendously* hard work. Underline it. Boldface it. Tattoo it on your forehead. Any marriage that has achieved intimacy through the years has been *worked* on. It's a truth, though, that very few understand. So the moment marriage isn't easy or smooth, a lot of couples begin to think, *We must not be right for each other. Otherwise we wouldn't have to work so hard.*

As strange as it sounds, I'd argue that hard work in marriage often suggests you married the right person. The hard work reflects the fact that all of us have a lot of things we need to improve in order to be better people. Isn't it amazing how often a person will complain that he has married someone who seems to "bring out my worst"? But I wonder if that isn't the beauty of it? Someone bringing out our worst can lead to enough pain and unhappiness to make us more serious about working on "our worst."

Lately, I've been seeing a couple in therapy who fit this scenario. Cheryl and Stan have been married less than a year and fight about something almost every day—large things, small things, anything. They have few interests in common and feel bored with each other. They spend little time together talking about how they feel because they find it painful. And their attitudes have spilled over into their sexual life, which is cold at best. They'd call it quits except that they're both afraid to be alone and worried about how their friends and family would react.

They habitually sit in the two single chairs in my office, a king and a queen sitting regally, rigidly in their individual thrones—Cheryl, self-assured and immaculately dressed, Stan slouched and always in slacks and a rumpled sport shirt. Typically, they start each session blaming each other and wondering out loud if they're hopelessly mismatched. I've tried to coax them to back off and look honestly at their personal styles.

"I know how frustrated you both must be with the problems in your marriage," I said one day, "but I don't think it necessarily means that you are wrong for each other."

"Well, if it doesn't, what else could it mean?" Stan shot back.

"Well, one thing your problems could mean is that both of you have serious flaws. Your fights are a symptom of how much both of you have to work on."

Stan rolled his eyes. "What do you mean?"

"Well, Stan, you two fight over how often you watch sports, right? Is it possible that you are being somewhat selfish in how much time you spend doing that?" I knew he didn't want to hear me say something like that.

He stiffened. "I love watching football. It helps me relax. You're not asking me to give that up, are you?"

"Of course not. It's not my place to ask you to give it up. It's more important whether you think you should cut back some to help your marriage. It's got to come from you. I'm just trying to get you to entertain the possibility that the fight you two are having over this issue could mean that you have some flaws to work on."

"I have flaws. I know that! It just seems to me that our marriage ought to be easier than this. Why do we even fight over things like me watching sports on TV? That seems so stupid!" Stan groaned. "There has to be someone out there who it would be easier with."

"Maybe, but all marriages are hard work," I observed. "Looking for someone that it would be easy to be married to is an escapist fantasy. The painful truth is that your marriage brings out areas in both your lives that need to be changed. You'd just be taking those same flaws into your next marriage I believe that you can grow the most in the marriage you are in." And with that, I noticed neither of them was looking at me anymore.

For the time being, they are chewing on what I had to say. Their pain is so acute, their anger so intense, I worry they'll divorce before the work they need to do is started, much less finished. I constantly remind them that their problems signal not that they should leave each other, but instead that they need each other's help to work out respective flaws.

The apostle Paul was right when he said, "Those who marry will face many troubles in this life."[3] The wisest couples use marital problems as an impetus to work even harder, not as an excuse to bail out. If your marriage is hard work, you have a golden opportunity to use that reality to make needed changes in who you are. You do not want to pass up that opportunity.

"My Spouse Can and Should Meet All of My Emotional Needs."

Another unrealistic notion is that a spouse will completely, totally, consistently, and wonderfully meet all of our emotional needs (such as attention, acceptance, appreciation, approval, affection, affirmation, comfort, encouragement, respect, security, support, understanding). We often walk down the aisle thinking we have found the person who can do that and look forward to perfect wedded bliss. Within twenty-four hours of saying "I do," the person we thought would meet our every need may hardly be meeting any of them. We become bitter and resentful, and "The War" is on. You'd be amazed at how stubbornly some people hold on to this idea, though. I've seen couples in my office who have been married thirty years and still believe that their spouses should meet their every emotional need. Lies die hard!

George and Sue came to see me after their tenth anniversary. They had hardly celebrated it at all because each was so hurt and angry with the other. George was the strong, self-sufficient type. Sue, just the opposite, was the bubbly cheerleader type who had always had someone "stronger" to depend on. She even admitted that when she and George first started going together, he was her Prince Charming who rescued her from all of her problems. Now, after a decade of marriage, George was growing a little tired of being Prince Charming.

"Dr. Thurman, Sue expects me to be there twenty-four hours a day to meet every need she has!" George blurted out.

"I do not. I just expect you to be there when I need you," Sue quickly answered.

George sighed. "Do you realize what you're saying? I can't be there every time you need me! I can't meet your every need! Nobody can do that!"

Sue frowned, looking intently at her husband. "But," she began, "if you don't meet my needs, who will?"

"Sue, that is an important question," I said. "Who will take care of your needs if George can't or won't?"

Sue's eyes began to water, and she looked a bit scared. "Well, I don't really have any friends or family to rely on, like George does."

"That leaves you having to depend on George for everything, doesn't it?" I pressed.

She paused. "I have to admit," she said in a quiet voice, "that outside of George I don't feel that I have anyone I can turn to. When we first met, George seemed to want to meet all my needs, and I was glad to let him."

"That's true," George added. "I wanted to then. It made me feel important and needed. Now I just feel smothered and used."

"Things have changed," I said.

"Yes. Frankly, I'm tired of her depending upon me for everything. It can't keep going like this. I find myself running away from her rather than moving toward her."

She thought a moment. She straightened her dress and crossed her legs. "I guess I need other people and other things in my life to take some pressure off him. To be honest, it scares me to think about all this," Sue confessed.

"Sweetheart, it's not that I don't want to meet your needs. It's just that I can't meet them all," George said, trying to reassure her.

The reality of any relationship is that no one person can be the perfect "need meeter" for another person. Our needs are too many and can be met only through a variety of people and activities. People who depend solely on one person or thing usually haven't developed other resources—a best friend, hobbies, satisfying work, a close relationship with God. So rather than identifying this as the problem, they turn to their spouses and say, "Here's my life. You take care of all my needs."

In healthy marriages, there is a mutual commitment to meet each other's emotional needs as much as possible. In healthy marriages, neither spouse depends completely on the other for all of the emotional needs to be met. In healthy marriages, each person has other people and activities to turn to in a morally responsible manner for emotional needs to be met. In healthy marriages, both spouses make every effort to be honest about when they are not meeting each other's emotional needs and try diligently to do better.

When you have emotional needs that are not being met in your marriage, you can basically do the following: (1) remind yourself that having emotional needs is healthy and it is okay to feel hurt when they are not met; (2) identify what emotional needs are not being met (see the list given earlier); (3) ask your spouse if he or she would be willing to meet them (be specific as to which ones and how you would like them met); (4) affirm and appreciate your spouse for meeting your emotional needs when he or she does; (5) keep meeting your spouse's emotional needs as best you can, even if he or she is not willing to do the same for you; and (6) look for other morally appropriate ways for your emotional needs to be met (a close friend, an interesting hobby, volunteer activities, ongoing education, church involvement).

There is nothing wrong with having emotional needs—we are made that way. All human beings have them. Problems occur, though, when we expect our spouses to meet all of our emotional needs. That puts too much pressure on them and damages the marriage.

"My Spouse Owes Me (for All I Do)."

Remember when you first started dating the person who became your spouse? You were happy to do anything for him or her and didn't really want much in return other than his or her company.

What's your relationship like now? If you're like most couples, you have fallen into a "green stamp" marriage style. For everything you do for your spouse, you build up a certain number of green stamps. Taking out the garbage might be worth ten green stamps, picking up the dirty clothes might be worth twenty, listening to your spouse complain might be worth seventy-five, and doing something with him or her that you don't want to do is worth a hundred green stamps. Then whenever you feel like it, you dump out your truckload of green stamps and say, "Here, I want to cash these in for fifteen minutes of your undivided attention," "I want to redeem these for a trip to Hawaii," or "You owe me a romantic night out for these." This style of marriage is destructive and is rooted in the lie that our spouses owe us for everything we do and should pay us back however and whenever we want them to.

Melissa and Burt epitomized this lie. They constantly had their "radar" up for what each owed the other, and both became very hostile when they felt they were paid less than what they were due. It had become so bad that they were never at peace with each other. Our sessions revolved around and around the "you owe me" theme until, one day, we came to an insight that triggered a turn-around in their marriage:

"Look," said Burt, leaning toward me, "I've worked hard to give her what she wants, and all I ask in return is that she do the same thing for me."

"You feel that she owes you for all that you have done for her?" I asked.

"Well, I wouldn't put it that way exactly, but, yes, I do expect something in return for all that I do," he said, leaning back.

Melissa almost exploded out of her chair. "Well, what about all the things I've done for you?"

Burt crossed his arms. "Like what?"

Melissa began counting on her fingers, "Helping put you through graduate school, keeping the house clean, putting dinner on the table every evening, pay-ing all the bills so you don't have to mess with them, taking care of our kids while you work. *Need more?*"

"Wait," I said. "Both of you sound convinced the other owes you more than you owe the other. Okay, then. Burt, whose efforts are worth more, yours or Melissa's?"

"I feel that I do more for her than she does for me. But I'm sure she feels the same way. I guess nobody can really decide who has done more," Burt admitted.

"Exactly," I said. "No one can ever honestly assess what his own actions and his spouse's actions are worth."

Melissa said, "I haven't ever thought about it that way."

"Me neither," added Burt.

"Most spouses 'green stamp' each other, usually without even realizing it. In doing that, they tend to overestimate the value of their own actions and underestimate the value of their partner's so that, by the end of the day or end of the week, they feel like they are so far ahead in the 'look what you owe me' race that their spouses will never be able to do enough to pay them back. It is a killer of a way to conduct a relationship," I said.

"So, what is the alternative?" Melissa asked.

"To meet each other's needs as best you can without keeping score. To help each other out because it is the right thing to do instead of using what you do to manipulate something out of your spouse in return. To acknowledge that when you do something for your spouse, it was your choice to do so, and nothing is owed to you in return. To be grateful when your spouse is loving and helpful—to accept it as a gift to you. To quit thinking of a marriage as a business relationship that operates on a quid pro quo basis and start having a grace relationship where you do things for each other whether they were merited or not."

"Nothing like setting the bar a little high, Dr. Thurman," Burt joked.

"Well, a couple's reach should exceed their grasp, don't you think?" I answered. "Both of you would agree, I think, that your current way of being married sets the bar far too low, right?"

"You got that right!" Melissa agreed.

Please keep in mind that I am not suggesting that we should quit *wanting* or *desiring* things from our spouses. I *want* my wife to be loving and faithful, to help around the house, to keep a balanced checkbook, and so on. I'm just suggesting that she doesn't *owe* me those things, even if I do those things for her. The minute I start demanding these things from her as if they were my marital "birthright," I am allowing the "you owe me" lie to ruin our marriage. And ruin our marriage it will.

You are owed absolutely nothing for all you do in your marriage. The "payment" for what you do for your spouse is getting to do it! The reward is in the giving, not what your partner does in response. If your spouse appreciates your actions and returns the favor by doing something loving, that is simply the icing on top of the cake.

"I Shouldn't Have to Change Who I Am to Make Our Marriage Better."

When I was a teenager, a song I liked had a line in it that went, "I am what I am and that's all I ever will be." I hear couples say this very thing in defending why they can't (really, won't) change. "I've always been this way and can't do anything about it. If you really loved me, you would just accept me for what I am and not try to change me."

What malarkey! *Of course,* we need to make changes in who we are to strengthen our marriages. We don't enter marriage "okay" so that we should be content to stay who we are. The issue isn't, "Should I change to make my marriage better?" It is, "*What* should I change to make my marriage better?" When we marry, all of us have defects that need to be corrected. Pulling off an intimate marriage requires that we work on our weaknesses, not wrap ourselves in the "accept me as I am" flag and hope our partners salute.

Let me give you an example that is too close to home. My wife, Holly, is better at emotional intimacy than I am. I, on the other hand, tend to be more analytical and emotionally distant. During the early years of our marriage, I often felt uncomfortable when Holly wanted to be emotionally close—say, take time to share our deeper feelings. I just didn't feel like doing it. My reluctance was very frustrating for her, understandably so. To be honest, I wished at times that she would just accept me as I was and not expect any more emotional intimacy than I wanted to offer.

I remember one specific instance when all Holly wanted was to sit down and talk about how we were both feeling about things going on in our lives at the time. At that moment, all I wanted was to do some work and be left alone. I didn't feel like relating emotionally. But in my gut, I knew that what Holly wanted was appropriate and that I needed to change. I needed to be open to her, not run the opposite direction. It hasn't been easy, but I'm trying to break through my fears of intimacy and make some needed changes. I may or may not ever be as comfortable with emotional intimacy as Holly is, but her influence is making me a better person. However uncomfortable it has been, I'm glad she pushed me to be more than I was when we first married.

"One flesh"—that's what Genesis calls a married couple.[4] Becoming one flesh is impossible if one or both spouses refuse to change. Please don't misread me here. I'm all for individuality, and I don't condone blind conformity to whatever a marriage partner wants just to keep him or her happy. But when something about who we are hinders intimacy, it's best to change. When both spouses have that kind of mentality, everyone wins because both become more complete—all while becoming "one."

"My Spouse Should Be Like Me."

This lie is a second cousin of the previous lie. The belief here is that your way of being a human being is the "best" and that your spouse must think, feel, and act like you in order to be loved or accepted. People who fall into this lie tend to see the world in black/white, right/wrong, all/nothing terms. They often arrogantly assume that because they think, feel, or act a certain way, their spouses are wrong if they don't think, feel, or act the very same way. To put it bluntly, these people want more of a clone than a partner.

Carol and Joe, our original couple, believed this lie, and it was one of the many destructive misconceptions causing their marital problems. Both felt that their own personal view on any issue was the best, smartest, wisest, and most accurate, and when they clashed, they clashed in a big way. For instance, one summer Carol "knew" that a vacation to the beach would be best and had all the logical reasons to back it up. At the very same time, Joe "knew" that a vacation to the mountains was the best choice, and he had just as many good reasons. Unwilling to back off their separate opinions, they spent countless hours arguing about what to do. Finally, they became so angry with each other, they didn't go on a vacation at all.

The truth of the matter is that if each of us was married to someone who thought, felt, and acted exactly as we did, life would be boring. We are unique. It's good that we are all different, even if that leads to tension or conflict. Conflict related to the fact that we think, feel, and act differently can lead us to be more well-rounded, complete people, something we would have missed otherwise. The Bible is right when it says that is not good for people to be alone, but it is also not good for people to be exactly the same. Variety is the spice of life!

Growthwork

So far, we have covered two levels of the A-B-C model. We have identified "A" as the "event" level where things happen to us. We have also identified "C" as the "response" level of the model where we react to events physiologically, emotionally, and behaviorally. Unfortunately, far too many of us stop with these two levels of the model figured out and make a fatal mistake.

The mistake we make, and it is a deadlier one than most of us realize, is to fall into "A causes C" thinking. With "A causes C" thinking, we blame our reactions at "C" on the event at "A" that occurred. In other words, we blame our feelings and actions on some external event as the cause. Here are some examples of "A causes C" thinking:

- "That guy riding my bumper ('A') is making me mad ('C')."

- "What my supervisor said in the meeting today ('A') hurt my feelings ('C')."

- "Flunking that exam ('A') depressed me ('C')."

- "You kids ('A') are driving me crazy ('C')."

- "Well, I wouldn't have thrown the dish at you ('C') if you hadn't thrown the cup at me ('A')."

As we have discussed earlier, no one can "make" you feel a given emotion or make you act the way you do. That is a critically important truth for you to take with you from this book. Events ("A") do not cause reactions ("C"), period!

Now, let me remind you that I am *not* saying you shouldn't feel angry or sad or hurt or depressed about things. These can be very appropriate emotional reactions to certain events. What I am saying is that you cannot afford to blame your emotional reactions on external events if you want to have emotional health, develop good relationships with others, and be mature spiritually. "A causes C" thinking and those three are like water and oil—they don't mix and never will.

Here is your assignment for the week. I want you to keep a record in your journal of all the times you fall into "A causes C" thinking. Anytime you find yourself blaming your feelings or actions on some person or situation, write it down. Put it in your journal any way you choose, but you might want to make each entry in sentence form: "The cleaners didn't have my shirts ready as they promised ('A'), and that really hacked me off ('C')," or "The Longhorns winning last Saturday ('A') made me happy ('C')," or "A guy cutting me off in traffic today ('A') made me so upset that I had to honk my horn at him ('C')."

The purpose of this assignment is to help you realize how often you tend to blame external events for what you feel and how you act. Believing that "A causes C" is one of the most destructive lies of all because it puts you in the helpless victim role. If you think an event made you feel and act a certain way, the event now has the power to control you. You are no longer in control of your emotions or behavior; circumstances are. That is no way to live.

The more aware of "A causes C" thinking you become, the better chance you have of moving from victim to victor. We live in a world full of victims who always seem to be able to blame their reactions on someone or something. If we ever hope to be emotionally healthy, intimate with others, and spiritually mature, this blaming has to stop. Begin that process now by monitoring "A causes C" thinking for a week. Be prepared to be humbled. You do it more than you realize!

5

■

DISTORTION LIES

> *The less clearly we see the reality of the world—the more our minds are*
> *befuddled by falsehood, misperceptions, and illusions—the less able we will*
> *be to determine correct courses of action and make wise decisions.*
> —M. Scott Peck[1]

Do you ever blow up over small things?

Do you take things too personally?

Do you tend to use words such as *always* and *never*?

Do you sometimes miss the "big picture" because you focus too much on specifics?

Do you tend to predict the future from the past?

Do you allow your feelings to be more important than the facts?

Be honest. How did you answer each question? Each one reflects a distorted way of thinking that will wreck your emotional health, your relationships, even your faith. When we distort reality, we are, in effect, lying to ourselves. We have turned reality into something it isn't. Like looking at something in one of those warped mirrors at a carnival, distorted thinking turns reality into something it isn't.

The truth of the matter is that all of us distort reality in various ways. Borrowing from the work of psychiatrist David Burns, I want to explore six of the most self-destructive ways we distort reality.[2] Let me forewarn you—you do all six, you do them a lot more than you realize, and you are paying a huge price for doing so. On that encouraging note, let's take a look into these six misshapen "mirrors" and see how they cause us to distort the truth.

"Magnification: Making a Mountain Out of a Molehill"

Jill was dragging by the time she reached the door of her home. It had been a very, very long day. Almost nothing had gone right at work. As she opened the

...om the garage, she glanced into the den. The place was still a wreck her son's video-watching party the night before.

"This place is a mess!" she said at the top of her voice.

At that inopportune moment, her son walked in the door.

Jill exploded. "You promised! You promised me this morning you'd clean everything up before you went to school! This is all I need to see after a day like today! You're grounded for a month!" And then leaving her son standing speechless, she stomped off to the bedroom, slamming the door behind her.

Jill is suffering from distorted thinking called *magnification*. In this way of thinking, an event is made much bigger than it really is. By reacting the way she did to the mess left by her son, she made a mountain out of a molehill. And when she did, she was lying to herself. By lying to herself, Jill turned up the volume on her emotions.

Odds are, you've been through a scene like this. The tendency to magnify is one of the more common ways we distort reality. We often take small, 5¢ events and react to them as if they were huge, $500 events. (The flip side of magnification, taking an event and minimizing it, is equally unhealthy.) But the emotions don't fit the situation. The more we magnify, the more emotional we get. The more emotional we get, the more likely we are to act badly.

I, for example, have a tough time keeping my cool in traffic. Someone's failure to give a turn signal, as small as that is, can yank my chain. Given that it is impossible to go out on the highway without seeing someone doing something wrong, my tendency to magnify can make driving a frustrating and anger-provoking experience. Then on top of overreacting, I mentally point my finger at the offending motorist as if he is the real culprit for the feelings I am having ("A causes C" thinking). I do all this rather than admit my tendency to magnify was the real reason I'm so downright irritated. Ugh!

As our lives unfold, we will experience thousands of 5¢ irritations (for example, a person with twelve items in the ten-item checkout line), hundreds of $250 events (for example, not getting a well-deserved raise), and more than a few $500 tragedies (for example, the death of a loved one). Total up these events, and you get a very difficult life. A person who makes each event even bigger mentally causes his life to be almost unbearable. No one is built to cope with a life that feels that big all the time.

How should Jill have handled that "one too many straws on the camel's back" mess her son left in the den? She needed to (1) see that she was making a big deal out of something relatively minor; (2) count to ten (count to one hundred if you are *really* angry); and (3) assert herself with her son to get him to clean up. When you feel like wringing someone's neck, recognizing you are making a mountain out of a molehill is easier said than done. Yet if you hope to achieve mental health and have reasonably healthy relationships with others, you have to learn to see molehills as molehills and mountains as mountains.

"Personalization: Taking Everything Personally"

"He comes home late every night from work," Cindy was saying in one of our sessions. She and her husband, Paul, were seeing me for marriage counseling.

"Why do you think he does this?" I asked her.

"It's obvious," she said, folding her arms. "He comes home late because he doesn't have the least bit of respect for me. He doesn't want to be with me. He doesn't love me anymore."

Cindy's reaction to Paul's lateness is a style of distorted thinking called *personalization*. In this style of thinking, a person overestimates the extent to which an event is related to him.

We all do it, don't we? Whether the event is someone looking at us "funny" or cutting us off in midsentence or forgetting an appointment with us, we often interpret the action as a reflection of us or about us in some way.

Couples tend to personalize quite a bit. If the husband leaves his dirty socks in the middle of the bedroom floor, criticizes too much, or never wants to talk, the wife takes it personally. If the wife is always with her girlfriends, spends too much money, or doesn't wear the perfume he bought her, the husband takes it personally. Like little kids, we think egocentrically (self-centeredly) as if everything that happens around us is about us.

I'm not suggesting that we should react with indifference to what people do or that their behavior is unrelated to how they feel about us. I'm only suggesting that our tendency to personalize their actions makes us overreact, which only makes the situation worse. You can't handle things well when you take them personally. Not only is the original problem still there, but unnecessary resentment and bitterness are added to the mix.

Cindy took Paul's lateness as a personal affront rather than as a statement about Paul—how overinvolved at work he is, how he runs from intimacy, how he can be insensitive to other people's feelings, and so on. By taking his actions personally, she ended up paying the price, becoming bitter, distraught, and unloving. I responded to her as I respond to most of my patients who personalize things.

"Cindy, could there be other reasons for his continual lateness?"

She frowned and said, "I guess it's possible, but I sure can't think of any offhand."

"In any given situation, let's assume there are at least four explanations for someone's behavior. Try to name four things that might explain Paul's lateness beyond that it has anything to do with you," I said.

She sat silent.

"Cindy, come on, give it a try," I finally said.

She made a face. "Okay. I guess he could just have a problem with being late. You know, he doesn't manage his time well. He does tend to struggle with that. But he used to be only ten or fifteen minutes late, not an hour or more."

"Okay," I said. "That's one."

"I suppose he could be caught up in wanting to impress his boss."

"That's possible," I said. "He could be feeling a lot of pressure to keep his boss happy."

"Mmmm," she answered. "Maybe."

"How about a third one?"

"He doesn't know how to say no," she said, teeth clenched. "You know, somebody comes by to ask him an important question or talk about a problem right before he is ready to leave, and he doesn't feel comfortable telling the person he needs to go."

"That could very well be true," I said. "And the fourth?"

She looked me in the eye. "He doesn't want to be home with me," she said defiantly.

"C'mon, a fourth reason that has nothing to do with you. Does he have trouble with intimacy?" I asked.

"Well, yes, he does. He rarely talks about his feelings. I always have to pull everything out of him."

"His lateness could be about that. Intimacy could be scary for him. He may feel safer at work where he's more in control. So he stays there later and later."

She pursed her lips, then nodded. "Maybe. But I still think he doesn't want to be home with me."

"That can be a self-fulfilling prophecy, you know," I said.

"What do you mean?" she asked.

"If you react badly to his lateness because you are taking it personally, he may begin to think of you and home in the very way you don't want him to. And he might stay at work even longer."

Cindy didn't reply, but it was obvious from her face that she understood the truth of what I said. Of all the explanations for Paul's lateness, she had chosen the only one that had to do with her personally. The possibility that his lateness had nothing to do with her had never really crossed her mind.

"Wait a minute!" you may be saying. "Paul's lateness is rude and insensitive to Cindy's feelings. She *should* be mad at him for neglecting her!"

Of course, there is some truth to that. But take a minute to think this through. If Cindy takes Paul's lateness personally, she will react too strongly and probably browbeat him in order to get him to change. With her reacting that way, do you think Paul will want to change? If he does change just to get her off his back, do you think the changes will last?

In my experience, situations such as Cindy and Paul's don't get resolved when one or both people take the other's actions personally. Taking something personally makes you resentful toward it, resentful people do mean things, and mean actions don't lead to intimacy.

Instead of personalizing the things that happen to us, then, we need to stop and ask a very important question: *Is what the other person did a reflection of me or the other person?* Etch the answer on your brain: *people's actions are always a reflection of who they are.* When someone treats you badly (or nicely), that is a statement about who he is as a human being, not a statement about you. We have to learn to see things this way if we hope to get through life reasonably sane.

If someone intentionally rides my bumper in traffic, I can think, *He doesn't respect me and is trying to ruin my day!* or I can think, *He has little respect for other drivers, and I happen to be the person he is disrespecting at the moment.* This may sound like splitting hairs, but these two views create totally different emotional responses. The first way of thinking makes what he is doing a slap in *my* face. The second is an objective observation about the other driver, and the emotional response to that bit of truth is more appropriate.

It reminds me of a humorous quote I like. *At age twenty, we worry about what others think of us. At forty, we don't care what they think of us. At sixty, we discover they haven't been thinking about us at all.* People act the way they do because of who they are, not because of who we are. We can't afford to lose sight of that fact, given that people will sometimes treat us badly.

The next time someone swerves in front of you on the highway or doesn't return your phone call or leaves the newspaper all over the couch, try to remind yourself that what he did is not a reflection of you but a reflection of him. Let it be.

"Polarization: Making Everything Black or White"

"Everything is so black and white to you! You hardly ever see any shade of gray!"

Have you ever had this criticism thrown your way? If so, you are being accused of a style of distorted thinking called *polarization*. The polarizer takes reality and cuts it into extremes of black and white (all or nothing, great or awful, never or always). Whatever the shade of gray may be in a given situation, the polarizer has a hard time seeing it.

One of the most serious forms of polarized thinking is scum/saint thinking. More than a few of my clients view themselves morally as either completely scummy or completely saintly, or they flip back and forth between the two extremes. Along these lines, I once read an interview with actor Daniel J. Travanti, best known for his portrayal of Captain Furillo on the television show *Hill Street Blues*. When asked about his struggle as a young actor with alcoholism, he described himself as having been an "egomaniac with strong feelings of inferiority." Basically, he was saying that he flipped back and forth between black/white extremes—feeling like a scum or feeling like a saint. His alcoholism may have been, in part, a way to numb the pain of such radical highs and lows.

Now don't get me wrong. We *do* scummy things, and we *do* saintly things. But no one *is* a scum or a saint. No one on this planet is as awful as he could be, and no one is as good as he could be. There is not one perfectly saintly person or one perfectly scummy person on earth. To label ourselves as scum or saint or to stick either label on others is to miss seeing the whole person. When aimed inward, the label of scum breeds self-condemnation and depression, while the label of saint breeds arrogance and pride.

The saints are an interesting group. I have had hundreds of people in my office who never in their wildest dreams had thought they would do the things they did. The truth about us as humans is that we are capable of doing almost anything. The saints do not—cannot—believe this truth. When they "fall," they are in shock about the impossibility of their actions. Usually, it takes a tremendous amount of work to help such people see the arrogance behind their assumption that they were somehow too saintly to do such things.

Though she'd never admit it, Sally saw herself as a saint. All her life she'd played the role of the "good girl." She grew up in the church and was taught a strong value system, so she became a highly moralistic adult and an avid churchgoer. Two years ago, if you'd asked Sally whether she would ever commit adultery, she would have either laughed or sniffed indignantly. Yet that is exactly what she did. She had been friends with a man at her office for years. One night Sally and this man were still working after everyone else had left. And the unthinkable happened.

"How could I have done this? How could I let this happen?" cried Sally in one of our first sessions. How could she be such a scum? That was what she wanted to ask. How could she, of all people, commit such an act?

"I feel so ashamed. I've come this close to suicide!" she said, holding her thumb and forefinger a quarter of an inch apart. "How could it have happened?"

"You didn't think you would ever do something like this," I observed.

"Not in a million years," she cried.

"Why not?" I asked.

"What do you mean?" she asked, sounding hurt.

"Why did you think that you would never do something like this?"

"Well," she stammered, "it's just not something that I thought I could ever do. I guess I thought I was a more moral person than that. I'm ashamed to say it, but I thought only immoral people had affairs."

"You thought you were too good to have an affair," I suggested.

"I don't like the sound of that. I don't like to admit that I think I'm better than others, but I guess I do," she confessed.

"We all have blind spots—things about ourselves we don't see that are, nevertheless, true," I observed. "You thought you were incapable of certain wrongs, didn't take an honest look at the possibility, and got blindsided."

"Yes, but me of all people. I just don't think I can live with what I have done."

"Me of all people" is the exact thinking that helped trip her up—a good example of "pride goeth before destruction." Why? Have you ever noticed that if you know you're weak in a certain area, you're more careful about it? For instance, if know you are a weak swimmer, you wear a life vest or are more careful in the water, right? Often, those who drown are the ones who overestimate their ability to swim, not underestimate it.

Perhaps a better analogy would be your car's blind spot—a point where the side view and rearview mirrors miss what's coming behind you. If you know your car has a blind spot, you don't trust the mirrors as much. You turn your head to see what's coming. Failure to do so can have serious consequences. We, like Sally, have blind spots. We fool ourselves into thinking that we are somehow better or worse than we are, and we end up having a major crash of some kind.

The pride involved in thinking too highly (or even too lowly) of yourself can set the stage for committing immoral acts you never thought you would because you didn't watch out for your blind spot. You're saying you don't have one. That's exactly what happened to Sally. Going all the way back to her unloving father, she had needs for male attention and affection that were never met. She married a man much like her father, and her needs continued to go unmet. She filled this void with work, kids, home decorating, and volunteer activities. In a moment she didn't see coming, she tried to get her needs met in an immoral way—with a man whose company she'd enjoyed for years. Her neediness overwhelmed her strict moral sense. And like a car in her blind spot, it overtook her because she didn't turn to look.

The challenge here is to be humble enough to see the shade of a situation properly, reading black as black, white as white, and the in between as whatever shade of gray it is. There are definitely times to think about things in all-or-nothing, never-always, great-awful, black-white terms, but it is also true that they are infrequent. We need to think about many people and situations in terms of grayer shades of reality where words such as *sometimes*, *frequently*, *often*, *occasionally*, and *good* are more honest and appropriate.

Are you a great parent? I doubt it. Are you an awful parent? I doubt it. Are you a horrible tennis player? I doubt it. Are you an awesome tennis player? I doubt it. Do you always mess things up? I doubt it. Do you never mess things up? I doubt it. Are you a scum? I doubt it. Are you a saint? I doubt it. Are you some shade of gray related to these various areas of life? I don't doubt it.

Splitting hairs? Word games? Semantics? I don't think so. Just ask yourself if there is any difference for you emotionally between someone telling you that "you never do anything right" and telling you that "you sometimes mess things up." It's not a word game anymore, is it?

"Selective Abstraction: Missing the Forest for the Trees"

An offshoot of the polarization lie is one called *selective abstraction*—the "can't see the forest for the trees" way of distorting reality. We focus so much of our attention on a small part of something that we can't see the bigger picture. For instance, have you said something fairly goofy in a crowd at a party and spent the rest of the night worrying about your remark? Now, let's assume you handled the better part of the evening with great social grace and skill. But if you are a selective abstracter, all you focus on or think about is your goofy statement.

Rick, a friend of mine, had just gotten a nice promotion. The promotion, though, involved added pressure he wasn't sure he could handle. One day I ran into him, and I could tell he was upset.

"I blew it! I know I'll lose this job," he exclaimed. "You should have seen it. There I was, making a presentation in front of my boss, and I knocked the overhead projector over. It made a noise you wouldn't believe. Broke the dang thing, so we had to stop the meeting for a few minutes and find another one. What an absolute idiot I am. Everyone got really quiet, and I stood there feeling like a complete imbecile! I have never been so humiliated in my life."

Rick went on like that for another few minutes. Finally, I said, "Rick, did anything *good* happen?"

"If you call laughing 'good.' That's what my boss did. He told me after the meeting that I had done a good job on the presentation and not to worry about breaking the overhead, but I'm sure that he thinks I'm a total loser and that he made a mistake in promoting me."

"Rick, it sounds like everything worked out fine. You might even have humanized the whole meeting."

"What? How? It was awful!"

In spite of all that had gone right, Rick could focus only on the one thing that had gone wrong. I helped him see that he was "missing the forest for the trees" in paying attention to the one thing that went wrong and what it was doing to him emotionally. Rick somewhat resisted my efforts, but he did come to see that knocking the overhead over was the only "dead tree" during his presentation and that the "forest" looked pretty good.

As a university professor, I used to teach an introductory psychology class with an enrollment of about one hundred students. During my lectures, I would often scan the auditorium and notice the students who were not listening to my lecture. Out of the hundred students in front of me, only five or so were not paying attention, yet I would often catch myself focusing on those five to the exclusion of the ninety-five who were paying attention. I'd end up feeling anxious and depressed about the class and myself as a professor. My own "forest for the trees" problem made me feel bad about something that was, overall, quite positive.

Examples of selective abstraction in everyday life are fairly common. A person works hard all day but remembers only what he did wrong. A homemaker exerts a tremendous amount of effort to clean up her home, yet when the day is over, she sees only the things she didn't do. A tennis player hits hundreds of good shots during a match but thinks only about the ones he missed. A parent ignores a child when he is behaving and pays attention only to his misbehavior. "Missing the forest for the trees" happens all the time.

No matter how many bad things may be going on in your life, positives are in there somewhere. You may have to work pretty hard to see them, but they are there. If we are to avoid becoming depressed and hopeless about life, we have to make sure that we don't lose sight of the good things just because there are bad things. If we focus on every negative that happens, it is no wonder we become emotionally troubled. Although the statement may sound trite, even the darkest cloud has a silver lining in it.

"Overgeneralization: History Always Repeats Itself"

Larry was coming to see me for his weight problem. A compulsive eater, he would eat when he felt sad or lonely or hurt, which led to despair, which led to more eating, which led to being overweight. A vicious cycle!

"I'm never going to be able to stop this," he moaned. "I've always been fat, and I'll always be fat. Let's face it."

Larry's prediction that he will "always be fat" is a style of distorted thinking called *overgeneralization*. In this distortion, any event, such as failing an exam or fighting with a spouse, leads to the lie that the future will inescapably hold more of the same. History, supposedly, *always* repeats itself.

Many of my clients tend to overgeneralize about their mental health. They worry that they will never get better, some going that extra fatal step and becoming sure of it. When they reach this decision, they typically leave my office and go the route of the self-fulfilling prophecy by keeping up the same self-defeating styles of thinking and acting that made them troubled in the first place.

Making negative predictions about the future has a hidden agenda underneath it. If I predict a negative future, I don't have to do all the hard work it would take to make things better. For example, let's say I'm a college student and I make an F on my first exam in Biology 301. Let's also say I then predict that I will make Fs on all the future Biology 301 exams. It then becomes more likely that I will drop the class. The hidden agenda of predicting Fs on all my future exams in Biology 301 is that this prediction allows me to get out of all the hard work it would have taken to do better on the next exam.

Overgeneralizing is a common style of thinking for many married couples. "We have never gotten along, and we will never get along," couples conclude, and they fall back into the same old destructive patterns of interacting with each other. Doing that ensures they will never get along with each other. When this prophecy fulfills itself, the couples say, "See, I knew we would never get along!" It's almost as if they'd rather be right about their prophecy and stay miserable than wrong about it and have a good marriage. The hidden agenda is that they do not have to do any of the hard work that it takes to have a good marriage.

"Larry," I said to my overweight client, "let me ask you something. In the last few years, have you had to learn a new skill?"

"What do you mean? Like learning that stupid computer at work? I thought it would kill me," he said, rolling his eyes. "I would never have even started trying to learn how to operate that crazy thing if my job hadn't been on the line. Took me forever."

"Okay," I said. "Did you think before you started that you'd never be able to work the computer?"

"Are you kidding? I didn't even know how to type!" he exclaimed, throwing up his hands. "I knew I was going to be demoted."

"When you first tried to learn it, did you think you'd never make it?" I asked.

"I thought I'd *never* get it," Larry groaned. "The first month was a killer. I thought of giving up a thousand times and packing it in."

"You thought you'd never handle it. You thought you'd always be a computer illiterate. You thought it so much that the task seemed to grow into a mountain. Every day you just knew you'd fail, but every day you kept trying, right?"

"Well, yeah, that's what happened," Larry agreed.

"And then what happened?" I asked.

He shrugged. "Gradually, I began to get it. I started understanding more, and now I handle computers just fine."

"You broke through that negative prediction, didn't you?" I said.

Larry, a bit surprised, smiled and answered, "Yeah, I guess I did." Then as if a light bulb went on in his head, he looked sideways at me and said, "And now you mean I can break through this one too?"

"You did it once, didn't you?" I pointed out as I watched Larry getting used to the idea.

Although he continued off and on to tell me his eating problem was different, Larry and I knew that his argument was hollow. He couldn't ignore the fact that he'd overcome a supposedly impossible problem once, and he knew that meant he could defeat others. After a few weeks, he began doing better with his overeating.

The simple truth Larry experienced was that the cards we are dealt (or deal ourselves) don't have to be the cards we end up with. That F on the first exam doesn't have to become the final grade in the course. That bad start with a coworker doesn't have to turn into a bad relationship. The loneliness we feel now doesn't have to turn into a lonely life. History doesn't have to repeat itself. The future can be better if we really want it to be. We *can* change.

"Emotional Reasoning: Feelings Equal Facts"

"I'm worthless," Angela said to me during one of our sessions together. In her late thirties, Angela had gotten a divorce ten years ago and was now considering remarriage. "I know I'll mess up this new marriage, like everything else I do. I tell you I'm worthless."

"Prove it," I blurted out, much to her surprise.

"How far back do you want me to go?" she said quickly. "In high school, I lied to my best friend about going out with her boyfriend. I did that a lot. In college, I did drugs. And I not only kept lying about going out with other people's boyfriends, but I slept with most of them. Then I flunked out of college. Then I got married to this guy I didn't love just because he had money, and when I got tired of him, I started running around with other men until he divorced me. Shall I go on?"

"All you've given me so far is proof that you have done a lot of wrong things. I want proof that *you're* worthless. Does doing wrong things make people worthless?"

"Well, no, not when you put it that way," she said, but I could see that she was not completely convinced.

"Then why do you think what you've done makes you worthless?" I asked.

A little of the defiance went out of her manner. "I guess because I feel worthless. I did some pretty worthless things. You gotta admit that," she said.

Angela feels worthless; therefore, she is worthless. That's what she said to me, and in her mind, that settled the matter. Her situation is a perfect example of *emotional reasoning*. It is a distortion that says, "Because I feel something to be true, it must be true." Emotional reasoning makes feelings equal to, if not superior to, facts.

Feelings, though, are just feelings. They change quite a bit, they are hard to predict, and they often spring from irrational and unrealistic ways of thinking. Our feelings can actually be completely at odds with the facts. In our culture, though, we *worship* feelings. How many pop psychology books teach that "you can trust your feelings" and "your feelings are your best guide"? What nonsense.

What would your life be like if you did nothing but follow your feelings? If you're like me, you'd buy everything in sight, shoot people for cutting in front of you on the highway, and run off to the Bahamas with someone twenty years younger. A feeling-based life would be, at best, a chaotic mess.

Don't get me wrong. I am not suggesting that we should ignore our feelings. We are feeling human beings, and we need to take our feelings into consideration when we are dealing with things. But we can't afford to let our feelings run the show. The main consideration needs to be the facts.

Sometimes couples considering marriage come to my office and trigger my concern that they are making their decision on the basis of feelings alone. They declare, "We love each other so much! We can't imagine having any problems!" I often am tempted to say, "Well, imagine it because it will happen. Once the glow dims, you'll wish you hadn't let your feelings dictate your decision."

In the premarital counseling I do, we spend time looking at the cold, hard facts: Do you communicate well? Do you resolve conflict properly? Do you have interests in common? Are you good at meeting each other's emotional needs? Has becoming a couple made your spiritual lives stronger? The facts that emerge from the answers to these questions need to guide a couple's decision about whether or not to marry, not just how much they feel "in love" with each other.

Unfortunately, when people turn their feelings into facts, they become much harder to help. Angela, for example, had turned her feelings of worthlessness into fact, so she had locked herself into a position that made helping her almost impossible. After all, who can argue with "facts"? All the immoral things she had done led her to feel worthless, so she decided she was. I tried to approach her problem from that perception.

"Angela, have you ever had a feeling about something that proved to be wrong?" I asked.

"What do you mean?" she answered.

"Well, a friend of mine once lent me a book. Months later he asked me if I had finished it. I was convinced I had already given it back to him. He said I hadn't, yet I *felt* very strongly that I had. Turns out, I had the book after all. I found it under the passenger seat of my car. I was certain I had given it back to him, but I was dead wrong."

"I see what you mean. Well, yes," she admitted, "I have done that before."

"Give me an example," I asked.

"Well, one time in high school I felt certain that a guy I was attracted to wasn't at all interested in me. Ten years after graduating, our senior class had a reunion. He was there, and we got to talking about the 'good old days.' I was a little embarrassed, but I just had to ask him about whether or not he was at all interested in me during high school. Turns out he was very interested but just didn't have the nerve to let me know. I misread him completely."

"So, you felt something pretty strongly that didn't turn out to have any truth to it?"

"Yes, that's right," she admitted. She sat there in silence for a short time, and I could tell the wheels were turning in her head. "I think I see where you're going with this," she added.

"Tell me what you're thinking."

"You are trying to get me to see that just because I feel a certain way about something doesn't mean I'm right. Sometimes my feelings can be off base about things, right?" she stated as much as asked.

"You got it. Your feelings seem to be not only running your life but also ruining your life. You felt like lying to friends of yours about whether or not you were dating their boyfriends, so you did. You felt like sleeping with these guys, so you did. You felt like doing drugs, so you did. You felt like marrying your ex-husband because he had money, so you did. You felt like that guy in high school wasn't interested in you, so in your mind, he wasn't. You feel worthless, so you are. See any pattern?" I asked.

With her eyes beginning to fill with tears, Angela replied, "It looks like I have spent my whole life letting my feelings dictate everything, and it has cost me friendships, a marriage, and my self-respect. Dr. Thurman, I don't want to live that way anymore. I'm tired of it all."

Reason without passion is boring; passion without reason is scary. In living out our lives, we must have both. We must reason things out with the facts but also allow ourselves to have strong feelings. But the bottom line is this: *if the facts of a situation are at odds with how we feel about it, our feelings need to change.*

Feeling something to be true doesn't make it true. We cannot afford to let our feelings run the show! Pop psychology be darned—our feelings are not our best guide. The truth is our best guide.

Growthwork

So far, you have been asked to do three things with the A-B-C model. First, you were asked to keep track of the "trigger events" at "A" for a week and assess their relative "value" as well as judge who was responsible for their occurrence. Second, you were asked to monitor your reactions at "C" for a week, paying special attention to any emotions and behavior that occurred fairly often. Finally, you were asked to note any "A causes C" reactions where you blamed your feelings and behavior on external events.

You are now ready to move on to the most important part of the model, "B." In the "B" part of the A-B-C model, your "self-talk" occurs; that is, what you think comes into play here. Self-talk, very simply, is "private mental dialogue" where you think about (perceive, judge, evaluate, analyze) an event that has taken place at "A." Your self-talk, as we discussed in Chapter 1, consists of all the "tapes" that play in your mind related to the things that happen to you.

The A-B-C model says that first, some kind of event ("A") takes place (your child spills grape juice on your new carpet). Then, your self-talk ("B") kicks into gear, and you mentally analyze the situation (*I told him not to bring his drink into the family room. He never listens to me. Now my carpet is ruined!*). Finally, you react ("C") physiologically (increased heart rate, shallow breathing), emotionally (frustration, anger), and behaviorally (yell at your child, spank him).

The A-B-C model says that events ("A") do not cause your reactions ("C"); your self-talk ("B") does. In other words, how you think about an event—not the event itself—determines how you react to it. The Greek philosopher Epictetus, writing in the first century, put it this way: "Men are disturbed not by things but by the view they take of them." That is the A-B-C model in a single sentence. "Men are disturbed" refers to "C," "not by things" refers to "A," and "but by the view they take of them" is the "B" part of our model. A modern restatement of Epictetus's statement is, "People become upset not because of the events that happen to them but because of how they think about those events."

Before I give you your next assignment, I want you to stop for just a minute and ask yourself if you believe what Epictetus wrote almost two thousand years ago. Do you really believe that how you think about something determines how you react to it, or do you still tend to believe that events can cause you to feel and act the way you do? Spend a couple of minutes chewing on that.

If the A-B-C model is correct, far more important than what happens to you is how you choose to think about it. Using our previous example, much more important than whether or not your child spilled grape juice on your new carpet is how you mentally evaluated it.

If we think about events unrealistically, our lives will be in constant turmoil. The idea of "garbage in, garbage out" comes into play here. If our self-talk is "garbage" (faulty, irrational, untruthful, distorted), then we can't help ending up with "garbage" emotionally and behaviorally (depressed, enraged, worried, addicted, phobic). Since we can't totally control what happens to us at "A" each day, our only real hope for achieving emotional health, intimate relationships, and a meaningful life is having the "right" tapes in our minds ready to go for whatever life may throw our way.

Now, to get you started down the path toward developing the "right" tapes, I want you to do the following growthwork. For one week, I want you to keep an A-B-C journal. In your journal, make as many entries as you can from your life where you break things down into the three parts of the model. Here is an example of how you could do this:

"A" (Event)	"B" (Self-Talk)	"C" (Response)
Late to work because of an accident on the highway.	*Why aren't people more careful! Now I am going to be late because some idiot wasn't watching what he was doing!*	Muscles tensed; felt angry and anxious; honked my horn and bit my fingernails.
Spouse forgot to pick up dry cleaning, left me without any clean shirts for important meeting next day.	*Why can't she ever remember stuff like this! I can't depend on her for anything! If she cared about my needs once in a blue moon, I would die of a heart attack!*	Breathing got shallow; became irritated and frustrated; slammed my briefcase down and stomped off.
Neighbor complimented me on how nice my yard looks.	*That was nice of her to say that. All the hard work I have been doing is paying off!*	Physically relaxed; felt proud and happy; patted myself on the back.
Friends couldn't meet me for lunch as we had planned.	*I was really looking forward to seeing them. Well, maybe next time.*	No noticeable physiological response; felt disappointed; got lunch at a fast-food place.

The purpose of this assignment is to get you to use all three parts of the model and become more aware of how they are connected. Specifically, I want you to become more conscious of the fact that what you tell yourself at "B" plays a significant role in how you react at "C." As you do your assignment, pay special attention to the events that you become upset over or feel that you mishandled. These are the scenarios where your tapes are most likely to be faulty, something we will work on in future chapters.

6

■

RELIGIOUS LIES

Our minds are stuck in a rut, a pattern of thinking that is antagonistic to the will of God. Successful Christian living depends on getting out of that rut and establishing another one that is characterized by biblical values and ways of thinking.
—Doug Moo[1]

Diane is an "average" Christian. When she was a child, her parents took her to church every time the doors were open. She accepted the "do's and don'ts" of Christianity, learning her Bible lessons well. As she grew older, though, she found church less uplifting, more like a duty. Sometimes she even wondered if she was really saved. When she came to me, she wanted to talk about God.

"God feels pretty far away," she said during our first session.

"Tell me more," I said.

"Well," she said with a frown, "I don't feel very close to Him or that He really loves me."

"Have you ever?" I inquired.

"When I was a little kid, maybe. As I have gotten older, less so. I know I don't always live my life the way that I should, the way that He wants me to. I'm sure that's a large part of it. But His love for me doesn't seem as real anymore," Diane admitted.

"Sounds like there is a connection between how you are living your life and how close you feel to God."

"Well, yes, I guess so," she said. "I know that when I do things right, I feel closer to Him and that He loves me more."

"How do you feel when you aren't living right? Do you feel that He hates you?"

Diane didn't answer for a moment, then she mumbled, "Hate is probably too strong for it. But, yes, I do feel He loves me a lot less. When I feel that, I run from Him, I guess."

I looked at her a bit quizzically.

Diane knew she'd have to explain, but she looked as if she didn't really want to. Finally, she said, "I mean, I run by not going to church, not reading my Bible, not praying. I avoid being around all my Christian friends, especially the gung-ho ones."

"You try to hide from God—is that it?" I said.

"Yes," she admitted.

I thought a second, then asked, "Do you feel any better when you do that?"

"No, not really. In fact, I end up feeling worse."

I paused. She looked uncomfortable. "Diane, has being a Christian ever felt good?"

She looked surprised for a second. Then with a pained look on her face, she answered, "No, not really. Many times I find myself wishing I had never become a Christian. If anything, my life seems more unhappy and troubled since I became one."

Diane is suffering from one of the most resilient types of lies we tell ourselves— a religious lie. Somewhere along the way, she'd been taught a destructive view of God and Christianity, and it had stayed around to haunt her to the point of making her wish God had never become part of her life. The sad thing is, her experience is too common. Too many Christians end up holding unbiblical beliefs that ruin their spiritual lives.

Why are religious lies perhaps the toughest of all lies to let go of? First, like most lies, they are usually taught to us when we are quite young. We accept more readily anything that we are told early in life, and letting go of it later in life is more difficult. Second, these lies are taught to us by people we trust, so we don't typically feel much freedom to doubt them. If you can't trust what your parents, pastor, or Sunday school teachers say about God, who can you trust? Finally, these lies are taught to us as what "God says," and who has the nerve to question something if God said it? Not many of us are willing to dis- agree with God.

Whatever factors make religious lies hard to let go of, we end up in a classic catch-22 because of them. If we dispute these lies, we fly in the face of things "God said," which we learned from people we trusted and we have believed for years. If we continue to believe these lies, our spiritual lives die. Either way, we lose.

Religious lies make us spiritually ill. Without spiritual health, none of us can be whole. Whether it feels good to do so or not, we have to overcome these lies in order to have a healthy faith. The first step, as always, is to see these lies for what they are, so let's look at the most common religious lies people believe.

"God's Love Must Be Earned."

"Diane," I said, "why do you think you've never found your faith in God to be a source of comfort or joy?"

"Would you if you always felt you were trying to measure up and never making it?" she challenged me.

"No, I wouldn't. You know, what you are describing is something a lot of Christians seem to struggle with, and it stems from their view of God. How do you view God?"

"I see God as a harsh judge with all these rules who loves to punish people when they break them," she shot back.

"Where do you think that view came from?"

"I guess my parents and even my preacher back home. All they seemed to focus on about God was hellfire and damnation. I think my image of God must come from that."

"Was God's *kindness* or *grace* ever mentioned?" I asked.

She laughed. "If it was, I can't remember. I just remember being very frightened about God."

"Any other images that pop into your mind?"

"Well, yes," she said. "Of me as a kid, getting punished. My father was strict. He yelled and screamed at us a lot. He showed little, if any, compassion. He'd spout the Bible at us fairly often and then proceed to verbally blast us if we messed up."

"And do you see God that same way?"

"Yes, I guess to some degree I do. Isn't that what God is like? Isn't He all about keeping us on the straight and narrow path?"

You probably see the problem in Diane's thinking. She has been conditioned to think that God is a mean-spirited Father who just loves to beat His children when they break the rules of the house. Maybe her parents, even her pastor, taught her that about God in subtle and not-so-subtle ways in their efforts to make sure she never did anything immoral, and the teaching stuck.

In our counseling sessions, Diane and I uncovered many instances when her parents withheld their love after she made mistakes, but interestingly enough, Diane could think of no specific time they overtly taught her that their love was conditional. What parent would? Perhaps she saw such an attitude in their actions, and she ended up seeing God the same way—God loves me only when I am living right.

Diane believed that her actions affected whether or not God loved her. The worse the sin, the more God hated her. And you can guess the next step. If her sins were ever bad enough and frequent enough, God would hate her intensely and forever. He would wash His hands of her, and she would be forever grounded.

When I was an undergraduate at the University of Texas, I was convinced of the very same lie. My on-again, off-again relationship with God was based on whether or not I sinned. I never felt secure in His love since hardly a "sinless" day went by. God rarely seemed close or real. Soon, my unbiblical version of religious faith led to burnout, and I backed away from God altogether. I didn't go to church; I didn't study the Bible; I didn't pray. When you believe that God's love has to be earned and that it takes being perfect to earn it, giving up altogether seems the only viable option.

About a year into my efforts to run from God, He found me in the laundry room of the dorm where I was living. I was doing my laundry one evening, and a guy I had never seen before came into the room. He asked if I would be interested in hearing a talk about God in one of the study lounges a little later that evening. I said yes more out of trying to please him and not wanting to look like a complete heathen.

The talk that night introduced me to a God I had never known before as well as people who believed in God that were different from other Christians I had grown up around. I heard about a God who can't *not* love me. I heard about a God who wants me to live a righteous life but who doesn't withhold His love when I don't. I heard about a God whose love for me wasn't so shallow that it depended on my actions in order to be there. I met some Christians I really liked and could identify with. They were different, and I wanted to be like them. Even though I had been a Christian since I was eleven, God used that evening to give me a whole new view of Himself and what it really means to follow Him. It was truly a life-changing night, one for which I will always be thankful.

Can God's love be earned?

Absolutely not.

Do many Christians feel and act as if it has to be earned?

Absolutely!

The primary challenge for the Christian battling this lie is to confront it, not with feelings, but with what the Bible says about the issue. Christians in Ephesus were obviously living this lie when Paul wrote them, "For by grace you have been saved through faith, and that not of yourselves; it is the gift of God, not of works, lest anyone should boast."[2] He wrote Timothy that God called us to a holy life—not because of anything we have done but because of "His own purpose and grace."³ And if we think God turns His back on us because we sin, we only have to look at Paul's words to the Romans about God's love: "God demonstrates His own love toward us, in that while we were still sinners, Christ died for us."⁴

Memorizing—and then meditating on—these biblical teachings that are so contradictory to the "God's love must be earned" lie is the first step toward overcoming it. The second step, I believe, is becoming involved with a community of mature Christians so that God can help you experience His love through them. Apart from intimate relationships with other committed Christians, it is doubtful that any of us will ever come to fully understand and appreciate how much God loves us. The third step to defeating this lie is noticing how often God does loving things, even when we are not living our lives properly. The job He helped us find, the illness He helped us heal from, the traffic accident He protected us from, the vacation He enabled us to take—these all have God's fingerprints on them as ways that He expresses His love for us.

One of my favorite songs as a kid attending Sunday school is pertinent here. However embarrassing it might be, I want you to sing it to yourself every day if you have to, but make sure you don't get too far from its truth: "Jesus loves me, this I know, for the Bible tells me so." God loves you unconditionally. Nothing you can do will ever change that. Set your mind on this, and don't let yourself ever think otherwise.

"God Hates the Sin and the Sinner."

A second cousin to the lie that God's love must be earned is that God not only hates sin (which He does) but also hates the sinner for committing the sin. In other words, God isn't deep enough or smart enough or wise enough to separate who we are from what we do. He equates the two.

When we buy into this lie, we make turning away from sin more difficult. Why? Because the energy it takes to turn from our sins is used up by all the self-hate we waste on ourselves. It's like an athlete being so self-condemning about the play he just messed up that there is no energy left over for doing any better the next time.

Janice struggled with this lie. She is a married mother of three and has been a Christian a long time. She and Dan had been dating for several months when she became pregnant. She felt extremely torn about what to do. Her Christian values and beliefs told her to keep the baby and marry Dan. Yet neither of them felt certain they should marry.

Janice, with Dan's urging, decided to have an abortion. Having an abortion so violated her conscience, though, she became guilt ridden and depressed. And she remained that way for years. She and Dan did finally marry and began having children. But Janice still hated herself for what she had done years earlier. She could not shake the guilt she carried from having an abortion and was convinced that God would never forgive her or love her again. On top of believing that God hated her for having an abortion, she believed that she should hate herself.

During our sessions, I found it painful to watch her struggle. She had buried so many feelings, and she suffered from so much self-hatred.

"I can't forgive myself for what I did," she said on more than one occasion.

"You feel you don't deserve to get on with your life—is that right?"

She nodded, then looked down at a crumpled tissue in her hand. "I don't deserve to be let off the hook for it."

"So," I answered, "you keep punishing yourself with guilt and depression."

"Surely God doesn't want me to act as if nothing happened!" she exclaimed. "I can't believe that He wants me to forget this."

I stopped for a moment, letting her think about it. Then I asked, "Do you really think that putting a destroyed life on top of an aborted one is what He wants?"

"What do you mean?" she asked, starting to sob.

"Do you believe in a God who wants you to throw your life away because of a grievous sin you committed years ago?" I replied.

"Well, no," she cried, "but it seems too easy. Somebody has to pay for what I did, and that's *me*."

"Christ paid for what you did, Janice."

"What?"

"Christ paid for your abortion with His life. You could never do enough to make amends to God for what you did, so Christ made amends for you. Now, are you willing to let what He did be enough?"

She shook her head and continued to sob. "What I did was so wrong! I hate myself for doing it! God hates me for it!"

"Janice, God doesn't hate you. It isn't in Him to hate you. He hated what you did, but it was forgiven when you turned your life over to Christ. God wants you to be thankful for that rather than reject it. He wants you free from self-condemnation. He doesn't want you to spend your life making yourself pay for something that has already been paid for. Are you willing to accept that?" I pressed.

She turned her head toward me with the same blank look on her face. "It sounds too easy. I will never be able to forgive myself for what I did."

Janice wouldn't let go. She chose sackcloth and ashes over grace and forgiveness, and I'm sad to say she still hates herself for what she did. With freedom from guilt and self-hate there for the taking, she settled for being in bondage to both.

The biblical story of the woman caught in adultery is a powerful example of God's thoughts about "the sin versus the sinner" issue. You'll recall that the Pharisees and teachers of the law were acting as religious cops for God, rounding up moral lawbreakers. They grabbed the adulterous woman and dragged her before Christ, whom they probably saw as some kind of morals sheriff.

According to Jewish law, the woman should have been stoned to death for committing adultery. Knowing this, the teachers and Pharisees asked Christ what should be done—a trick question if there ever was one. His reaction: "He who is without sin among you, let him throw a stone at her first."[5] Of course, no one dared move, though I would guess a few of them wanted to. What was Christ's point? All people sin, and we don't help sinners by beating them up or putting them to death. When He spoke to the woman, He responded with grace and then a challenge: "Neither do I condemn you; go and sin no more."[6]

Sin is usually its own punishment in terms of the natural consequences it brings. If I overeat, the natural consequence of that sin is gaining weight. If the natural consequences of sin don't get our attention, a loving God will discipline us as well. To heap on top of all this our additional penalty of self-hatred and the miserable life that goes with it is to be masochistic and unbiblical. As one of my colleagues vividly put it, that's like treating a sprained ankle by pounding on it with a crowbar.

What will it be? Are you going to go Jill's route of not accepting God's forgiveness and continuing to pay for sins that have already been paid for? Or are you going to go the route Christ offers where sins are forgiven and where you show your appreciation by dedicating yourself to "go and sin no more"? If you think you are letting yourself off the hook too easily by choosing Christ's route, let me suggest you give it a try. Christ's route will cost you everything.

"Because I'm a Christian, God Will Protect Me from Pain and Suffering."

Jerry was one of those Christians who praised God when things were going well but who felt bitter toward Him when things went wrong. When he lost his business and faced bankruptcy, things were obviously not going well. And Jerry was very bitter. When he came to me for counseling, his overriding question, session after session, was, "How could God let this happen to me?"

"You seem to be assuming that a loving God wouldn't let bad things happen to you," I said.

He looked at me with a funny expression on his face. "Well, how can He be loving if He lets bad things happen to us?"

"Let me throw that question back at you. What do you think?"

He didn't have a quick answer. Finally, Jerry said, "Could be He's getting me back for some sin in my life."

I waited. "Then all of us would be toast, wouldn't we?"

"You're right. I suppose that's not it. But what else could it be?" Jerry looked genuinely puzzled.

Being a Christian always means joy, peace, and contentment, we are told. We childishly misinterpret that to mean a Christian will never have problems or pain, at least not the more serious versions. We foolishly believe that God will protect us from losing our jobs, suffering serious illnesses, or having other bad things happen to us. We want to believe it, so we do.

I've seen many Christians like Jerry whose "faith" becomes a source of bitterness and resentment the moment life turns sour. We spew all the venom in our souls at God when He doesn't come riding to our rescue as if He is some heavenly knight in shining armor. We, as the earthly damsel in distress, expect Him to save us from the fire-breathing dragons of life because we think being a Christian is some kind of guarantee that life will never harm us.

The bottom line is that life is difficult for everyone, Christian and non-Christian alike. Having faith in God doesn't mean you won't have problems. If anything, being a Christian means more troubles for two primary reasons: (1) you are asked to die to your own selfish desires and live for God on His terms; and (2) you will be persecuted for standing up for Christ by a world that rejects Him. Dying to self and suffering for the cause of Christ are two inescapable realities of the Christian life that make it a difficult life to live.

The ultimate comfort of Christianity isn't that it ensures that our lives here on earth will go well. They surely won't. The ultimate comfort of Christianity is that however bad life is down here for us, we have God's help in time of need and eternal life in heaven waiting on us when we die. Both give us real hope.

But don't we Christians deserve less pain and suffering just because we are Christians? No! A thousand times no! Anyone coming to Christianity for an easier ride through life has missed the point altogether. Christ Himself came out of heaven and suffered greatly here on earth. If anyone *deserved* to be protected from life being painful, it would have been Him. Christ was not spared life's slings and arrows, and neither will those called by His name.

Jerry and I talked about this.

"Jerry, I'm truly sorry about what happened to your business and the bankruptcy you are facing. I wouldn't wish that on anyone. I know you are in a lot of pain over it, and you should be. What concerns me is that your spiritual life seems to be suffering as a result."

"What do you mean?" he asked.

"It's one thing to go through tough times. It's another to be resentful toward God about the situation. I get the feeling that as long as things were going well for you, God was a great guy and you praised Him to the mountaintops. But when your business failed and your fortune went with it, the first person you felt bitter toward was God."

"You're telling me I should just put a happy face on all this and 'count it all joy,' like the Bible says?" he replied.

"Well, no and yes, actually. Put a happy face on it? No, that isn't what's called for, nor does it help. It would be lying to yourself and others to act as if you feel happy about what has happened. No one would feel that way about a painful situation, and no one should. But 'count it all joy'? Yes, that is what you are supposed to do. Do you know what that really means?" I asked.

"Well, I thought it meant we were supposed to be happy about everything. I take it from what you've just said that it doesn't mean that, right?"

"Right. That verse of the Bible means that whatever happens to you and however bad it may be, put joy together with it. In other words, couple your suffering with joy—joy based in the fact that God is still God, He still loves you, He is more powerful than any circumstance that you come up against in life, and that regardless of what happens to you down here, you are still going to heaven someday where all the misery will end."

"So, Christians aren't supposed to whitewash the bad things that happen to them, just not lose sight of the good things that remain true. Is that it?"

"Yes, that is exactly it. Christ didn't 'pretty up' the bad things that happened in His life. He wept over them, got angry about them, felt hurt over them. He always went to God the Father and received comfort and help. He didn't get bitter and stomp off."

Jerry looked caught. He heard what I was saying, and it stung him. He realized that he did expect God to protect him from bad things. He realized that he felt bitter when God chose not to. Jerry came to see that he was choosing to resentfully "stomp off" from God over his problems rather than turn to God for help. Seeing all this enabled Jerry to allow God to comfort him in his time of need instead of choosing to give God the royal stiff-arm for allowing bad things to happen to him in the first place. Jerry was on his way to a healthier faith and dealing with his problems constructively rather than destructively.

"In this world you will have trouble," Christ once said,[7] summing up the great truth that counters the "God will protect me from pain and suffering" lie. If we demand that life be pain-free, we will almost automatically be bitter when it isn't. And we will take it out on God, the very person who wants to help us when we are hurting.

"All My Problems Are Caused by My Sins."

Ever since the days of Job, people have been hearing and believing that a person's problems are always caused by his sins. Harold was the victim of that same old lie.

"I know why I'm having such trouble," he said. "I'm being punished." Harold was a distinguished older man I'd been working with for only a short time, and he opened one of our sessions with this statement.

"Punished? By whom?" I asked.

"God," he quickly replied.

"For what?" I asked.

"Well," he hedged, "I don't know for sure. But I'm sure it's something we can figure out. It's the only thing that makes sense."

"Harold, do you believe that people have problems only because they have sinned?"

"Yes, it makes sense."

"Then bad things happen only to bad people? Good people never have any troubles?"

"Well, no, that's not what I said. Good people seem to have troubles . . ." He thought about that for a second, then clicked his fingers, "But maybe they're not as good as they seem to be!"

"And bad people who get away with awful crimes, they're not really bad?"

"No, no, no. Look, I don't know. There's some explanation for that, I'm sure," he said, with a wave of his hand.

We humans like to explain things. We like to explain the universe to one another, to have some tiny grasp of it all. Everything must happen for a reason, we believe. If we just know that reason, we can feel more in control somehow. To believe we cause all of our problems is a very easy lie to believe (the opposite lie, that all of our problems are caused by others, is also very easy to believe). If it's true, then all we have to do to avoid problems is to be good. Yet even when we are "good," we still have problems.

Of course, as always, this lie has a toehold in reality. When you sin (lie, steal, commit adultery), problems will result from the act. But other people's sins can cause our problems too. If your business partner decides to funnel off revenue into a Swiss checking account rather than use it to pay bills, you will suffer.

Sometimes we have problems and no one sinned! For example, our friends' home was struck by lightning. It burned a hole in their roof, fried some of their electrical wiring, and ruined some appliances. They had a lot of problems as a result of that strike, and no one had sinned. Yet even in a situation like that, some Christians would fall into thinking, *They must have done something wrong because otherwise God would not let that lightning strike their house.* If God used lightning to get back at us for our sins, every house in this country would have been torched long ago!

We can see this truth, once again, in the ministry of Christ. His disciples must have believed that people's problems are always caused by sin. When the disciples saw a man blind from birth, they asked Christ, "Rabbi, who sinned? This man or his parents? Who caused his blindness?"

"Neither this man nor his parents sinned," said Jesus, "but [this happened so] that the works of God should be revealed in him."[8] What an amazing statement—the guy was blind and nobody's sin was the cause! The man was made blind so that God could demonstrate His power in giving him sight.

Whatever the cause of a personal problem may be, the main truth we can grasp here is that God can bring good out of it. That's the truth behind the passage "in all things God works for the good of those who love him."[9] If I inflict a problem on myself because of sin in my life, God can use it for my good. If someone else's sin causes me a problem, God can use it for my good. If no one sins but I still have a problem, God can use it for my good.

The challenge we face here is to examine honestly the root of a given problem. If the root is personal sin, then we need to repent of that sin. If a problem is the result of someone else's sin or no sin at all, then we need to let ourselves off the hook of responsibility and focus on solving the problem with God's help as best we can. The alternative is to feel guilty over something we didn't cause, all because of a lie.

Harold started to understand this in our work together.

"Harold, as I understand it, the problem you are dealing with has to do with being laid off recently. For the last two months you have been unable to find work. Your company gave you three months' worth of salary as severance pay, but you are going to have to make some significant life-style changes if a new job doesn't come through soon. Is that right?" I asked.

"Yes, that's right. Seventeen years of hard work and dedication, and they thank me by letting me go. I've got one more month of income left, and there is no job in sight."

"And you're convinced that some sin in your life caused all this to happen?"

"Right."

"What sin?" I asked.

"I don't know," he answered somewhat defensively.

"You have a guess, don't you?" I prodded.

"Well, I occasionally drink too much. I wonder if it might be related to that."

"Anything else?"

"I struggle with watching things on TV that I shouldn't," he confessed.

"R-rated movies?"

"Yes."

"Very often?"

"Every so often."

"Anything else?" I asked.

"I lose my temper sometimes and let some words fly around my wife that are wrong."

"Anything else?" I kept on.

"Well, sure, there are other things I do that I'm not proud of, but the ones that concern me the most are the drinking, watching R-rated movies, losing my temper, and cussing," he asserted.

"And you believe that God made you lose your job as a way to punish you for these things?"

"Yes, that's how I feel," he replied.

"Do you think everyone else in the company who was laid off was similarly being punished for sins in his life?" I asked.

"Well, everyone sins . . . ," he stammered.

"Yes, I know, but do you think that all of the people who were laid off got laid off because God was punishing them for their sins?"

"I had never thought of that. No, I don't guess that would be the case with everyone."

"So, why did some people get laid off if personal sin wasn't the issue?"

"Actually, the company made some bad business decisions years ago, and the layoffs are tied to them. The company is laying off people in order to survive."

"You might say that the sins of those who run the company have led to some people getting laid off?"

"Yes, I guess so," he admitted.

"Any other reasons that people might be losing their jobs unrelated to sin in their own lives?"

"Well, the computer field itself is a competitive one, and we, like a lot of other companies, are running into the fact that the need for the computers we make isn't as great because so many companies are making them. So, the lay-offs are partly tied to the fact that our profits have been lower and may continue to be."

"Harold, let me throw a thought or two at you. I'm not saying God isn't disciplining you for your sins by taking your job away from you. The sins you are struggling with could be the reason you are out of work. I think, though, that it is just as likely that you lost your job through no fault of your own and that this isn't about sin in your life. God is probably dealing with your sins some other way, more likely than not. Otherwise it would be hard to imagine a Christian who would have a job."

"So, I might be right. I could have lost my job because God is trying to discipline me?"

"Yes, but make sure you hear the other things I said. It seems unlikely to me that He is doing that and more likely that your company's bad business decisions and the downturn in the market for computers are the actual candidates. In saying that to you, I am not trying to make you less concerned about the sins you mentioned. I just think you might be falling into a very unbiblical way of thinking that could leave you at odds with God and lacking any hope that He wants to help you find a new job."

"What do you mean?"

"Well, given your line of thinking, if God took you out of a job because of those sins, it would only make sense that He wouldn't help you find a new job until you repent of them. Do you think He leaves people who want to work without food, shelter, and clothing in an effort to get their attention about sin?"

"Probably not. Otherwise, like you said, there would be a lot of homeless, hungry, naked Christians."

"I think you are starting to see the light."

Yes, personal sin causes personal problems. We can lose a job because we act irresponsibly in it. But other people's sins can cause our problems too. And we can have pretty bad problems at times when nobody sinned. The challenge in all of this is to try to keep in mind that the rain falls "on the just and the unjust"[10] and not assume that anytime we have a problem, it must be all about us. Job's "friends" accused him of something along those lines, and they were dead wrong.

"It Is My Christian Duty to Meet All the Needs of Others."

Bob, a pastor friend of mine, is a bright, articulate, kind, and caring man who loves people a great deal. During his thirteen years in ministry, he has helped literally thousands of hurting people. One day, he dropped by my office, and I soon found out that he was the hurting person. His eyes were hollow, his shoulders hunched. He looked depressed. All the signs of burn-out were there.

"Bob," I said, motioning for him to have a seat, "how's it going?"

"I didn't get much sleep last night. For that matter, I haven't slept much all week. My phone rang almost every night, once in the middle of the night. I ended up running over to some people's homes to offer some help," he said, slumping into my couch. "The thing is, I don't have time during the day to catch up on the rest I need or the things I've fallen behind on. We're still looking for an assistant pastor, and my youth pastor just left. I sometimes think that I should wear running shoes to work," he said, with a sigh.

Well, his sense of humor isn't totally gone, I thought.

He went on. "Today, though, I didn't want to get out of bed. I just couldn't move. I didn't get up until noon. So, I dropped in to see you."

Bob was in trouble. In his efforts to serve God, he was suffering from a pretty severe case of physical, emotional, and spiritual burn-out, all of which made it impossible for him to carry on his ministry. He was, as the saying goes, "so heavenly-minded, he was no earthly good." Bob worked so hard to please God and everyone else that he had worn himself out.

Bob suffers from the "Christians never say no" lie, and it's a tape a lot of us play and replay every day. I play it too. A woman from our church phoned to ask me to call on a family in our neighborhood who had visited our church recently. The request was appropriate, but my head and heart told me I did not have time to be the one to do it. Since I would have felt guilty saying no, though, I said yes. I'm embarrassed to say that the family's name and address sat on my desk for two months yelling, "Chris, you said you'd do this!" Guess what? It never got done. By failing to be honest about my priorities and limitations, I said yes when I needed to say no—all because of that faulty tape in my head that says, "A good Christian never says no."

God calls us to labor on His behalf, to "bear one another's burdens," but we are also told that each person is supposed to carry his own load. We are supposed to do some things to help others, but we are not supposed to do other things. Many of us forget that we can do only *our part* to meet the needs of others.

We tend to forget that Christ said, "Come to Me, all you who labor and are heavy laden, and I will give you rest. Take My yoke upon you and learn from Me. . . . For My yoke is easy and My burden is light."[11] Christ had the most important job of anyone on the planet, and yet He described His burden as "light." Amazing! In spite of those words, many of us turn Christianity into something heavy and burdensome by trying to be everything to everybody—a life nobody of sound mind would want to live.

I always think of the story of Mary and Martha when I hear my clients struggling with the "never say no" lie. In her efforts to be the perfect hostess to Jesus, Martha was scrambling all over the place busily preparing things for her important guest. Mary, on the other hand, sat quietly at Christ's feet, listening to Him and enjoying His presence. Martha, as many of us would, began to gripe to Christ about Mary's failure to help. "Don't You care that my sister has left me to do the work by myself? Tell her to help me!" she almost shouted at Jesus. She was upset with Mary and with Jesus as well.

Remember Jesus' answer? "Martha, Martha, you are worried and troubled about many things. But one thing is needed, and Mary has chosen that good part, which will not be taken away from her."[12]

I think we can take an important life lesson from this—Christ does not want any of us to be so preoccupied with *doing* that we fail at *being*. Martha was getting all the urgent things done; Mary was getting the most important thing done. One woman was frazzled, frustrated, and fed up. The other was calm, cool, and collected.

Bob, a minister of all people, had lost sight of this. He was so busy serving Christ that he had quit sitting at the feet of Christ. He was so busy saying yes to people that he had said no to God. He was so busy helping others that he failed to appropriately help himself. The warning signs that something was wrong were everywhere, and Bob was starting to notice.

"You know, you said something interesting that I think explains why you are depressed and feel that you can't keep going," I suggested.

"Really? What was it?" he asked.

"You said you thought that you needed running shoes to keep up with everything at work. That's a pretty insightful thing for you to say," I said, trying to affirm him.

"Well, that is exactly how I feel. I run from one thing to another to another, and it never slows down. I am absolutely exhausted by the end of the day! I can't keep going like this," he admitted.

"You know, I don't remember the Bible ever saying that Christ ran anywhere, do you?"

"What do you mean?" Bob asked.

"Oh, I think you know what I mean," I replied.

"Christ was never in a hurry, right?" he acknowledged.

"You tell me. You're the theologian," I responded jokingly.

"Okay, Shrink, I get it. I'm running around wiping myself out all in the name of the Lord as if I have to be everything to everybody. I think that I need running shoes because I'm too busy."

"Hey, pal, you'd make a pretty good client. Yes, you are too busy and burned out because of it. You are acting like Martha when you need to be more like Mary," I suggested.

"You aren't telling me I need to get in touch with my 'feminine' side, are you?" Bob said, showing he could be a funny guy too.

"No, but I am telling you that unless you slow down, start saying no to people, and quit carrying the whole world on your shoulders, you will never make it as a pastor. It is time to rest and balance your life whether you want to or not and whether your church members like it or not," I challenged him, knowing that this would be easier said than done for Bob.

"Can you write me some 'doctor's orders' so that I can show my church that you told me to do this?" he replied with a laugh.

"Gladly."

There is no magic formula for when to say yes and when to say no in life. I wish there was one. Deciding which to say requires the wisdom of Solomon at times. That is why we need to wear our knees out praying to God for help to make the right decision. The point here is that you are not supposed to say yes to every request, however legitimate it may be. Christ didn't always say yes. He didn't meet every need that He saw. He didn't try to please everybody. As a result, His burden was light. He never ran.

Are you running? Are you always in a hurry? Are you carrying more than your load because you believe the lie that a good Christian never says no? Learn to say no. Take off your running shoes.

"A Good Christian Doesn't Feel Angry, Anxious, or Depressed."

Imagine, if you will, that you are crossing a street and a car comes barreling out of nowhere, right at you. At that moment, you experience a strong fight-or-flight reaction. Your body gets a surge of adrenaline, your pupils dilate, your breathing becomes shallow, and your muscles tense. Emotionally, you feel extremely anxious as you dive to get out of the way. At that moment, would you say that your faith in God is weak?

Now imagine again. Your phone rings, and you pick it up to hear your best friend's spouse crying on the other end of the line. He has called to let you know that your best friend of twenty-five years was killed in a head-on car accident that morning. You immediately feel overwhelmed with sadness and grief, and you hang up the phone feeling more depressed than you have ever felt in your life. At that moment, would you say that your faith in God is weak?

Now imagine one more time. You come home after a long day at work, open the front door, and step inside to find that your home has been burglarized. Everything is turned upside down, numerous things are broken, and many costly items have been stolen. You feel angry. At that moment, would you say that your faith in God is weak?

I ask you these questions because many Christians suffer from another lie. It is the lie that anytime you have a negative or painful emotion about something, you are automatically sinning and showing that your faith in God is weak. In other words, if you ever feel anxious, depressed, or angry, you are messing up and lacking faith.

Malarkey!

God made us emotional beings, and He gave us a broad range of emotions to feel. Some of the emotions are the ones we like—peaceful, joyful, content, and happy. But He also gave us emotions that we don't like to feel that much— angry, sad, depressed, and anxious. They all come in the same package, and you really can't have the "good" ones unless you are willing to also have the "bad" ones.

In certain homes and churches, however, the message you get is that if you are feeling negative emotions, something is wrong with you. If you feel angry, there must be some sin in your life. If you are depressed about something, you must be lacking faith. If you feel anxious, you better have more faith and get your act together. In especially unhealthy churches and homes, these emotions are trained right out of us, and the only ones we are allowed to feel are the ones that others don't feel threatened by.

The belief that we shouldn't feel painful emotions often results in "stuffing." Stuffing is taking what we feel and suppressing it so that we don't feel it. The feelings don't really go away, though. They may stay buried awhile, but they are ready to come out when we tire of the effort expended to keep them stuffed or some kind of external crisis triggers them. Ultimately, when too many feelings get stuffed, there are two bad results. One is a very depressed, withdrawn, and hopeless person. The other is a person who, after stuffing for too long, erupts like Mount Saint Helens and is very hostile, enraged, and aggressive.

Well-meaning Christians can actually encourage us to stuff if they aren't careful. Maybe they can't handle seeing us in pain, so they try to make it go away. Or maybe they don't think we ought to be in pain. Whatever is motivating their actions, they can end up offering us platitudes like these:

- "You needn't be depressed. God hasn't forgotten you. Cheer up!"

- "It must be God's will, so be happy. Everything will work out."

- "If you really trusted in God, you wouldn't be feeling so angry."

- "Why are you feeling anxious? God is still in control!"

Well, God hasn't forgotten us, but that doesn't mean some things aren't worth getting depressed about. Yes, it may be God's will that a certain thing happened, but that doesn't mean we have to be happy about it. Even if we trust God, there are things worth getting angry about. And, yes, God is in control, but if someone is walking toward me with a menacing look on his face and a gun in his hand, I am going to feel anxious. The point here is that some events are worth being troubled about, and becoming troubled about them doesn't mean we are mentally ill or lack faith in God.

I get quite a few "stuffers" in my office. They come to me because they have stuffed so long, they are emotionally sick from it. Ann, who was in her forties, was a perfect example. She sat on my couch and nervously nibbled away at her fingernails for the first few minutes of every visit.

"Ann," I would finally say, "how are you doing?"

Usually, she told me small things, never much about the real reason she'd finally come to me—that she had been diagnosed with cancer. She'd felt anxious, depressed, even angry, since being diagnosed, but she had put a happy face on it and acted as if everything was fine. But during one of our sessions, she cut straight through her smaller concerns to the heart of her problem. She acknowledged that having cancer had turned her life upside down, but as a Christian, she felt that she should "count it all joy" and "be anxious for nothing" and not be upset about it.

"Ann, there's nothing wrong with feeling angry and sad and scared about having cancer," I countered.

"If I really trust God, I don't think I should feel those things," she replied.

"Ann, we are wired by God to feel strong emotions in the face of serious situations like the one you are in," I said quietly. "Allowing yourself to be sad about having cancer is healthy. Letting yourself feel angry about it is good. Being scared about what is to come is normal."

"As a Christian, I'm supposed to be thankful about everything, joyful about everything. Isn't that right?" she asked.

"Well, yes, even in the worst circumstances there are still things to be thankful for and joyful about. But you seem to have taken that to mean that it isn't okay to feel troubled at the same time."

She crossed her hands in her lap and looked at me. "Are you saying you can feel upset about something and still be thankful and joyful?"

"Yes, although that is no easy trick."

"Well, it doesn't seem right to feel angry or sad and thankful at the same time," she admitted.

"It isn't easy, but it is possible. Look, Ann, when Christ was here, did He react with strong emotions to things?"

"Yes, of course."

"Did He always react with 'positive' emotions to things?"

"No, I don't guess He did."

"So, what does that tell you?"

"That it must be okay to feel upset."

"Do you think Christ was able to be sad or angry or hurt and still be content and thankful and even joyful?"

"I guess."

"Okay, so here is the lesson: 'A Christian can feel painful emotions and still be thankful, even joyful.' How does that sound?"

"Well, it sounds good, but . . ."

If painful emotions are a sign of a weak faith, then how do we account for the times Christ expressed strong, painful emotions? He wept when Lazarus died. As He prayed in the Garden of Gethsemane, He told His disciples, "My soul is overwhelmed with sorrow to the point of death."[13] He shouted and overthrew tables when He was angry with the money changers in the temple. Pretty strong emotions, wouldn't you say? If strong, painful emotions are a sign that you are immature, mentally ill, and faithless, then Christ must have been all three.

Now, allow me to speak out of the other side of my mouth. While it is good and healthy to feel sad, angry, and anxious at times, it is also true that we sometimes (oftentimes?) have versions of these emotions that may very well suggest that we are immature, are emotionally unhealthy, and possess a weak faith. How can we tell the difference? Let me suggest that you ask yourself three questions: *How* often *do I feel these emotions? How* intense *are these emotions when I feel them? How* long *do these emotions last in me?*

Painful emotions that show up *frequently* should make us question what's going on. For example, some Christians are anxious all the time, regardless of the circumstances. Such chronic anxiety reflects a lack of mature faith in the fact that God does control the universe and that He will never allow us to have problems too big for us to handle with His help. Painful feelings that occur too frequently are a warning signal that you have a problem.

Emotions that are overwhelmingly *intense* may be a sign of psychological problems and an immature faith that needs tending to. If I lose my job and become so intensely depressed that I cannot function, I probably do not really believe that God is in control and has the ability to help me find a new job. Emotions that are so intense you can't function normally are a warning signal that you have a problem.

Painful emotions that last *too long* may signal psychological and spiritual problems. If we stay anxious, depressed, or angry about an event for, let's say, three years, we probably need some help. I can't tell you exactly how long you should feel a certain emotion—no one can. How long, for example, should someone be deeply grieved over the death of a loved one? I don't know. But most of us have an internal timer on these matters that tells us when it's time to move on, and listening to that clock is wise. Emotions that stick around too long are a sign you've got problems.

"Ann, your feelings about being diagnosed with cancer are strong and painful, and they should be. Stuffing them isn't going to do anything but cause you more pain," I suggested.

"So, letting all this out is okay? I don't have to feel that I am some kind of horrible person or that my faith in God is weak?"

"No, of course not. If Christ wept, you should weep. If He got angry, you should get angry. If He felt sad, you should feel sad. Where we do have to be careful is that we are sad, angry, and grieved over the right things. Sometimes we weep or get angry over things that don't warrant it."

"Like what?" she asked.

"Well," I replied jokingly, "sometimes I feel like weeping over the Texas Longhorns losing a football game, or I feel really angry over being out of milk when I was really looking forward to having some with my favorite cookies."

Ann laughed, one of the few times she did so in our sessions. "I get it. Some situations don't warrant certain reactions."

"Right. As another example, it would be inappropriate to be happy about someone falling down a flight of stairs. That would be the wrong emotion for that situation. That's one issue. The second issue here is that even when we feel the appropriate emotion toward something, we may feel it too strongly or too often, or it may last too long. It would be appropriate to feel sad over being laid off a job you love, but if you become clinically depressed and can't function for the next ten years, you have gone too far."

"So, even when you are appropriately feeling angry or sad about something, you still have to be careful not to become overly hysterical about it all," she acknowledged.

"You got it. And in the case of your diagnosis of cancer, I would say that warrants some pretty strong feelings, don't you?"

"Yes, I guess so. What you are saying makes sense. Maybe I do need to let myself feel some things about having cancer that I have been keeping stuffed down inside."

Ann did "get it" and was able to let herself cry about having cancer, feel angry that it had happened, and be appropriately scared about what the surgeries and chemotherapy would involve. As a result, she faced her cancer as a much healthier person emotionally, and I believe that was a significant factor in the success of her treatments.

Feel sad. Feel happy. Feel angry. Feel peaceful. Feel depressed. Feel content. Feel grieved. Feel joyful. Feel scared. *Feel!*

"God Can't Use Me Unless I'm Spiritually Strong."

I want to conclude this chapter with a short discussion about a very widespread lie. As a college student, I remember playing this tape over and over. I would want to tell friends about Christ, but I felt my life was such a mess that God wouldn't want to use me. I was convinced people would look at my life and say, "Hey, you aren't any great shakes of a human being. Why should I listen to *you*?" Even today, I'd love to tell some close friends about God, but I find myself still playing that same old tape in my head: *How can I tell them about God if my life doesn't show shining proof of all I'm talking about?*

Yet one of Christianity's paradoxes is that through our weaknesses, God can show His power. Through our imperfections, He can be glorified. Through our sin, God can show that He is God. God has chosen to implement His plans through very flawed people, and He wants to use us even if we are not as together as we should be.

Yes, God wants His people to be mature and practice what we preach in front of others. He doesn't want us to be hypocrites. The world has enough of those. The world will never be the same because of Jesus Christ; He was the only One—the only One—to ever walk the planet who perfectly practiced what He preached. I'm just saying that if any of us wait until we are just like Christ before we make ourselves available to be used by God, we will wait a whole lifetime.

The apostle Paul is a good example of what I am trying to say here. By his own admission, he was not a striking figure. He was not a great speaker. He was not anything that would have impressed us. He called himself the "chief" of sinners, so he obviously didn't have his act together. Yet it is hard to think of anyone in Christianity who has had a bigger impact. God certainly used Paul greatly in spite of his flaws. In his letter to the Corinthians, Paul captured the paradox of it all when he said, "For when I am weak, then I am strong."[14] When we admit to being weak, flawed, and insufficient, we quit thinking it is all about us and realize it is all about God working through us to do great things.

I've come to realize I don't have to be a spiritual giant to tell people about God. In fact, my being honest about my weaknesses and struggles gives those I tell a healthier, more realistic picture of Christianity—one, I hope, devoid of lies. As Christ said, it's not the healthy who need a doctor, but the sick.[15]

The bottom line is that we are all "sick" and in need of the Great Physician. We are always going to be less than perfect representatives of Christianity, no matter what level of Christian maturity we ultimately attain. Pretenses otherwise are hurtful and unhealthy. What better favor can we do non-Christians than to allow them to see the reality of who we are, be honest about how we struggle, and point them in the direction of the true help we have found in Christ?

Growthwork

We have reached the end of our discussion on the various lies we believe that destroy us emotionally, relationally, and spiritually. I'm sure it has been painful at times to read about these lies and realize the damage they have caused in your life. I want to pat you on the back for your efforts so far. You have shown a great deal of commitment and courage to have been willing to face these lies.

For your growthwork, I want you to participate in Track a Lie Week. Think back through all the lies we have covered, and pick one that troubles you the most. Once you have decided on one, I want you to keep an A-B-C journal for a week focused on that one lie. In your journal, write down any situation you were in that triggered that specific lie and what the emotional and behavioral consequences were for thinking it.

Let's say that you chose the "I must have everyone's love and approval" lie for Track a Lie Week. With that lie as your focus, you would write down any A-B-Cs that had to do with your need for approval getting triggered and what reactions you had. Your journal might look like this:

"A" (Event)	"B" (Self-Talk)	"C" (Response)
Coworker was upset with me when I was late for a meeting.	*I can't stand it when he is mad at me. I want him to like me and approve of me as a person and worker.*	Tense, heart raced; felt anxious; bit my fingernails.
Spouse didn't like what I was wearing.	*I want him to approve of how I look.*	A little muscle tension; felt angry; changed into something I knew he would like.
Waitress acted upset/ irritated when I told her my meal was cold.	*What have I done wrong? Why is she upset with me? I need her to accept me.*	Breathing got shallow; felt worried and angry; left her a large tip to soothe her feelings.

This assignment is designed to help you see the role that one lie can play in causing emotional turmoil, relationship problems, and spiritual conflict. Whatever lie you choose to focus on, try to identify as many situations as you can where that lie reared its ugly head and damaged you. Chances are that you will see how often just one lie plays into your life and the horrendous cost of believing it. That alone can motivate you to overcome this lie in your life.

PART 2

TELLING OURSELVES THE TRUTH

7

■

THE TRUTH ABOUT THE TRUTH

Seek the truth,
Listen to the truth,
Teach the truth,
Love the truth,
Abide by the truth,
And defend the truth,
Unto death.
—John Hus

Men don't usually like to reveal their deeper feelings. When they finally decide they can't keep things to themselves any longer, they often seek out another man to "talk things over with."

But when the problem runs really deep—deep enough to shake their world—they will bypass their golf buddies, work cohorts, and even their best friends. Instead, they turn to someone like me.

Bill's world was shaking. He called for an appointment and came to my office on a hot July afternoon. He dropped into an armchair and combed his fingers through his hair. His eyes were bloodshot. The fresh nicks on his face were indicative of the hit-and-miss shave he had given himself that morning. There were bags under his eyes. He had the haggard look of a man too exhausted to keep trying, yet too terrified to close his eyes and sleep.

"How may I help you?" I asked.

Bill was quiet for a few seconds, expecting me to say more. Instead, I just eased back in my chair and waited. Whatever he needed to talk about I knew he had rehearsed dozens of times before ever phoning me. I'd let him explain in his own time, in his own way.

"I'm losing it," he finally blurted out. "I don't know if I'm cracking up or falling apart or what! I'm wiped out, and if I don't get myself pulled back together soon, I don't know what's going to happen to me. I need some help."

"Tell me more. I'm listening."

"I've never had a time in my life like this past year," he said in a low voice. "It's like a black cloud is floating over my head all the time. I'm constantly depressed. Every day is a burden. I toss and turn at night, and I don't want to face each day. I can't seem to shake this feeling of hopelessness."

"Things seem pretty bad all the way around," I said, stating the obvious, hoping he would say more about what was bothering him.

"Yeah, everything seems pretty bleak. I thought something might be wrong with me physically, so I had our family doctor give me the once-over. He couldn't find anything wrong with me. No symptoms. No headaches or stomach cramps or fevers. He thought it was stress. He talked me into trying to rest more often and get some exercise. It didn't help, though. I'm still walking around like a zombie. I went back to see him again. I asked him for some sleeping pills, but he said I needed something else. He said I needed to talk to a guy like you. You know . . . a . . . a . . ."

"A listener?" I suggested.

Bill grinned ever so slightly. "Yeah, a listener."

"Well, I'm glad you decided to come. Let me ask you, was there anything that triggered all this?"

"I don't know," said Bill, waving one hand limply before his face. "Just a bunch of stuff. At work . . . at home . . . it all adds up after a while."

"Tough times at work, you say?"

"Aw, yeah, work has been a real bummer since we lost a government bid back in February. It was my project all the way. I had every angle figured. Our plans were the best. Our prices were the lowest. Our guarantees were the most dependable. Anyone with half an ounce of sense would have seen in an instant that our company should have been awarded that contract."

"But . . . ?"

"But we didn't get it. Our main competitor did, although I have no idea why. I did my best, but we lost. And losing that contract meant losing millions of dollars and years of steady work for everyone in the company! Nobody said anything, but I had this feeling that everybody felt that it was my fault, that I had blown it somehow and now everyone else was going to suffer because of my failure. I could feel their eyes on me when I went to work each day."

"Losing the contract was a big disappointment for you and your company. I take it that this isn't the first big contract that your company has lost out on."

"No, no, that's true. But it came at a time when I needed something positive in my life. I didn't need any new troubles. My son—the middle one—was having trouble in school. He's the sweetest kid you've ever met, but he just can't read very well. They worked with him all through last school year, but it was slow going. He just couldn't keep up with the other kids his age."

Bill stood up and walked to the window, blinking back tears in an effort to appear strong. I gave him a moment of silence as he collected himself and recalled events from the previous year.

"They told us before last year to hold our son back a grade," Bill continued, "but I resisted it. I should have listened. Midway through the school year he was way behind the other students in everything except math and physical education. My wife and I told the teacher to help him as much as she could and we'd let him repeat that grade this year."

"You felt bad about that, didn't you?"

Bill nodded. "It tore my heart right out of me. The kid tried so hard, but there I was breaking the news to him that he'd be in that same grade again this year," he replied, tears again welling up in his eyes.

"It was almost as if you had failed that grade along with your son, wasn't it?"

"I failed him, that's for sure. And it came when I failed the company too."

"The double whammy," I said, trying to console him.

Bill smirked, turned from the window, and moved back to his chair. "The triple whammy. My wife and I started having some marital problems about then. She started in again with this 'thing' she's always had about wanting to buy her dream home. Well, that dream home has a nightmare price tag. I put my foot in my mouth when I promised her we could buy it. I got her hopes up."

"That was back when you were certain your company was going to land the big government contract," I surmised.

"Yeah. And that would have meant a big bonus for me and probably a raise too. We could have handled the new mortgage payments with that kind of money. But when the bonus and raise didn't materialize, my wife still wanted the new house. She told all her friends we were going to build it."

"I assume you and your wife have discussed your financial situation?"

"Hey, I tried. Believe me, I tried. But she wasn't in a very receptive mood . . . and that's putting it mildly. I may have to go ahead and buy that new house if she keeps on like this. It doesn't look like I've got any other choice if I ever want any peace with her again. How I'll pay for it is anybody's guess, though. It's crazy. My whole life is crazy. Maybe *I'm* crazy. What do you think? Am I nuts or what?"

I smiled reassuringly. "No, Bill, you're not crazy, just hurting and confused. You're hurting over some painful situations that would be tough for anyone to deal with. Also, you're confused about the truth of your situation."

Bill's head jerked up. His eyes narrowed as if I had just called him a liar. "Hey, I'm not making any of this stuff up. What I told you is true!"

"Bill, I believe you're telling me the truth as best you understand it," I suggested, "but there's a lot more truth to your circumstances than you realize. Have you ever heard the expression, 'You shall know the truth and the truth shall set you free'?"

"Yes."

"Well, in our work together, I hope to show you just how true that statement is. Knowing the truth and being set free by it are what counseling is really all about. Here in this office, you and I are going to play our own version of 'To Tell the Truth.' We are going to find out the real truth about the situations troubling you. Are you willing to try?"

Bill looked a little dubious, and he shrugged his shoulders.

"Look," he finally agreed, "I'm open to anything if it will help."

"All right, Bill, let's look at the truth of the situation with your son," I began. "Why wouldn't you let him be held back last year when his teacher suggested it?"

"Because I was stupid," said Bill. "I should have listened to the teacher and trusted her suggestion."

I shook my head. "No, you didn't make that decision because you were stupid, Bill. The truth is, you aren't stupid. I'll ask you again: Why wouldn't you let your son be held back last year?"

Bill look full-faced at me, blinked a few times, then stammered, "Because . . . because I hoped my son would do better without having to face the pain and embarrassment of being held back. I didn't want the other kids to make fun of him as if he were stupid. I kept hoping for some kind of a miracle where he'd wake up one morning and just start to do better."

"And now? Why are you willing to let him be held back now?"

"Because it's best for him. I can see that now. He was in over his head, and he always will be unless we can do something now to help him out. As painful as it will be for him, keeping him back a year will help him learn to read better and catch up on what he has already missed."

I nodded my head in agreement.

"You're a good father, Bill. Better than you realize. You let your pain for your son get in the way of doing what was best for him at first, but you saw your mistake and corrected it. You saw the truth that the only way your son would really learn to read was through the pain of repeating the same grade. While it hurt to admit it to yourself, you faced the truth 'there is no gain without pain.' Seeing that truth helped free you up to do what was right for your son. But *you* seem to be missing an important truth that might help you out a little."

"You've got my attention. What truth am I missing?" he asked.

"One you have heard a thousand times before but seem to have quit applying to yourself, that 'to err is human.' As trite as that may sound, it is one of the truths you need the most right now. You aren't cutting yourself much slack about what you did regarding your son or what happened at work with the contract not coming through, and you are feeling like a failure as a father and a worker when you are actually pretty good at both."

Bill slowly sat back in his chair. He massaged his face with his hands, then relaxed his shoulders. I could hear a soft sigh ease out of him.

"I see what you are after. I really don't allow myself to make mistakes with my kids or at work, either. I guess I have forgotten that making mistakes is pretty normal."

"It's a truth that's easy to forget, but it's emotionally deadly when we do. Truths such as 'to err is human' and 'there is no gain without pain' are the building blocks of emotional health. If we get away from them, we emotionally suffer in ways that could have been avoided. The suffering you have been experiencing isn't so much tied to your son's reading problems or the job setback or the struggles with your wife as it is tied to your having gotten away from these and other basic truths."

"That sheds a new light on things. When you mentioned that the truth sets people free, I guess I kind of blew that off as one of those platitudes that counselors say that doesn't mean much. But it really is true. How about some more?"

"Sure. Let's look at that situation with your wife and the new house. You said you don't feel that you have any choice in the matter, that you have to buy the house whether you can afford it or not."

"Uh-huh."

"Well, what about that? Is that really the truth? Do you have to buy the house? Can your wife force you to buy that new home?"

"Well . . . not literally force . . . that is, she can't actually make me sign the . . . what I mean is . . . uh . . ."

"What you are saying is that you do have a choice," I injected, pushing him to confront the situation squarely. "No one—not even your wife—can force you to do something you know is careless and irresponsible. Isn't that true?"

Bill's forehead furrowed in thought. He turned serious.

"Yeah," he agreed. "Well, of course, I have a choice." He paused, then added, "I don't have to buy the house my wife wants. I guess I tell myself I have to and end up feeling trapped by that. Maybe I trap myself."

"I think that's right. We often tell ourselves, 'I have to do this' and 'I have to do that,' only to feel trapped. We end up doing things that we either don't want to do or know to be wrong to do, or both. In a very real way, we trap ourselves with a *have to* mind-set when the real truth is that we don't have to do anything we don't believe is right to do. You and your wife have a tough decision to make together regarding whether or not to buy a new home, but it is important for you to realize that you don't *have to* buy one. That truth may free you to pursue what you feel is wisest rather than give in to keep her pacified and then resent the whole thing once it's finished."

"This truth stuff is starting to make some sense," Bill admitted. "I guess I didn't realize that I had gotten so far off in my thinking about all these things. I can see how some of the emotional strain I have been under is related to all this. I have a feeling, though, that there are some things about truth you haven't told me yet."

Bill was right. There are certain realities about truth—the truth about the truth—we hadn't discussed yet. For any of us to become whole people, we must understand certain things about the nature of truth. We need to know what we are getting into before we start. Failure to understand the truth about the truth sets the stage for disappointment and failure in our quest for healthy lives.

"Yes, there is a lot more about truth that we haven't even scratched the surface of yet. Where do you want to start? What about the truth do you want to know?" I asked.

The Truth Comes Piece by Piece

"Why does the truth sometimes seem so unclear? Why can't I just 'get it'—see the whole truth about a given situation all at once?" Bill responded.

"Truth isn't something we 'get' all at once," I explained. "Understanding truth is more like trying to put a thousand-piece puzzle together. We find truth piece by piece and try to fit it together with the other pieces we already know. The more pieces we put together, the more of the whole picture we get to see. Doing that is hard work."

My daughter, Ashley, who has loved doing puzzles since she was a child, can tell you that. One mental picture I will always have of Ashley is her at a table intently hunched over her newest puzzle, patiently looking for the next piece she could press into place. I don't recall that she ever sat down in front of a puzzle and put it together easily or quickly. And whether we like it or not, discovering truth and putting it together with other truths to form a clearer picture of reality are never done painlessly or rapidly.

"What makes the pursuit of truth even more difficult," I added, "is that mixed in with the truthful pieces of the puzzle are lie pieces that don't fit. We pick up these pieces, think they are part of the truth puzzle, try to fit them in somewhere, only to find that they don't fit and that we wasted valuable time on them. Picking out and discarding the lie pieces require hard work, which also slows down how fast we can assemble the truth puzzle."

"I never could finish one of those puzzles," he muttered. "What else?"

The Truth Isn't Ours

"There's another sobering truth about truth," I told him. "While we are here, we don't have all the pieces of the puzzle available to us. If the whole truth is a thousand-piece puzzle, we have only a hundred or so pieces to work with. Even if we put all one hundred pieces together, we get to see only a small part of what the whole puzzle looks like."

"Why? Who has the other pieces?" Bill asked.

"God," I replied. "I believe that God knows all one thousand pieces of the puzzle and is the only One who does. Like it or not, the whole truth is God's possession, not ours. Fortunately, even though we can't know the whole truth while we are here, He makes the most important truths available to us if we genuinely want to know them."

"Okay, okay," Bill interrupted. "But you've never come out and said what truth *is* or how I find it."

"Simply put, truth is reality as it really is," I said. "As far as finding it, there are three main ways. First, we can learn truth through our own experiences. Second, we can learn truth through the experiences of others. Third, some truths—the most important pieces that go beyond human experience—must be revealed to us supernaturally by God and accepted on faith."

"So, let me get this straight. Truth is unvarnished reality. I can learn some of it on my own, some of it through others, and God can reveal some to me."

"Right."

"If God has something to do with it, where does the Bible come into all of this?" he asked.

"Although not everyone agrees on this point, some of us believe that God supernaturally inspired certain people to write the Bible and that it is *the* book of truth. If we accept the Bible as such, we have available to us the most important textbook for knowing the truth about God, ourselves, and the way to live healthy, meaningful lives. The Bible itself even says, 'All Scripture is given by inspiration of God, and is profitable for doctrine, for reproof, for correction, for instruction in righteousness, that the man of God may be complete, thoroughly equipped for every good work."[1] If the Bible is what it says it is, then we need to take it seriously and use it as the primary book we study when we want to know what reality is."

"Yes, but isn't the Bible pretty unclear? Can't it be used to say anything you want it to say?" Bill asked.

"Yes, it can be difficult at times to understand exactly what the Bible really says. And, yes, people misinterpret the Bible all the time. That is why we have a responsibility to study it for ourselves and work diligently to know what it really teaches."

The Truth Is a Prerequisite for Personal Growth

"You're giving me a headache, Dr. Thurman," Bill said, rubbing his temples. "If knowing the truth takes this much hard work, why would anybody even try?"

"Because our lives depend on it," I replied. "The Bible isn't kidding when it says that 'the truth shall set you free.'[2] Without the truth, we aren't free. Without the truth, we are in bondage to emotional problems, troubled relationships, and spiritual turmoil. Without the truth, we are lost and our lives are a mess. That is why knowing the truth is worth whatever effort it takes."

"So, without the truth, we will be miserable and life wouldn't be worth living," he said.

"Think of it this way. Truth is the best food for your soul. Truth has all the right vitamins and minerals and nutrients in it. Without the truth, your soul dies from malnutrition."

"Sounds like a person who doesn't eat right," he observed.

"Actually, that is a pretty good way to put it. Telling yourself the truth is like eating a meal of grilled chicken, rice, green beans, wheat bread, low-fat milk, and frozen yogurt pie—it's good for you. Telling yourself lies is like eating a dinner of chicken fried steak (smothered in gravy, of course), onion rings, French fries, butter-drenched rolls, beer, and a chocolate fudge sundae. 'Eating' the truth leaves you better off, healthier. 'Eating' lies, while they may 'taste' good, leaves you sick."

"Thanks for making me lose my appetite!" Bill joked.

"Sorry, but if it gets my point across . . ."

The Truth Has Barriers

"Okay," he interrupted, "but it still sounds as if we can miss the truth altogether, even though we know all this stuff. What gets in the way of knowing the truth?"

"There are numerous barriers to knowing the truth. Two seem to be the biggest," I said, hoping he would take the bait.

"Which two?"

"Prejudice, for one. Prejudice is a barrier to knowing the truth because our minds are already made up. We decide ahead of time how to view something and won't let anything change our minds. Once we have made our minds up, the truth could bite us on the nose, and we wouldn't see it. Ever been there?" I asked.

"A couple of million times," Bill admitted. "I used to think that all rich people were snobs until I became friends with someone who had a ton of money but was the nicest, most decent person I have ever known."

"Good for you."

"What is the other barrier to knowing the truth?" he asked.

"Pride. In being prideful, we arrogantly believe we know the truth, whether we do or not, and we refuse to look at the possibility that we may be wrong. Pride truly goes before our own destruction. That ever happened to you?"

"Boy, I'll say. Once, my wife wanted to explain something to me about our computer. I got my nose all bent out of shape that *she* wanted to teach *me* something, so I didn't let her. I ended up doing the wrong thing and lost a whole night's worth of work because I was too proud to let her show me how to do it."

"I have to plead 'guilty' to being prideful too. I'm the stereotypical guy when I'm lost on a highway. I'll drive around forever, pridefully convinced that I can figure out where I'm going without anyone else's help."

"You, too, huh?" he replied.

"Real men don't ask for directions," I said with a smile.

The Truth Often Leads to Pain

"Hmmm," Bill replied. "I can see, though, that knowing the truth is not easy. Pride and prejudice are pretty difficult things to overcome. Is there anything else I should know about the truth?"

"Well, brace yourself. Another sobering thing about the truth is that it sometimes hurts."

"What do you mean?" he asked.

"Well, just as we sometimes lie to others to avoid painful consequences, such as lying to a policeman to avoid a ticket, we also lie to ourselves to avoid pain."

"Give me an example."

"Well, let's say that a man is a pretty bad parent and that he is emotionally damaging his children. Facing that would be painful. So, he runs from the pain through self-protective lies. He might tell himself, *I have done everything a loving parent can do—I just have rotten kids,* or *The world we live in is such a horrible place—that's why my kids are so messed up,* or *If teachers did their job right, my kids would be fine.*"

"So, instead of facing the truth that he is a poor parent, he lies to himself by making it all about his kids or the culture or the school system," Bill said.

"He may feel better at that moment to think that way, but in the long run, he and his family are going to be damaged by his unwillingness to face the truth and let it hurt. You've heard the expression, 'The truth hurts.' Some people run from that unpleasant reality at great personal expense."

The Truth Means Being Willing to Doubt

"I tell you what I find hard," Bill said, gazing past me. "I find it difficult to doubt some of the things I was taught growing up as a kid even when the 'adult' part of me knows I should. Is that bad or good?"

"Doubting is not only good. It is a necessity," I answered. "We need to be willing to doubt things in order to know whether they are really true. I believe the ability to doubt is from God Himself. He doesn't want us to blindly accept what people say just because they say it."

"So whatever I was taught to think and whoever may have taught it to me originally, it's okay to doubt it."

"Yes, with one minor addendum," I added.

"What's the addendum?" Bill asked.

"Remember Thomas, the 'doubting' disciple in the Bible?"

"Yes, I do."

"Well, he was from Missouri, the 'Show Me' state. Everyone was telling him that Christ had risen from the grave, and Thomas was sitting there thinking, *You guys need some counseling! I am not buying any of this nonsense unless I see Christ myself and touch His wounds with my own hands.* Christ appeared to Thomas and gave him the evidence he asked for. Then what did Christ demand of Thomas?" I asked.

"That he believe," Bill said quietly.

"Exactly. Once He gave Thomas proof of His resurrection, Christ demanded that Thomas believe. Doubt is good to a point. However, anyone who needs repeated proof of the same truth doubts too much and may never make a commitment to truth at all."

"You have to land on one side of the fence or the other. Otherwise, doubt is more of a hindrance than a help," he observed.

"You got it. Once the evidence is in, you have to quit doubting."

The Truth Will Stand Forever

"Is there anything else about the truth I need to know?" Bill asked, sounding as if he was ready to stop and try to digest all that he had heard.

"Yes, there is one final truth about the truth I want to throw at you."

"Fire away," he said.

"When all is said and done, the truth will still be standing. The truth existed before you and I got here, and it will be here long after you and I are gone."

"So, truth has a life of its own? People come and go, but truth remains the same?" he asked.

"Right. In our world, more and more people believe that truth is relative. In other words, something can be true for you but not be true for me. I agree with that notion if we are talking about personal preferences but not if we are talking about truths that are absolute," I said.

"What do you mean?"

"The 'truth' for you may be that mint chocolate chip ice cream is the best kind, whereas the 'truth' for me is that cookies 'n' cream is the best kind."

"I see what you're saying. Some matters of 'truth' have to do with individual taste," he acknowledged.

"But certain truths are true for everyone. These truths are absolute. They have been around since man first appeared on earth, are true for everyone, and are true for every generation," I said.

"Like what?" Bill asked.

"Let's talk about that next time."

Bill and I had covered a lot of ground about truth during our first session together. It was time to stop and let him "chew" on what we had discussed. In the session, Bill came to realize that you have to tell yourself the truth to be mentally and spiritually healthy. He also came to appreciate that truth, like a diamond, has many facets—it comes piece by piece, it's God's possession, it's required for personal growth, pride and prejudice get in its way, it can cause pain, we need to be willing to doubt in order to believe it, lies are often more attractive, and the truth will last forever. (See Appendix D for additional teachings about truth.)

Before you go any farther, I want to ask you a couple of questions. First, do you believe that telling yourself the truth is necessary for your life to be emotionally and spiritually healthy? Second, do you agree that the various facets about the truth I shared with Bill are true? Take a few minutes to "chew" on that yourself. If you can't swallow all of this, the rest of the book won't do you much good.

Growthwork

You have come a long way. At this point, you have self-assessed the lies you tell yourself, read in-depth about these lies, learned the A-B-C model, used the model to become more aware of how telling yourself these lies ruins your life, and learned some critically important truths about the truth. Congratulations on making it this far!

As we focus more on the role that telling ourselves the truth plays in helping us to have better lives, it is time for more self-assessment. In this section is a simple questionnaire that I want you to complete. Using the scale provided, respond to each statement in terms of how much you agree or disagree with it. Answer as honestly as possible. Please *do not* answer in terms of how you think you should think. What I am looking for here is an honest, gut-level response that reflects how you *really* think. Also, if at all possible, try to avoid using 4 as your answer. I want you to land on one side of the fence or the other in responding to each statement.

1	2	3	4	5	6	7
Strongly Disagree			Neutral			Strongly Agree

_____ 1. To err is human.

_____ 2. You can't please everyone.

_____ 3. You don't "have to" do anything.

_____ 4. You are going to die.

_____ 5. The virtue lies in the struggle, not the prize

_____ 6. You are not entitled to anything.

_____ 7. There is no gain without pain.

_____ 8. Emotional pain is good.

_____ 9. Life is difficult.

_____ 10. You reap what you sow.

I believe each statement is a vital truth—an absolute truth that is true for every person all the time. (See Appendix C for biblical support for each of these ten truths.) If you gave any of these statements a 1, 2, or 3, you disagreed with what I consider to be a truth we must believe if we hope to achieve emotional health, intimate relationships, and spiritual maturity. Look back through your answers and put a check mark by any statement that you gave a 1, 2, or 3.

How many check marks did you end up with? Even if you had only one, it means you don't believe something to be true that is true. It means you are at odds with reality. It means you have a "tape deck" problem that needs to be corrected. It means you are not as healthy as you could be.

There is one other thing I would like you to do before you move on to the next chapter. For each statement that you gave a 1, 2, or 3, answer the following questions about it in your journal: Why do you disagree with the statement? What about the statement makes it untrue? Could it be true? If the statement is true, what's the evidence that it is? How would your life be better off if you believed this statement?

In the following chapters, I will attempt to help you understand why each of the statements is true and how your life would be significantly better off if you lived by these truths. Read with an open mind, yet be willing to doubt—both are required for these truths to set you free.

8

■

TO ERR IS HUMAN

If at first you don't succeed, you're running about average.
—M. H. Alderson

To err is human. You've heard it all your life. But I would be willing to bet you don't really *believe* it. My guess is that you go out each day trying to be perfect or semiperfect and then feel disappointed, if not outright annoyed, whenever you make a mistake. Deep down in your private stock of hidden beliefs, you probably are still hanging on to the notion that in all you do, you should hit a home run every time you step to the plate.

Most of us hate to make mistakes. And it's not just because they require time and energy to correct. It's because they are evidence of something we don't want to face: the fact that we are flawed. Many of us try in vain to be flawless, all in an effort to stiff-arm the basic truth that we are anything but. Something about accepting the fact that we are imperfect irritates us, maybe even is an affront to our pride. We keep trying to be perfect, even though we cannot be.

Don't get me wrong. I'm not against the fighting spirit of "never say die" if the cause is worthy. I cheered every time Rocky Balboa got up off the mat after being knocked down. We love and admire the person who goes the distance. What worries me is when we go from getting up off the mat after a knockdown to thinking we should have never been there in the first place. That is dangerous.

"How," you may ask, "is it dangerous?"

A person who believes "to err is stupid" will make a mistake and immediately start into a self-abusive song and dance. As if making the mistake itself wasn't bad enough, he starts beating himself up for making it! He starts telling himself things like these:

You stupid idiot! What's wrong with you? How could you have ever done something so imbecilic! No one else on the planet has ever done anything this ignorant. You are the only person dumb enough to have pulled this off. Great work, chump! Everyone around you must think you are the biggest moron ever born. You deserve the miserable life you're leading because you are nothing but a loser from the word go. Hang your head in shame, you loser.

Feelings of self-condemnation, anxiety, shame, embarrassment, and depression go sky-high with this commentary going on in his mind. Imagine the damage it does to his sense of competence and value. Its devastating effect on his ability to relate to others is immeasurable.

Someone who believes "to err is human" approaches mistakes and failure differently. The minute he messes up, his internal reaction is something like this:

I just messed up. I don't like it, but I did. This will take some time to correct, so I'd better get started. I see people make this sort of mistake all the time. This isn't the end of the world. After all, I am only human. What can I learn from making this mistake so I don't make it as often in the future?

The emotional volume control for "to err is human" people stays at a reasonable level, a level that doesn't get in the way of correcting mistakes and moving on. These people don't inflict unnecessary pain on themselves just because of a mistake. The mistake itself was painful and costly enough. Creating further damage via emotional self-abuse makes no sense. These people are not at odds with human frailty; they face it, even accept it, and then move on. And that's emotionally healthy.

"To err is stupid" people feel so bad about themselves, they believe the only way they can conquer their problem is to go to the other extreme: to try to be perfect. Of course, trying to do this only exacerbates the problem. They can never be perfect, and each new mistake they make underscores this point. They become even more self-condemning, and their emotional turmoil intensifies. The cycle is vicious and endless.

Mistakes and Anger: Frequent Bedfellows

Alicia, one of my clients, struggles on a very deep level with accepting the truth that to err is, indeed, very human. She has spent her whole life believing just the opposite and, thus, hating herself every time she makes any kind of mistake. By exploring her past, I learned she was severely criticized as a child whenever she made a mistake. Her parents indoctrinated her to believe that personal errors were intolerable. Now as an adult, she has continued to follow that early, destructive path.

Problems with anger and depression caused Alicia to seek counseling, but she often used our sessions to defend her belief that mistakes could be the norm for everyone but her. I challenged her on this as often as I could, hoping to knock down the wall she had built to hide her humanity. Here is an example of how one of our sessions went:

"What would you like to talk about today?" I asked.

"I've been feeling really angry this week. Toward everything. The littlest thing can set me off," said Alicia.

"Tell me more."

"Some things at work haven't been going well. I messed up a letter I was supposed to do for my boss. That was really stupid. Then when I got home, I yelled at my husband for not doing something he said he would do for me."

"What do you think is causing your anger?" I prodded.

"I don't know. You're the doctor. You tell me," Alicia answered half jokingly, not really wanting to look at herself.

"Come on, Alicia, give it a try. I think you know what's going on, don't you?"

"You want me to admit that I don't let myself or anyone else around me make mistakes and that when I do, or they do, my anger explodes. That's what you want me to say, isn't it?"

I shook my head. "What *I* want you to say isn't important. The point is, what's the truth? Isn't that what we're really after in these sessions?"

"I guess so," she said reluctantly, "but it seems to me that making mistakes is really stupid and completely avoidable. I just can't stand it when stupid things like that happen."

I looked directly at Alicia. "I think we both know these ideas about mistakes being stupid and inexcusable were trained into you a long time ago."

Alicia rolled her eyes upward. "All roads lead home, eh?" she ventured. "All right, yes, I got it from my parents. They never let up on me. They were constantly on my case. I could never measure up to their yardstick, and they would beat me with it when I didn't."

Suddenly, bitter tears formed in her eyes.

"The way they treated you hurt a lot, didn't it?" I responded, hoping to keep the tears flowing. She needed the emotional relief.

"Yes. A lot," Alicia replied.

"It seems to me that your parents used a standard with you that no one could have measured up to, but you've never realized that. You've continued to use that same yardstick ever since then."

"I guess I have. I certainly never seem to measure up, and for that matter, no one else seems to be measuring up to my yardstick, either," she admitted.

"I'll tell you what I think. When no one measures up, it's time to change the yardstick."

"Could be," she answered, not really sounding committed to the idea.

"Alicia, I believe that *if* you're willing to take a truthful look at the yardstick you were handed by your parents—the one you've been using ever since you left home—you'll see that you need to throw it away and replace it with a more realistic and humane one. Your parents taught you that to err was stupid, inexcusable, and unforgivable. Like all other children, you believed your parents. Unfortunately, in this area, they were wrong. You need to recognize that. You'll never get over your chronic problems with anger and depression until you allow yourself and others to make mistakes—even some big ones."

"I will never accept the idea that making mistakes is all right," she defiantly replied, replaying the mental tape her parents had put inside her.

"Then you will never get better!" I said, just as defiantly.

"You're telling me I have to *like* my mistakes?"

"No," I replied. "Accepting mistakes and liking them are two different things. I'm just telling you that if you keep refusing to accept the fact that making mistakes is part of life—yours and everybody else's—you won't ever become emotionally healthy and you won't get along with others. You certainly don't have to like your mistakes, but you need to accept them as part of being human."

"Sounds like an awfully fine line between accepting and liking."

"Maybe. But it's a fine line worth distinguishing."

Alicia shrugged. "I'll tell you straight out, I don't really want to do what you say. Still, I know I need to do something. I'll give it a try and see how it goes."

"That's a start," I encouraged her. "I'm confident you can pull this off."

How Human Is Making Mistakes?

Is making mistakes human or not? Your decision about this, like Alicia's, will be crucial. If you decide that making mistakes is stupid/dumb/inexcusable/

avoidable/intolerable/idiotic, you'll be in for a lifetime of self-abuse and emotional misery. If on the other hand, you can see the truth that making mistakes is inescapable/human/normal/tolerable/frequent/understandable, you will experience a lifetime of growth and peace.

Now, again, let me emphasize that believing "to err is human" does not mean we have a license to make mistakes all over the place or not to try to correct our mistakes. You can't expect to succeed in life if you have the attitude, "Well, since I can't be perfect, I might as well be imperfect all over the place and not worry about it." Not being concerned about doing well is just as grievous a mistake as trying to be perfect. Both are failures to deal with the truth. We are imperfect, but we are capable of quality and improvement. Yes, we'll all make mistakes. But making them out of indifference or carelessness isn't healthy. As Jerry Jenkins humorously put it, "To err is human, but when the eraser wears out ahead of your pencil, you're overdoing it."

Growthwork

At the end of each chapter, I have given you an assignment (you *have* been doing them, haven't you?). The purpose of these assignments has been to help you see the lies you tell yourself and how they are destructive to you and your relationships with others. Now, as we focus more on telling ourselves the truth, I want to add to our A-B-C model to help you go even farther.

In the A-B-C model, recall that "A" stands for the "event," "B" stands for your "self-talk," and "C" stands for your "response." To extend our model, let's add the letters "D" and "E." "D" represents "new self-talk," and it is here that you tell yourself the truth needed to counter the lies you told yourself at "B." "E" represents "new response," and this is the part of the model where new (healthier, more appropriate) emotions and behavior will begin to replace the unhealthy, inappropriate reactions you've been having at "C."

Let's take real-life "A" and run it through the A-B-C-D-E model:

"A" (Event): At the express (ten-item or less) checkout line, the person in front of me has more than twenty items.

"B" (Faulty Self-Talk/Lies): She's got a lot of nerve! What an inconsiderate person! Why do I always get behind people like this? I ought to give her a piece of my mind! Doesn't she think about anybody but herself? Why do people do this to me!

"C" (Response): Muscles tighten up, breathing becomes rapid; feel irritated, angry, resentful; slam my seven items down, one by one, let out a noticeable grunt, and give the person a dirty look when she turns around.

"D" (New Self-Talk/Truth): I'm choosing to let what this person is doing bother me. That's my choice. She is being inconsiderate, but it isn't the end of the world. She isn't doing it to me personally; she is just doing it. I can choose to say something, or I can choose to let it slide—that's up to me. This is a small thing. I need to keep it that way."

"E" (New Response): Less physical tension; reduced feelings of anger; pick up a magazine and start reading it until it is my turn to be checked out.

The challenge is adding steps "D" and "E" to start using the truth to defeat the lies you tell yourself at "B." Don't worry if your initial efforts result in less-than-immediate improvement in your attitude or emotions. Lies are hard to change, and hard work over time is the key to making significant changes.

Let's run a tougher situation through the A-B-C-D-E model just to see what it's made of:

"A" (Event): My spouse and I had our worst argument in the last ten years. Both of us said some pretty mean things. The argument reached a boiling point, and my spouse cursed at me, stormed out of the room, and slept in the guest bedroom that night.

"B" (Faulty Self-Talk/Lies): How dare he talk to me like that! He never thinks he does anything wrong! It will be a cold day in Hades before I apologize to him! I should have never married him in the first place! Now I'm stuck with someone I don't even like half the time! I hate being married and hope he dies in an accident on the way to work tomorrow!

"C" (Response): Heart raced, breathing rapid and shallow, muscles tight; felt extremely hurt, angry, and hopeless; went into the kitchen and ate a half-dozen chocolate chip cookies and watched television until one o'clock in the morning.

"D" (New Self-Talk/Truth): That was our worst fight in years. Both of us were out of line and didn't really listen to each other. My spouse was wrong to

curse at me—that is never acceptable. But I still need to forgive him for that. I need his forgiveness for some of the things I said too. We hardly ever fight like this anymore, a sign that things are getting better in our relationship. Just because we blew it pretty badly this time doesn't mean we have gone back to square one or that this relationship isn't a good one. Yes, I don't always like everything about my spouse, but he doesn't like everything about me, either. I really don't want him to die. I just feel very hurt and angry. We need to talk again and try to resolve this—swallow our pride and give it another try.

"E" (New Response): Calmer; still hurt and angry but not vindictively so; called spouse at work to say that I was sorry for my part in last night's fight and that I would like to try and figure out what went wrong and solve it.

Now, here is your assignment. I want you to spend the next week keeping an A-B-C-D-E journal. Make entries in your journal about situations you felt upset about and/or didn't handle very well. Specifically, I want you to write about any situations that have to do with the battle between the "I must be perfect" lie and the truth "to err is human." A journal entry might look like this:

"A" (Event): I locked my keys in my car.

"B" (Faulty Self-Talk/Lies): What a stupid idiot I am. Only I would do something this idiotic! What kind of moron locks his keys in his car at a time like this? Incredible! Now I'll miss my appointment, and everybody will end up mad at me. What a complete jerk I am!

"C" (Response): Muscles tensed up; breathing rapid; heart raced; felt angry, humiliated, ashamed, anxious; pounded on the roof of the car.

"D" (New Self-Talk/Truth): Okay, this is inconvenient, but lots of people make the same mistake every day. I'm not the first guy to lock his keys in his car. This doesn't make me an idiot. I'm not happy about it, but then again, it's not the end of the world. If people get mad at me for being late, I'll tell them exactly what happened. No doubt they've done the same thing.

"E" (New Response): Less physical tension; heart slower; felt less angry, embarrassed, more at peace; went inside to call security for assistance.

Consider another example:

"A" (Event): I spilled a greasy, red-sauced hors d'oeuvre down the front of my shirt at a *very* important company event with the boss watching.

"B" (Faulty Self-Talk/Lies): *You stupid idiot. Only a socially ungracious slug like you would do something as stupid as this. No one else at this party did something this stupid. You look like a clown with no circus to go to. Every eye in the place is on you. You will be lucky if you ever get invited to another social event the rest of your life.*

"C" (Response): Heart started to race, muscles tensed up, began to sweat; felt anxious, humiliated, embarrassed, uncomfortable; immediately covered up the stain with my hand and hurriedly walked to the rest room where I feverishly worked on getting it out.

"D" (New Self-Talk/Truth): *Hey, you just made a mistake. It isn't the end of the world. Nobody really noticed, and even if people did, they probably felt some compassion for you. Maybe you can even make a joke out of it to put everyone at ease (tell the host and hostess that not only did you enjoy the hors d'oeuvres but your shirt did too). Be thankful it wasn't battery acid you spilled on yourself. Now, go clean yourself up and get back to enjoying the party.*

"E" (New Response): Physically calmed down, breathed easier; felt less embarrassed, anxious; able to laugh about it.

A second assignment I want to give you is to do something imperfectly on purpose this week. I want you to do something "good enough" but not perfectly. For example, let's say you are an obsessive-compulsive "neat freak" when it come to cleaning up the kitchen after a meal. Instead of spending an hour making everything perfect in the kitchen (i.e., making the floor so clean you could eat off it), spend fifteen minutes making it clean enough. Or instead of putting everything "in its place," leave some things lying around. Find something this week that you usually try to do flawlessly, and purposely permit some flaws in how you do it.

The main purpose of all this is to get you to fight the "I must be perfect" lie you tell yourself at "B" with the "to err is human" truth you need to tell yourself at "D" in order to react more maturely and appropriately at "E."

Again, be patient. Old "tapes" are hard to change, and you may find it diffi-cult to come up with new ways of thinking.

Think of the lies you tell yourself as speaking your native language. Fighting back with the truth, then, is like learning to speak a whole new language. Just as you can learn a foreign language with enough effort and practice, you can learn to speak fluent "truth" if you will do the same.

A quick story. When I was an undergraduate at the University of Texas, I had to take four semesters of a foreign language in order to get my degree. Because my parents were stationed in Germany at the time, I decided to take German. Big mistake! My first day of class in my first semester of German was, how should I put it, a disaster! The professor began the class speaking German. I dropped the class in a heartbeat because it was just more than I could handle. It took me four years of college to finish four semesters of German because I kept dropping them when they got tough.

I say all this just to let you know that learning to tell yourself the truth will be as hard as learning to speak a new language. I'm not saying this to discourage you but to help you be more realistic about what you have gotten yourself into. To become fluent in a new language is a time-consuming, laborious process. Hang in there—don't drop the class. It will be worth it!

9

■

You Can't Please Everyone

In 1975 singer Rick Nelson recorded a song entitled "Garden Party." It tells of an actual event from his life. He was invited to be part of an "oldies" concert at Madison Square Garden in New York City where he and other popular artists from the fifties and sixties were to perform their hits. When he got on stage, he chose to sing his newest songs, not the ones for which he was famous, such as "Hello, Mary Lou" and "Traveling Man" and his other classics. The crowd registered their displeasure. They booed him. That wasn't what they had paid to hear.

Rick Nelson learned (relearned?) something at that concert. A line from "Garden Party" reveals what it was: "You can't please everyone, so you've got to please yourself." While I am not so sure about the "so you've got to please yourself" part (it sounds a little bit too self-centered for my taste—if all we did was please ourselves, we wouldn't be any better off), I do think the "you can't please everyone" line is one of the great truths we need to know and practice to lead emotionally and spiritually healthy lives. To some extent Rick Nelson must have come to this realization, for the last line in "Garden Party" is, "If memories were all I sang, I'd rather drive a truck."

Yes, I know. "You can't please everyone" is a one-liner you've heard a million times before. But hearing it and believing it are not the same thing. Most people (including you?) are out there every day trying to please everyone. Consider how much you worry about people not liking you. Why does it put a knot in your stomach whenever someone is upset with you? Why are you willing to do *almost anything* to ensure that people will be pleased with you?

The answer is that we all have a God-given need for approval that we take much too far. The need for approval itself isn't the problem—it is normal and human to want approval from others. In fact, if we *don't* receive adequate approval from people, we don't make it through life very well. The problem arises, however, when we live for the approval of others and try to get it from everyone. Approval becomes our god, and we emotionally wipe ourselves out looking for it in every nook and cranny.

Childhood and Approval

The origin of the need to please everyone, and thereby gain approval, often goes back to childhood where there was a real (or perhaps perceived) lack of love and approval from one or both parents. This critical missing element of personal development creates an internal "thirst" for love and approval that is very strong and hard to ever satisfy later on in life.

Brett, one of my clients who came to see me because of marital problems, struggled with an extremely strong need to please everyone and receive approval. During his childhood, Brett had been ignored by his father. Brett's father hadn't criticized him or hit him or yelled at him. He had just ignored him. His father was so caught up in his own world that he never took the time to enter Brett's. Brett never received one of the essentials for growing up a reasonably healthy person—a father's love.

Feeling rejected by the most important male in his life, Brett spent his adult years trying to make up for the love he had missed by doing his best to get everyone else to love and accept him, especially people at work.

"My wife and I had another one of those heated arguments the other day," Brett told me at the start of a session.

"What caused it?" I asked.

"Same as always. She thinks I work too much. I'm usually the last guy out of the office every night. That puts me home late. And even then, I have a brief-case filled with contracts to review, proposals to analyze, and ad campaigns to help design. My wife says she is so far down on my list of priorities, we might as well not even be married."

"What do you think about that?"

Brett shrugged his shoulders. "I guess if actions speak louder than words, she's probably right. She just doesn't understand, though, that I have a lot of responsibilities and a lot of people depending on me."

One glance at Brett showed that he was physically exhausted. He had bags under his eyes and a pallor to his skin. His posture was slumped and heavy.

"Looks like your work life is jeopardizing your relationship with your wife and ruining your health, Brett," I told him flatly. "Why do you think you continually get yourself involved in so many different things?"

Brett's eyes avoided mine. "I don't know."

"Do you remember our discussion last session about how you felt you never received any approval from your father?"

"Yes, sure, I remember."

"And do you remember how you decided that because of that, you developed a heightened need to have people like you and approve of you? You admitted last time that you were deathly afraid of anyone ever being displeased with you."

"Yes, I know," he said.

"Let me ask you this: Do you see any connection between how hard you work and the hurt you felt from being ignored by your dad?"

"That happened thirty years ago," said Brett, ducking the question. "What does that have to do with me now?"

"I think you know," I insisted. "You do know, don't you?"

"This is where I'm supposed to say that I'm still looking for my father's approval by working so hard," he said with a tone of indifference. "You want me to say that since I couldn't please my old man, I'm now trying to please everybody else I come in contact with. It's my unfulfilled need to find love and approval, right?"

"We both know that," I agreed. "But don't you see the irony in all this? In going 'all out' for everybody at work, you are ignoring your wife. And *she's* the one who wants to give you love and approval. You're treating her exactly the way your father treated you."

That struck a chord in Brett. He began to tear up and sat silently for nearly a minute weighing what I'd said. Finally, he spoke.

"The last person in the world I want to be like is my father. It never occurred to me that I have been doing to my wife what he did to me. It's just that . . . well, I've spent so many years trying to get people's approval, I don't know if I can change. I know that if I pulled back at work, I'd upset a lot of folks. The boss, especially, would really be angry with me. That worries me."

"Change is always hard. But listen to yourself, Brett. You're saying that at the expense of your marriage and your health, you're more concerned with trying to please everyone at work. Isn't that a rather high price to pay?"

At that, Brett began to cry. "What's . . . what's wrong with me, Dr. Thurman? When I hear you talk about my life, I see how stupid it is to be like I am, but then, I just go out and continue to live that way. Why am I acting like this?"

"Maybe you are addicted to approval?"

Brett's eyes widened. "*Addicted!* Can you be addicted to approval?"

"Sure. It's possible to be addicted to almost anything, not just alcohol or drugs."

"I would never have thought of it like that. But . . . it kind of makes sense, doesn't it? I'm like a drug addict. If I can get daily injections of approval, then I'm fine. But if I don't, it's like I go into withdrawal. I can't handle that. I need a 'fix' of approval on a regular basis. It's frightening to think of it like that. I'm addicted to approval. I've got to do something about this."

"How would you handle it if you were addicted to drugs?" I asked him.

"I'd . . . I'd quit," he stammered. "I'd stop taking that poison. I'd clean out my system. I'd purge myself of the addiction."

"It would be painful," I reminded him. "It hurts to go through withdrawal from *any* kind of addiction."

"But that would be a matter of life and death," Brett responded, a sense of genuine anxiety coming over him.

"So is your addiction to approval," I warned him. "The shape your marriage is in and the way you look right now, it's obvious you're headed for serious problems."

"You're right," Brett said seriously. "I'm hooked on approval, and I need to break the habit. Until today, I didn't want to see that."

A Cure for the Addiction

Can you relate to parts of Brett's confession? Although the truth is that we *can't* please everyone, a lot of us keep trying anyway. If you find yourself seeking everyone's approval, don't deceive yourself into thinking it is not an addiction. It is. For too many people, approval is the "drug" they crave night and day. But just as with any comparable street drug, the effects of approval are short-lived, and the addict all too quickly needs to "score" again so that he can feel good once more. It's a vicious, dangerous, and life-threatening cycle, but something that can be overcome.

My client, Brett, was able to make positive changes in his life related to try-ing to please everyone. He made changes with much "fear and trembling," but his sincere desire to break his addiction to approval motivated him.

I helped Brett create a list of priorities for his life. Right at the top he listed renewing his love for God. He realized that he had become so consumed with seeking people's approval that he had allowed his relationship with God to atrophy. Brett was spiritually wise enough to know that people's approval had become his god and that things were never going to get any better in his life until the one, true God became his God again. Second on his list of priorities was nurturing a close, intimate relationship with his wife. Brett knew he had run from intimacy with her for years, and he saw that it was time to stop running. Whether it felt comfortable or not, he needed to work on becoming her soul mate and learn to love her and accept her love in return. Third, Brett admitted that he hadn't had a close male buddy since college and that he should deepen his relationships with men. Specifically, he thought he might become good friends with a couple of guys who had asked him to play golf and go to some football games; it was time to find out. Finally, he made a commitment to balance his life better. He would have to cut back at work by going home earlier, get much-needed rest, do some regular exercise, and watch his diet. Along work lines, he focused on doing an excellent job for his employer but staying within the confines of *his* job description rather than trying to be everything for everybody. By sticking to these priorities, Brett saw his life take a significant positive upturn. He shifted from trying to please everyone to trying to love God and the people who really loved him for who he was. In doing so, he got his life back.

Yet Brett also ran into disapproval and rejection from some people at work for remaining true to his priorities. Some of his colleagues, being overly committed to work and pleasing the higher-ups, didn't like the fact that Brett was not working as hard as they were. They didn't like seeing him go home at 6:00 P.M. while they worked until 7:00 P.M. or 8:00 P.M. or later. They resented Brett's taking breaks during the day while they worked through their own. They felt Brett should plug away at work on the weekends, just as they often did.

Misery loves company, and these coworkers, probably without really being aware of it, wanted Brett to be as miserable as they were. In a very real sense, they resented his choice to be healthy as they chose to remain sick. As he quit trying to please them in order to get their approval, some of them liked him less. The boss wasn't thrilled with the "new" Brett, either. That was tough for Brett to accept, but he came to see that the only way to get his life back was to risk not receiving applause from others.

Rick Nelson was right—you can't please everyone. I would put it even more strongly—you are not on this earth to please people. It isn't your job. Nor are people here to please you. We are here to glorify God. That means being displeasing to others at times whether we like that or not. Christ is the ultimate example of what I am talking about. Christ was morally perfect, and people hated Him so much that they killed Him. That ought to tell us just how shallow and flaky people's approval and disapproval can be.

If you consider yourself to be a person who is addicted to approval, take some positive steps to "go straight." Begin by admitting you have the addiction. Admit that approval has become your god and that it is a god that will kill you. Nothing changes until you admit you have a problem.

Next, return home to the God who loves you as you are. He is ready to kill the fatted calf and throw a party for you if you will just come out of the foreign land where you have wasted your life. We are all prodigal sons and daughters in some way, and we need to come home.

Then, think of the people who accept you *as you are,* and work on being intimate with them. If there isn't anyone like that, try to connect with people at church or other safe places, and do what you can to allow relationships to form. As I said earlier, we all need approval, but it is impossible to get any if we don't allow people to get to know us well enough.

Finally, stay balanced. Work, play, rest, have fun, eat well, do hobbies, cultivate new interests, enjoy the arts—put your eggs in multiple baskets. Brett was a mess partly because he had allowed his need for approval to lead him into putting all his eggs in the basket called "work." All work and no play made Brett a very dull boy, and it makes us dull as well.

I'm sure you are thinking, *Chris, get real! I barely have time to brush my teeth at night before I drag my dead carcass into bed, much less do all the things you are talking about.* Well, I have only one thing to say to you: Bull! You have the time. You just don't use it right. Quit making excuses. Life is passing you by, and you are boring us all to tears with all your complaints while you're letting it. Get off the couch and reclaim your life.

Growthwork

If you have led a life like Brett's, I want to challenge you to do something right now to start breaking your addiction. If you feel that you need everyone's approval, I want you to do something that purposely leads to disapproval. Here are some possibilities to choose from:

- Yell out the time in the middle of a large store.

- Walk down a city street wearing Mickey Mouse ears.

- Express an opinion in a conversation at work tomorrow that is different from what the others are saying.

- If someone asks you to do something that is unreasonable, say no.

- If someone asks you to do something that is reasonable, say no.

- Wear a dress shoe and a tennis shoe out in public.

- Walk around in a shopping mall with a sign that reads, ADVICE, 25¢.

I am not encouraging you to do anything unkind, immoral, insensitive, or dangerous. I am just asking you to act in a manner that is consistent with the truth "you can't please everyone." I'm challenging you to find the courage to live a life that doesn't make pleasing everyone and getting universal approval the central focus.

Oh, and don't be surprised that life will go on, because it will. And better.

10

■

THERE IS NO GAIN WITHOUT PAIN

One cannot get through life without pain.
—Bernie Siegel

Imagine what your reaction might be if you saw a story in your hometown newspaper tomorrow morning that read as follows:

New Psychosurgery Procedure Makes
Mental Health Possible Without Any Effort

Unbelievable Press International (UPI)—Doctors at Happy Days Hospital in Nirvana, New York, have developed a new surgical procedure that creates mental health in a matter of minutes. The procedure involves removing all of the patient's faulty beliefs, attitudes, and expectations through laser surgery of a certain part of the brain. Patients who have undergone the procedure report the complete absence of emotional problems afterward, and they are now kind, self-controlled, patient, giving, selfless, and unconditionally loving people. Dr. I. M. Deluded, the surgeon who pioneered the psychosurgery technique, hails his discovery as, "What everyone has been looking for all along—all the benefits of mental health without any of the hard work!" Dr. Deluded has reported receiving thousands of calls from people all over the world asking about the availability of the new surgery. He stated that within ten years, it would be possible for the whole population of the world to have undergone the procedure and have complete mental health.

That sounds pretty attractive, doesn't it? Most people would love to undergo a procedure that would free them from all of their distorted thinking and the psychological misery created by it (except for those of us in the mental health profession who would be put out of work!). There is only one problem: there is no way to achieve mental (or spiritual or physical) health without painful effort on our part.

The idea that something can be done *to you* to help you achieve mental and spiritual health goes way back in time. One of the earliest treatments of mental/ spiritual disorders for which we have evidence was a practice in the Stone Age called trephening. Trephening involved using crude stone instruments to chip away an area of the skull of a disturbed person. This opening presumably allowed the evil spirit that was causing the illness to escape. Some people actually appear to have survived the surgery and lived for many years afterward.

The early belief that all psychological problems were the result of possession by evil spirits also gave rise to exorcism as a way to mental/spiritual growth. Exorcisms varied considerably, but most involved prayer, noise making, and the use of horrible-tasting concoctions. Extreme cases involved making the body of the possessed person such an unpleasant place that the evil spirit would leave voluntarily.

Another method used to treat psychological and spiritual problems through external means was the circulating swing. This approach, used in the early nineteenth century, involved strapping a patient in a chair that could be spun around. I assume the idea behind it was that the operator could spin a person's problems right out of him. The technique was believed to bring the disturbed person back to sound reasoning.

In our current age, many still continue to search for ways to achieve personal growth and maturity that are easy and painless. Too many hurting people even view medication that way. More than a few clients have come in just to have medication prescribed to make their emotional and spiritual pain go away, not to work on the underlying issues causing their pain. When I informed them that I was a psychologist, not a psychiatrist who could prescribe medication, some didn't return. All they wanted was a pill to make them better. Since I couldn't offer that, they went off looking for a psychiatrist who could.

The problem here isn't that people in emotional and spiritual pain turn for help where they think they can find it. Who doesn't? Pain motivates all of us to look for help, and it should. The problem is that we think some technique or procedure or pill can make us better people. Becoming a better person requires hard work on our part from the inside out, not something from the outside doing its magic internally. We may find relief from our pain through something external—medication, a warm bath, a trip to Maui—but relief is not the same thing as growth. Growth comes only from painful effort.

No Quick-Fix Solutions

Dan, a client of mine, truly wished for an external, painless solution to all his problems. He came to see me because of depression and anxiety related to problems at work and in his marriage. He was about to lose his job, and his wife was very close to walking out on him.

For most of his life, Dan had been dodging his problems, hoping they would just go away. Now, the consequences of his doing so were beginning to catch up with him in some undeniable ways. One session we had began like this:

"Have a seat, Dan. What's on your mind today?"

Dan shrugged his shoulders.

"Oh, I don't know," he responded, as if he didn't care.

"Why don't you start with what seems to be bothering you most," I suggested.

"Well, I suppose I still feel kind of depressed about everything," he confessed.

"During our last session, we discussed some things you could do to work on overcoming your depression," I reminded him. "Were you able to do them?"

"No, I wasn't," he replied, with little concern in his voice.

I kept pressing. "Any idea why?"

"I just didn't get around to them," he answered, as if to imply that it was no big deal.

"I'm not sure what you mean by 'just didn't get around to them,'" I stated.

"Well, it was a tough week, and I just didn't feel that I had the energy or time to work on what we talked about," he responded.

"Dan, let me be straight with you. I can't help you if you are not willing to do the assignments we agree on."

"What do you mean?" he asked, sounding hurt.

"You come here for help, but you don't do any work in between sessions. You're making it impossible to get better."

"I guess you're right," he said, pacifying me. "So what do you want me to do?" I detected some anger in his voice, which meant we were beginning to get somewhere.

"I want you to come to counseling with more than 'I guess' and 'I don't know' and 'I just didn't get around to it' as your replies," I responded, being more confrontational than usual. "I want you to make some effort in the direction of getting better rather than just sitting there with a 'Psychologist, heal me' look on your face."

"I . . . I'm doing the best I can," he defended himself.

"No, you're not. You know that and I know it. You aren't really trying in any area of your life, and that's why you're failing in your job, your marriage, and even our counseling." I wondered if I had gone too far in confronting him.

"You don't understand. It isn't that easy!" he continued in his defense.

"I'm not saying it's easy. Getting better is anything but easy. But you aren't putting much of anything into it," I told him frankly.

"I know it. I do that all the time, and I hate myself for it," he responded, trying the "pity me" strategy with me that he often used with his wife and boss.

"It sounds like you want me to take pity on you as you beat yourself up for avoiding your problems."

"I feel like a loser who will never amount to anything," he replied, still wanting me to pity him.

"Dan, you aren't a loser, but you are losing. By avoiding the pain of dealing with your problems head-on, you've made them worse. That doesn't warrant sympathy or pity." I countered.

"It sounds like you're disgusted with me," he interrupted.

"I'm not disgusted with you. I am disgusted with your style of wanting good things out of life without putting any effort into getting them. I care enough to confront you on that. I want you to get better, but I don't know how you can if you don't take more responsibility for facing your problems, even if it would hurt," I answered.

"I get the point," Dan said. "I've heard it before from my wife, the boss, my parents—from everyone really."

"I know you've heard it before. But that doesn't make it any less true," I responded, hoping he would take this lifelong message and finally do something with it.

"I'll consider what you have to say," he said, as if he was doing me a favor.

"I hope you will do more than 'consider' what I've said. Considering what I have said is just another way for you to run from doing anything. I'm telling you that you need to act on what I've said. There is a huge difference," I replied.

"You're pushing me where I don't like to be pushed—into doing stuff I really don't want to do."

"Dan, we can't always do what we want to do in life. Sometimes, like it or not, we need to do what has been asked of us. That means working hard to face painful things directly when we'd rather not. What we gain in the process is greater emotional health and less troubled relationships."

"Well, I sure want to be happy and to get people off my back," he acknowledged.

"But are you willing to do what it takes to achieve that?"

"I'll think about it," he replied.

I'm sorry to say that all Dan did was "think about it." He never did much of anything in counseling to put elbow grease into making himself a healthier person. In retrospect, I saw that Dan came to counseling to look as though he wanted to get better and to see if I had magic words or techniques that would produce mental health in him.

It Takes Some Painful Effort

Dan isn't all that different from the rest of us. He wants the nice rewards of a healthy life, but he doesn't want to do what it takes to get them. I can identify with that. I'm sure you can, too, at least to some extent. The lazy side of all of us wants the path to good things to be bump-free.

The fact of the matter is that the road to mental and spiritual health is paved with a lot of hard work. This truth—"there is no gain without pain"— is not new. It's one of those "been around a long time" truths that we always need to stay close to. If we want to achieve personal growth, we have to do it the old-fashioned way and earn it.

I am reminded of a couple who came to see me for marital problems, Scott and Ellen. They had been married for eight years, and most of that time had been unhappy. They were in a lot of pain when they came to see me and *appeared* to be willing to work hard to make their marriage better. Unfortunately, in their case, appearances were deceiving. After a few sessions, I gave them their first assignment to do. Here's what happened:

"Before you leave, I want to give you something to work on by next session," I said.

"Something to work on?" Scott asked, a twinge of concern in his voice.

"Yes, there is a marital intimacy workbook I want you to work on between sessions. It has sixteen chapters in it, and I would like you to do one a week. Each chapter takes about an hour individually to read and respond to study questions, and then you spend another hour talking with each other about your responses," I explained.

"So, we do each chapter by ourselves and then spend some time talking about it, is that it?" Ellen asked.

"Yes, that's right," I said.

"Dr. Thurman, I'm not sure we have the time to do something like that," Scott stated.

"Oh, sure we do!" Ellen quickly responded.

"Well, maybe you do, but I sure don't. I'm lucky to keep my head above water each day. There is no way I have time to spend two hours on this workbook each week," Scott said, becoming defensive.

"You have time to watch football every Saturday and Sunday," Ellen replied, just as defensively.

"Scott," I interrupted, "I know you are busy, but the work you do in between sessions is just as important as what you do when you are here in my office. If you are going to get the most out of counseling, you need to go through the workbook."

"Well, I'll try but . . . ," he said.

Over the next three weeks, Scott and Ellen continued to come to counseling, but Scott never got around to completing the first chapter of the workbook. Ellen had done a number of chapters, but she couldn't discuss any of them with Scott because he hadn't done them. That issue surfaced during what turned out to be our last session together.

"Ellen, you look upset today," I said.

"I am, Dr. Thurman," she replied.

"What are you upset about?"

"You told Scott and me that we needed to do this workbook as part of counseling. Every week for the last three weeks I have done a chapter in the workbook, but Scott has done nothing. We are supposed to have those 'staff meetings' you talked about where we discuss our answers, but Scott can't because he hasn't done anything. How am I supposed to not be upset about that!" she replied angrily.

"I have been busy!" Scott asserted, defending himself.

"You are *never* too busy to do what you want to do! You haven't missed playing golf with your buddies in three weeks! You haven't missed a Cowboys game on TV! You haven't missed *anything* you enjoy, but you can't seem to find the time to do this workbook and make our marriage better!" she exploded, tears streaming down her face.

"Look, I am doing the best I can! Isn't it enough that I am coming here to counseling every week?" Scott shot back.

"No, it isn't enough! If Dr. Thurman is going to help us, we have to do what he says! You show up in here for an hour a week and think that will somehow magically make our marriage better!" Ellen complained. Sometimes, clients do the confronting for you.

Ellen was right. Other than coming to the counseling sessions once a week, Scott wasn't willing to do any hard work to improve his marriage. He wanted gain without any pain. Ellen, on the other hand, "put her money where her mouth was" in that she had invested a fair amount of effort into doing the workbook so that she and Scott could discuss their answers and grow as a couple. Scott was using his golf game and keeping up with his favorite football team to run from the hard work his marriage required of him. And Ellen was understandably upset. Scott decided to quit coming to counseling after that session because he said, "It isn't helping me, especially getting jumped on for not doing the assignments."

Is it human nature to want something for nothing? Yes! Does it ruin our lives? Yes! The desire to grow without being willing to pay a price for it is a part of our nature that we must destroy. Scott gave in to his nature, and he and Ellen quit coming to counseling. Scott wanted a "fit" marriage, but he didn't want to spend any time working out in the "gym" to have one. Their marriage continued to be "out of shape" as a result.

There was a television commercial several years ago in which some college students were talking about how easily everything seemed to come for a friend of theirs. As they made these comments, scenes were shown of their friend studying late into the night, doing pull-ups at the gym, and closing down a pizza place after a long night of work. I liked that commercial because I think its message was honest: positive results are never easy, no matter how things may appear to be on the surface.

If we want anything to be easy, we have to work hard. If we want a quiz to be easy, we have to study hard. If we want a couple of hours on the tennis court to be easy, we have to train hard. If we want our marriages to be easy, we have to work diligently on them. If we want life to be easy, we have to put our all into it, painfully so.

When it comes to mental, physical, and spiritual growth, there is no gain without pain. Don't let anyone tell you otherwise.

Growthwork

Years ago, I was out of shape. I joined a health club in an effort to face that problem. I will never forget my first workout. I tried to lift some weights and found that I didn't have a whole lot of muscle strength. I got on an exercise bike and started pedaling but could last only a few minutes before my lungs and legs started to hurt. By the end of the workout, I thought I was going to die. I was so exhausted and dizzy that I had to sit on the floor of the shower stall in the locker room with cold water coming down on my head to keep from fainting. I wanted to quit. It was too painful.

Yet I stuck with it whether I felt like it or not. I showed up at the health club three nights a week and kept doing whatever I could. As time passed, I could lift the same weight a greater number of times. Then I could lift a heavier weight. I could get on the exercise bike and last ten minutes, then thirty, and ultimately an hour. After a few months, I had lost weight and felt better than I had in years.

I say all of this to remind you of what you already know—the first "work-outs" in any area of life where you need to improve yourself are always the hardest. If you can "gut it out," you will build up stamina that will enable you to reach a higher level of being "in shape" so that the workouts down the road are no longer that painful.

This is true in the physical realm of life, but it is also true in the emotional and spiritual realms. Our emotional and spiritual health depends on our willingness to "exercise" on a regular basis, however painful it may be. We are motivated by knowing that the personal gains will be tremendous if we will stick with the program long enough.

Now, here is your assignment. Write down on a piece of paper the areas in which you want "gain" but have been unwilling to do the "pain." Maybe you have wanted to lose weight but have been unwilling to exercise. Maybe you have wanted to get out of debt but have been unwilling to reduce your spending or cut up your charge cards. Maybe you have wanted deeper friendships but have been unwilling to call somebody to arrange spending more time together. Maybe you have wanted a closer relationship with God but have been unwilling to practice certain spiritual disciplines to have it. Whatever the "don't want to do the pain to have the gain" issue in your life has been, write it down.

Choose one item from your list, and *go face your pain*. Do what you have to do to get the results you want. Right this very minute, decide what you are going to do, how you are going to do it, and when you are going to do it. Do it right now if you can. Make sure you do not let this week go by without doing whatever it takes to face your problem.

Let me recommend two things that might help you here. First, tell somebody what you are going to do, and ask him to hold you accountable for doing it. Ask him to call you every day if necessary to encourage you to do what you agreed to do and make it more difficult to bail out of the effort.

Second, you may want to make getting to do something you like dependent upon whether or not you face your problem. Let's say you need to do your taxes but have been putting them off. Let's also say you love to eat out. I suggest that you don't let yourself eat out again until you finish doing your taxes. Whatever it takes to get it done, do it!

Do the pain; get the gain!

II

■

You Don't "Have to" Do Anything

People are always blaming their circumstances for what they are.
I don't believe in circumstances.
—George Bernard Shaw

Have you ever noticed how often people say the words *have to*? Have you ever noticed how often you say them? Here are some frequently heard "have to" statements. Do any of these sound familiar?

"I have to go to work tomorrow."
"I have to pay my taxes."
"I have to obey the speed limit."
"I have to visit my parents."
"I have to finish college."
"I have to take my kids to the park Saturday."
"I have to lose some weight."
"I have to clean out the garage this weekend."

I'm sure you've said most or all of these statements at one time or another. But here is the truth: you don't *have to* go to work tomorrow. You don't *have to* pay your taxes. You don't *have to* obey the speed limit. You don't *have to* visit your parents. You don't *have to* finish college. You don't *have to* take your kids to the park on Saturday. You don't *have to* lose weight. You don't *have to* clean out the garage this weekend. You don't *have to* do anything if you don't want to. That's how free you are.

But there is a not-so-small hitch. You don't have to do anything, but negative consequences may come your way if you choose not to do certain things. For example, you don't have to go to work tomorrow, but you may get in trouble with your boss or possibly be fired if you don't. You don't have to pay your taxes, but you may find yourself in trouble with the IRS if you don't (the agency has a way of wanting to hear from you each year). You don't have to obey the speed limit, but you may get a ticket if you don't. I think you see the quid pro quo going on here, right?

Now, why all the fuss about the words *have to*? When we say the words *have to*, we have lost sight of the truth that we do everything out of choice. In other words, we have *free will*. We *choose* to do whatever we do. The bottom line to all this is critical if you want to be mentally and spiritually healthy: a *have to* attitude toward life makes you a bitter victim while a *choose to* attitude makes you a healthy victor.

You Always Have Choice

Alan was a classic example of how a *have to* mind-set can destroy you. He came to see me about the tremendous bitterness he felt concerning how he *had to* get married. He and Sandra had dated off and on throughout college. Toward the end of their senior year, Sandra became pregnant with their child. As much as Alan loved Sandra, he did not feel ready for marriage. Yet he married her anyway, carrying into the relationship busloads of resentment toward Sandra, as if his choice to marry her was all her fault. During one of our sessions, Alan expressed how he felt.

"I don't know if I can ever get over this," Alan stated bluntly.

"The way you and Sandra got married bothers you a lot," I replied, trying to narrow the focus.

"I *had to* marry her," Alan replied, as if the need to discuss that issue was over. "I had no choice."

"Objectively speaking, that isn't really true, is it?" I asked.

"What do you mean?" he shot back. "I'm not the kind of person to ask a girl to have a baby out of wedlock, much less have an abortion."

"Nevertheless, those were some options available to you, weren't they?" I pressed.

"No, they weren't. I couldn't have asked her to do those things. They were not options for me," Alan stubbornly retorted.

"Alan, you keep saying that these options weren't really options. Yet they were. You just chose not to take them," I replied just as stubbornly.

"Dr. Thurman, they were not options for me. There is no way I would have asked Sandra to have our baby out of wedlock or to abort the baby!" He refused to budge an inch, and his eyes seemed to dare me to continue my line of conversation.

"Look, Alan, I think I know where your bitterness and resentment are coming from, but I'm not sure you are open to seeing it," I said gently, hoping he would let me open the door to truth just a crack.

His rigid posture relaxed slightly.

"Look, I'm here for your help," he said at last. "I'll try to listen to what you have to say."

I smiled reassuringly and then chose my words carefully.

"It seems to me that the bitterness you're carrying around about the way you got married has to do with your refusal to see that you did have some choices, both before Sandra became pregnant and afterward," I suggested. "Prior to Sandra's becoming pregnant, you both made the choice to be sexually involved. You and she also chose not to make certain she couldn't get pregnant.

"When she became pregnant, you both had some choices even then. Because of your values, though, abortion and adoption were options you were not willing to choose. So, you chose to get married instead—something you did not have to do. You and Sandra had choices. By not being willing to admit this and take responsibility for the choices you made, you now believe that you were forced into marrying Sandra by circumstances. And because you believe that you had to marry her, you resent her. You blame her, and you blame the circumstances you found yourself in for why you got married rather than take responsibility for the choices you made all along the way that helped create those circumstances."

Alan started to squirm in his chair. I could tell that he wanted to be open-minded, but his rigid notions about his situation were still too deeply ingrained in him.

"I just can't buy that! What would you have done if you were in my shoes? Would you have felt that you had a choice?"

(It is times like these that most of us therapist types feel like pulling our hair out and going into a different line of work—say, renting surfboards in Maui.)

"To be honest, Alan, probably not. But that just means I would be missing the truth too. The truth is, you had some options open to you, even if they didn't seem like options. You made the choice that best fit your values—what you believed to be right. Your wife didn't make you marry her. The circumstances didn't make you marry her. You *chose* to marry her!" I said this last statement with an exclamation mark in my voice. I wanted to make it stick.

"If that is true, how is it supposed to help me with the bitterness I feel about the whole thing?"

"If you accept responsibility for choosing to marry Sandra, your bitterness toward her will ultimately make no sense. What would there be to be bitter about?"

"Well, I would still be bitter that I had to . . ." His voice trailed off as he realized what he was about to say again.

"I think I see what you're after," he said, "but I feel light-years away from *really* believing that I didn't have to get married."

"I understand," I said. "But becoming emotionally healthy is tied to allowing the truth about all this to take precedence over how you feel about it and giving the truth enough time to do its job in your soul. The truth is, you chose to marry Sandra even though you didn't have to. She is not to blame for your choice. She owes you nothing for the decision you made. Your feelings of resentment are real, but you don't actually have a legitimate reason for being resentful toward her. These truths need to become a lot more important than how you feel right now."

One of the most difficult tasks we face is that of taking responsibility for how we feel and how we act. The natural human bent is toward blaming other people or things for the unhappiness we feel and the actions we take. Yet blaming somebody or something outside us for *our* feelings and *our* actions is a cop-out.

This was the struggle underlying Alan's bitterness over his marriage to Sandra. Alan didn't want to take responsibility for the choices he had made, so he fell into a *have to* mind-set that made it easy to blame Sandra. Once he had convinced himself that he had to marry Sandra, he was able to build up a mountain of resentment and bitterness toward her, as if she were the enemy. Doing that only added more problems to his real problem.

In both small, barely noticeable ways and big, glaring ways clients often fail to accept responsibility for the decisions they have made and for the consequences of those decisions. Helping clients take responsibility for both is a central task of effective counseling. Some clients choose to take responsibility; others choose to keep blaming. The former get better; the latter stay troubled and sick.

The unwillingness to accept responsibility for one's own problems is a primary reason that therapy doesn't "work" for some clients. A fair number of clients want to blame their problems on others. An example is a client of mine who sees the problem that brought him to counseling as "My company is the problem—my company is transferring me" rather than "I am having a hard time accepting the fact that I am being transferred." When the counselor doesn't join in on the scheme and dares to suggest that the client has a problem that isn't someone else's fault, the client sometimes becomes angry and stops coming to therapy. This is a more common scenario in counseling than you might imagine.

Clients who leave therapy this way often tell people, "Well, I did everything I could to deal with the problem, even went into counseling, and nothing helped!" The truth of the matter is that they didn't really do anything of substance to face the problem responsibly. It is a real battle at times to get clients to take any responsibility for their problems and for finding solutions to them. The beginning point for all this is helping clients see that *they* have problems and get them to accept responsibility for solving them.

Seeing Options, Accepting Responsibility

This, then, brings us back to Alan. The truth was, he did not *have to* marry Sandra. He did have other options, even if he didn't like them. But he found it easier to blame Sandra than to see his own problem. In counseling Alan, I focused on helping him recognize that he did have options in the situation he faced with Sandra and that he was responsible for the decision he made.

"It's hard for me to see how I could have opted for anything but marriage to Sandra once I found out she was pregnant," Alan insisted.

"Let's try another tack, then," I suggested. "Do you have to pay taxes?"

"Yes," he said. "It's the law."

"Just because it's the law doesn't mean people always pay their taxes, however, does it?"

"Well, no."

"It is a law that people are to pay taxes, but no one has to, if he or she is willing to run the risk of getting in trouble with the government."

"I'm not willing to run that risk." Alan chuckled.

"Me, either," I said. "But let's move this now from a question of legality to a question of personal standards. When the United States went to war against Mexico, Henry David Thoreau was so against it, he refused to pay his taxes. He was supposed to pay his taxes, but he didn't have to. He chose instead to face the consequences. He was arrested and put into jail.

"Thoreau's friend, Ralph Waldo Emerson, was also very much against the war in Mexico, but because Emerson believed in the democratic rule of the majority and obeying the laws of the land, he paid his taxes. He didn't *have to,* but he *chose to.*

"One day, Emerson went to visit Thoreau in jail. He looked through the bars and asked, 'Henry, good friend, what are you doing in there?' Thoreau immediately replied, 'A better question, Emerson, is what are *you* doing out *there?*'"

Alan nodded his head. "I see your point. Both men had a choice, but no matter which choice they made, it would bring consequences with it. Thoreau chose to disobey the government, and he wound up in jail. Emerson obeyed the government, but at the expense of his personal beliefs about the war."

"Exactly! The point here is not that one man was right or wrong in what he did. That isn't our concern. The only thing we are concerned with here is that both men had options. So if Thoreau were here today in my office telling me he had no choice but to go to jail over the war with Mexico, you and I would know that just wasn't true. He did not have to go to jail. He chose that option."

"Just like I didn't have to marry Sandra," Alan said, seeing the personal connection. "I just chose that option because it fit who I am and what I want to stand for the best."

"That's right," I said. "It was your choice. And to be bitter toward Sandra about something you chose to do isn't really honest or fair, is it?"

He shook his head. "I guess I've been using her as a scapegoat. I just didn't want to take responsibility for the choice I made. I suddenly feel like a real coward. I've been hiding behind my wife, using her as a shield against being responsible. I can see that there are a lot of things I blame her for, especially when it comes to the marriage itself."

"I know that seeing this is painful for you, Alan, and that the changes you need to make seem a long way off. But you are already on your way and farther along toward taking responsibility for your choices than a lot of people get."

At this point in our work together, Alan has taken more responsibility for his decision than ever before, but he occasionally lapses into a "look what you made me do" assault on Sandra. Now, though, he views his resentment toward Sandra as a problem he has—a struggle to see the truth more clearly. And struggle he does. As theologian Robert Munger so accurately put it, "All truth is an achievement." This was certainly true in Alan's case. Seeing that he didn't have to marry Sandra and that he was responsible for his choice to do so was probably the toughest achievement of his life.

I hope you will take the discussion in this chapter seriously. More than a few of us walk around with hundreds of *have to*'s dominating our thoughts and, much like Alan, feel pretty bitter toward people and life in general. We feel like victims, not victors. Alan had certainly built a huge case for what a helpless victim he was regarding how he got married, and he had a ton of bitterness and resentment to show for it.

The truth we all need to see is that we don't have to do anything. Even if someone has a gun pointed at your head and is demanding your money and valuables, you don't *have to* give him what he wants (although I would suggest that you *choose to*). That is how free we are. Seeing this leads to greater acceptance of personal responsibility for what we choose to do in life and, consequently, a lot less bitterness and resentment.

A quick thought out of the other side of my brain. If you want certain outcomes in your life, you can legitimately argue there are *have to*'s. If you want a healthy body, you *have to* exercise and diet. If you want a good marriage, you *have to* spend time working on it. If you want stable employment, you *have to* go to work consistently. But you don't *have to* want a healthy body, a mature marriage, or stable employment. The point here is that there are no real *have to*'s until you choose to want some specific result or outcome in your life. Then, the *have to*'s are real, but you still freely choose them.

Now, try out the following statements and see how they feel:

"I *choose* to go to work."

"I *choose* to stay married."

"I *choose* to love my kids and raise them properly."

"I *choose* to lose weight."

"I *choose* to be unhappy (or happy) in my life."

"I *choose* to get angry at the guy who rides my bumper."

"I *choose* to let things from the past continue to hurt me."

"I *choose* to allow people to treat me the way that they do."

"I *choose* whether or not to have a satisfying life."

If these statements have the ring of truth to them, you are on your way to living a healthier life. If they don't, you have a lot more work to do. Keep working, though; it will be worth it. It was for Alan.

Growthwork

For the next week, I want you to use the A-B-C-D-E model to keep as accurate a record as you can of all the times you tell yourself you *have to* do something. For example, let's say someone at work whom you don't like that much happens to like you a lot and asks you to have lunch every week. Using the A-B-C-D-E system to examine this, your entry might look something like this:

"A" (Event): A person I don't like that much asks me to have lunch every week.

"B" (Faulty Self-Talk/Lies): I have to have lunch with him, or his feelings will be hurt. I can't really say no, even though that is what I really want to say. Why do people do this to me?

"C" (Response): Tense physically; feel irritated and guilt ridden; avoid running into him at work.

"D" (New Self-Talk/Truth): I don't have to say yes. His feelings might be hurt, but that really isn't my responsibility. I can tell the truth, which is that I already have lunch partners. I could thank him for asking me to eat lunch—it is a compliment to have been asked. I could try to eat with him now and then, like once a month, just to show some kindness and interest. Whatever I do, it is a choice. I really don't have to say yes just because I was asked. I'll be honest and tell him that meeting regularly won't work for me, but that I will be glad to meet with him once a month.

"E" (New Response): Less tense; feel calmer, more at peace, somewhat anxious about having *the* conversation with him; called him on the phone to talk.

The thrust of this assignment is to help you fight your *have to*'s with the truth that you always have options, the freedom to choose from among them, and responsibility for what you decided to do. I encourage you to prove this truth in your life as often as you can. In the process, you will see more clearly than ever before that you don't *have to* be a victim in life or put up with the emotions that go along with being one.

Remember, you are about as free in life as you think you are.

12

■

THE VIRTUE LIES IN THE STRUGGLE, NOT THE PRIZE[1]

When the one Great Scorer comes to write against your name,
he marks not that you won or lost, but how you played the game.
—Grantland Rice

One day two women met on the street.

"Lucy, I haven't seen you in ages," said the first woman. "Your new pet store must really be keeping you busy."

"All the animals got sick from bad water," said Lucy. "They died and I lost the business."

"My word! How tragic. You and Ralph must be heartbroken."

"Ralph is dead. One of the dogs bit him, and he contracted rabies. Didn't last a month."

"Incredible," said the first woman. "Your son must miss him terribly."

"The shock was too much for him. He died of a heart attack."

"Your son too? This is just too much to believe. How dreadful!"

"Oh, but wait," said Lucy, starting to smile, "you haven't heard the good news yet . . ."

And just then a bolt of lightning struck her, and she fell dead on the sidewalk.

We all might laugh at this story, not because we enjoy sick humor but because we all can identify so strongly with the poor woman's problems. As you face each day, it can seem as though life is one problem after another. On Monday your electric bill arrives, and it's three times as much as you have left in your bank account. On Tuesday your child comes down with strep throat. On Wednesday your car dies. On Thursday your spouse tells you he or she is sick and tired of being married. On Friday you discover you have lost thousands of dollars in a poor stock investment.

And so it goes, never ending.

Maybe that's why we laugh so hard when we watch Wyle E. Coyote in his continuous efforts to catch the Road Runner. It's like watching ourselves. When something goes wrong for the coyote, it usually leads to a chain reaction of catastrophes. The boulder he rolls down the hill at the Road Runner circles up the opposite wall and comes back down and smashes poor Wyle E. . . . and then the cliff ledge he is on gives way and he drops down the canyon and smashes into the ground . . . after which, the same boulder falls on him again. Finally, he squeezes from under the boulder, staggers to his feet, only to be run over by a passing truck.

It's so stupid, yet for thirty-plus years I've watched those cartoons and laughed my insides out. It's fun. It's fun because even though we see the coyote squashed into an accordion, we know that ten seconds later he will be up and ready to try again.

There's a message in that. When we're laughing at that ridiculous coyote, we're laughing at ourselves, at the way we are, at the way life is. Pursuing the Road Runner gives meaning to Wyle E. Coyote's life. Catching and eating the scrawny little bird would almost seem anticlimactic after all those years of scheming and plotting for his capture. After the conquest, what next? It's the struggle that brings out the persistence and drive and ingenuity of the coyote. That's what makes us laugh—he is always getting smarter because he just doesn't know when to quit.

And neither do we, I hope.

The Need for Struggle

There is a lot of human nature in Wyle E. Coyote. We often love a struggle even more than the prize it offers us. It has always been that way. When Alexander the Great conquered the entire known world in 323 B.C., he sat down and wept. There were no more battles to be won. Hundreds of years later, just months after the July 20, 1969, date when Edwin "Buzz" Aldrin Jr. became one of the first two men to walk on the moon, Aldrin realized that, as a pilot, there were no greater achievements he could strive for in his lifetime, and he had a nervous breakdown.

A great irony of life is that people complain constantly about how hard it is to "get ahead"; yet when they no longer have to struggle, they seem to go stir-crazy and *make* work for themselves, or they lose their inner sense of purpose and develop emotional problems. Few people seem able to "stand success" and enjoy the "prize" once they have it.

This has been a recurrent theme of great literature. For example, throughout the novel *Les Misérables*, by Victor Hugo, a police inspector named Javert hunts the elusive criminal Jean Valjean. In the end, when Javert finally has a chance to capture and arrest Valjean after many years of pursuit, he cannot bring himself to do it. Instead, he hurls himself into the Seine River, committing suicide. The chase had given him a reason for living. For it to end was for life to end.

Consider the real-life parallels to that. Have you ever heard parents say that they can't wait to get their kids raised and out of the house so that they can have some time to themselves, yet once the kids are gone, these same parents nearly go crazy with all the time they have on their hands?

Have you ever heard a man say he couldn't wait until retirement so that he wouldn't have to work any longer, yet once retirement came, he became depressed, maybe even suicidal, because he lost his work-related identity? That was one of the themes in Joseph Waumbaugh's novel *The New Centurions*, which relates the story of a police officer who killed himself after he was retired from the force because he no longer felt he had a reason to exist.

The point of all this is to challenge you with another great truth that has survived the test of time: the virtue lies in the struggle, not the prize. It is the hard work we put into the trip itself that is our victory in life, not getting to the destination.

I have had my struggles with "the virtue lies in the struggle, not the prize" truth. My tendency is to be so prize-minded that my efforts along the way get little or no credit. Graduate school felt like that. I felt as if victory was to be obtained only when I got my doctorate, not in my efforts to get it. Postponing victory until after five years of graduate school was a long time to wait. Writing my first book felt the same way. I worked hard for more than a year to write it, but I didn't allow myself any feelings of victory until it was finished. The effort to write it seemed to have no virtue, whereas I put much of my sense of victory in the actual prize of finishing the book.

In each case, I cost myself a great deal. In retrospect, I can see that the virtue was in working on a doctorate, not in getting one. I can also see that the virtue was in writing a book, not in its finally coming out. This "scoreboard" mentality, where the effort on the field is considered unimportant and the final score is considered the only thing that matters, crushes a lot of us.

Accepting the Struggle

There is another spin on this issue: pursuing a dream but not achieving it. How many times have you felt like a loser because something you were earnestly trying to accomplish didn't come through? So many times, our efforts don't result in what we hoped they would. The salesperson invests tremendous amounts of time in making an important sale to somebody, but it doesn't come through. The athlete trains diligently for a major competition but doesn't place in the top three. Parents put their all into raising well-rounded, healthy children, yet one of them makes numerous self-destructive decisions totally out of keeping with the way he was raised. Life is full of these situations where our efforts aren't rewarded with a successful outcome or at least aren't as successful as we had hoped.

In these situations, most of us would feel that we had failed and that there was no value in our efforts. Our struggle would not feel worthwhile to us because the prize never came. As before, let me suggest that the truth we need to face is that the virtue is always in our efforts, not in what they yield.

Yes, I know this sounds trite, but if understood on a deeper level, this truth becomes very important. It creates more willingness to try and less resentment and bitterness if our efforts do not turn out so well. Let me take you into the counseling office again to show you the importance of this truth.

Hal was a full-blown perfectionist, which caused chronic feelings of depression and anxiety for him. Throughout his life, he struggled with a feeling that his performance was never good enough. In college, he made grades that most of us would kill for, but to him, they were mediocre.

He felt the same way about his performance in sports. He was an avid golfer, but he was chronically upset about his golf game because it was never "good enough." He might shoot the best round of his life, yet walk away upset because of the one or two holes he played imperfectly.

In our sessions together, Hal started to accept the "to err is human" truth discussed earlier in this book, and his depression and self-hatred lessened. However, in spite of this progress, Hal started to feel that his improvement should be coming faster. He wasn't going to be satisfied until he had his perfectionism "perfectly" cured. So we discussed this issue.

"Dr. Thurman, I'm getting very impatient with therapy. Things aren't going fast enough to suit me. I'm not getting better quickly enough!"

"You feel you should be changing faster?" I asked.

"Yes. I feel that I should be over this problem by now," he answered, as if not wanting to be challenged on it.

"Hal, it sounds to me like you're being perfectionistic about your perfectionism," I said.

"What! What do you mean by that?"

"Well, you have been perfectionistic since the time you were a very young boy, being that way day by day for more than forty years, and after twelve sessions of counseling, you feel as though you should be cured. How realistic is that?"

"Not very, I guess," Hal admitted. "But I can't really feel good until I whip this thing."

I shook my head slowly. "No virtue in the effort, just the prize," I mumbled, more to myself than to Hal.

"What's that?" Hal asked. "I'm not sure what you mean by that."

"You seem to take no satisfaction from the fact that you are trying to fight your perfectionism. Instead, you've decided that you can't claim victory until you completely defeat the problem."

"Well, that's true, isn't it? Until I defeat my perfectionism, there is no victory."

"I don't agree with you," I said bluntly. "The fact that you came here for help and are trying to be less perfectionistic is your real victory, your 'virtue,' if you will. It's not a matter of whether or not you've beaten it yet."

"That sounds nice in theory," he shot back, "but while I'm still struggling with perfectionism, I'm continuing to be depressed, angry, and unhappy. That isn't much of a reward for all this work I've been doing."

"But you're doing all that you can. Can't that be enough?" I asked, knowing full well that Hal wouldn't see it that way.

"No, it isn't enough. I'm not going to be content until I see some results for my efforts. That's just the way I am about things."

"But I thought 'the way you are about things' is why you've been so unhappy and why you came to see me for help," I countered. "You sound like you're making a case for staying the way you are."

"No, I'm just saying that it's hard for me to accept mere effort as the victory. What I want is the end result—that's the victory I'm after."

"I understand that, Hal, but I think this attitude often gets you into emotional trouble. So many times the reward for our efforts is way down the road, if available at all. In light of that, it seems to me that our effort to try to accomplish something worthwhile has to be the victory."

"Maybe, but what you want me to accept is pretty foreign to my whole way of thinking," said Hal. "I'm not sure I can buy into it."

"Believe me, I know what you are talking about. The idea that the effort is the key thing didn't always fit into my way of thinking, either. But I believe it to be one of the critical truths we need to live by if we are going to be emotionally healthy. Given that you play golf, let me put it this way. The virtue is not actually in breaking par but in making an effort to play your best. As simple as that sounds, it is the truth."

"So you are telling me to fight my perfectionism by letting my efforts to change be enough—at least for now—and to quit focusing so much on whether or not I whip this thing. That, I guess, will come by making the effort, right? Sort of like playing golf: just work on keeping your head down and left arm straight, and the ball almost *has* to fly in the direction you want it to."

"Yes, that's right," I agreed. "All we can do is make a good effort. That is our victory, our virtue. Then the ball goes where it goes."

Winning the Prize Is the Only Thing?

In my efforts to help Hal focus on effort versus results, an interesting piece of the puzzle emerged. When Hal was a youngster playing Little League, his father would take him out for a hamburger and a malt after a game only *when he played well*. On nights when Hal played poorly, his father drove him straight home. From the experience, Hal surmised that the bottom line was how well he performed, not how hard he tried. His whole life might have been different if his father had said things like, "I'm sorry you didn't do too well tonight, Son, but I'm proud of the effort you gave it. Let's grab something to eat and then get home in time to play a little catch before it gets dark."

As a youngster, Hal needed his parents to help him understand that "the virtue lies in the struggle, not the prize." He needed to know that however well or poorly he played, the important thing was that he gave it his all. Since he was not told that, he fell victim to the Vince Lombardi mania that says, "Winning isn't everything; it's the *only* thing." What rubbish.

Here's a better perspective for you to have on winning and losing. Teddy Roosevelt was shorter than most men. He had poor eyesight. As a child, he was often quite sick. He was married in 1880 to Alice Hathaway Lee, who died just four years later. He ran for mayor of New York City and lost. He ran for president in 1912 and lost. He organized an expedition in 1919 to explore the remote jungles of South America but died of a blood clot before getting very far into the jungle.

At a quick glance, it would seem that Teddy Roosevelt had a terrible life. But Roosevelt lived daily by the concept that the virtue lies in the struggle, not the prize. Here is how he expressed it:

> The credit belongs to the man who is actually in the arena; whose face is marred by dust and sweat; who strives valiantly; who errs and may fail again and again, because there is no effort without error or shortcoming; but who

does actually strive to do the deeds, who knows the great enthusiasm, the great devotion.[2]

Did this attitude help Roosevelt through those terrible phases of his life? You be the judge. Here is a brief summary of his life's accomplishments: commissioner of the New York City Police; assistant secretary of the U.S. Navy; colonel in the Rough Riders; governor of New York; vice president of the United States in 1900; at age forty-two, the youngest man ever to serve as president of the United States (1901–9); author of two thousand published articles, essays, and books; father of six children in two marriages; and winner of the Nobel Peace Prize in 1906.

Teddy Roosevelt was a winner every day of his life—whether he won an election or lost it, whether he made progress on a task or suffered a setback—because Roosevelt's personal definition of a winner was someone who made an effort. Making the effort and being "on the field" were what counted, not if you finished win, place, or show.

When Losing Is Winning

Champions in sports, business, politics, industry, and the arts know this truth: if you do your best at something, you end up a winner even if the scoreboard says you've lost.

I realize that sounds contradictory, but stay with me a moment and I'll show you how it works.

During the 1980 Olympics, an American athlete named Eric Heiden took all five gold medals for men's speed skating. In the first four events Heiden set new Olympic speed records: 38.03 seconds for the 500-meter race; 1 minute 15.18 seconds for the 1,000-meter; 1 minute 55.44 seconds for the 1,500-meter; and 7 minutes 2.29 seconds for the 5,000-meter. In the final event, the 10,000-meter race, Heiden not only broke the Olympic record, but also set a new all-time world speed record of 14 minutes 28.13 seconds.

As amazing as these victories were, they came as no surprise to those who had followed Eric Heiden through the years. Heiden had been winning every time he competed in an amateur race. He was recognized as the greatest men's speed skater who had ever lived. Sports writers knew it; coaches knew it; even Heiden's competitors knew it. The plain and simple fact was, no one could equal Eric Heiden when it came to speed skating.

Now, you may think that such knowledge would demoralize and deflate skaters who had to compete against Heiden. After all, what was the point of entering a race when you knew in advance you had no chance whatsoever of beating the champion? Depressing, right?

Just the opposite proved true. When Heiden won the 500-meter race, silver medal honors went to Evgeni Kulikov of the USSR, *who turned in his personal fastest time ever* for the 500-meter race. When Heiden won the 1,000-meter race, the runner-up was Gaetan Boucher of Canada, *who clocked his personal fastest time ever* for the 1,000-meter.

And so it continued in every race. The silver and bronze medalists who lost to Heiden actually achieved greater personal speeds than ever before simply because they were doing their best to be the equal of Eric Heiden. This phenomenon became known as the Heiden Effect, which now is defined as achieving new personal victories by striving to equal a competitor one knows one can never be equal to or surpass.

Would you call Evgeni Kulikov and Gaetan Boucher a couple of losers just because they finished second to Eric Heiden? I wouldn't. My feeling is that anyone who exceeds all of his personal best levels of performance is a winner, no matter what the scoreboard says. That is the way I am trying to bring up my three children. If they make a solid effort, they'll be winners in my opinion. And unlike Hal's father, I let my children *know* that their dad loves them—unconditionally!

The virtue lies in the struggle, not the prize. Memorize that truth. Meditate on it. Keep it available for those times you are working diligently on something and the reward is nowhere in sight. When you are fighting a weight problem and not making much progress, remind yourself that the effort to lose weight is your victory. When you are fighting being in financial debt, remind yourself that the effort to pay off your bills is your virtue. If your marriage is faltering and all your efforts to make it better seem to be failing, remind yourself that your struggle to make the marriage better is your victory. I hope "I'm giving it my best shot" can become a victory statement for you. More often than not, it will result in "I accomplished," which is icing on the cake.

Grantland Rice was right. It is how you play the game that really matters.

Growthwork

This chapter, as with the chapters preceding it, has challenged you to alter your old way of thinking about certain ideas you've heard or experienced all your life. Before you move on to the next chapter, I want you to do another growthwork assignment.

Specifically, I want you to take one of the truths we have covered so far and write down the pros and cons of thinking that way. What are the advantages and disadvantages of having that tape up in your head? Let me give you a little help to get you started.

Let's say you choose to do a comparison using the truth "to err is human." Here is how you might want to do this in your journal:

Truth: To Err Is Human

Advantages of Thinking This
- It fits reality.
- It allows for mistakes.
- It takes pressure off me.
- It allows me to focus on learning from mistakes vs. wasting time and energy being self-condemning.
- _____
  _____

Disadvantages of Thinking This
- It could lead to becoming indifferent about mistakes.
- It could be used to justify making mistakes: "After all, I'm only human."
- _____
  _____
- _____
  _____

The point of all this is to get you to use your common sense to assess the cost/benefit side of thinking a certain way. The truth will always have more benefit to it than cost; lies will always cost you more than they help you gain. Take a shot at this by choosing a truth that is especially important for you to grapple with, and compare the pros and cons of thinking it.

13

■

LIFE IS DIFFICULT

*Life is like playing a violin solo in public and learning
the instrument as one goes on.*
—Edward Bulwer-Lytton

Does the name Vinko Bogataj ring a bell? No?

Well, let me give you some hints about who this very famous person is. He drives a forklift in a factory that manufactures anchor chains. He lives a quiet life with his wife, two daughters, and mother-in-law. In his spare time, he paints and carves wood.

Any guesses yet? None? Well, let me give you more hints. Vinko Bogataj lives in Lesce, Yugoslavia, and is probably the most famous retired ski jumper in history. Still no guesses?

Even if you don't recognize his name, you've probably seen Vinko Bogataj. You see, Vinko happens to be the poor "agony of defeat" guy of ABC's *Wide World of Sports* fame. He was the guy who took an incredible head-over-heels fall while in a ski jump competition in Oberstdorf, Germany, in 1971. Unfortunately for Vinko, *Wide World of Sports* was there to capture every inglorious second of his spectacular fall. They have been broadcasting Vinko's fall at the opening of their show every week for years, permanently immortalizing him in the "Sports Hall of Shame." Jim McKay, the voice of *Wide World of Sports* for the thirty years it has been on the air, says that perhaps the single most-asked question about the show concerns this poor skier from Lesce.

I don't know about you, but I kind of understand how Vinko must have felt when he messed up for all the world to see. In my own not-so-glorious ways throughout my life, I have made some pretty spectacular falls. Mine weren't there for the whole world to see as was Vinko's, yet I still felt as though I had about the same amount of embarrassment and shame that went along with them. Hardly anything feels worse than these moments.

I remember one of those moments as if it were yesterday. I was in Michigan giving one of my "Thinking Straight" seminars before an audience of about three hundred people. I was covering some important material using an overhead projector. Thinking I was writing on a transparency, I actually wrote all over the clear glass plate that the light is projected through instead. I can't tell you how humiliated I felt when I realized my mistake.

There I was in front of three hundred people staring at an overhead projector with my scribblings all over the glass plate and no way to erase them. If there had been an exit door nearby, I would have slithered out as quickly as possible and never returned to the beautiful state of Michigan again. I felt like Vinko Bogataj sailing off the side of the ski jump. Talk about feeling like you have been walking around in public with toilet paper hanging out of your pants! Fortunately, the people in attendance found my plight extremely funny, and a member of the audience got me some wet paper towels to clean off the glass plate so that I could continue the seminar.

Maybe you have had a Vinko Bogataj moment or two in your life. Maybe you have found yourself gliding down the ski jump of life ready to take glorious flight, thinking to yourself, *What a piece of cake!* Only you lose your balance and go careening off in some disastrous direction. As you lay there emotionally bruised and bleeding from your mistake, you probably felt the complete loss of self-worth and confidence that goes with such moments. You might also have felt the cold stare of people who were there to observe that not-so-grand moment in your life.

Why all this fuss about our friend Vinko and his famous fall off some ski jump in Germany? Well, I want to use his experience, and our own like it, to suggest another important truth that we need to fully understand as we head down the ski jump that each day represents: life is difficult. Vinko found that out as he tried to keep his balance as an athlete. We find this out each day as we try to keep our balance as human beings.

It's a Difficult Life

Almost everyone on the planet seems to have a personal "life is difficult" story to tell. These stories are sometimes amusing, sometimes heartbreaking, often somewhere in between. But listen closely to how these stories are told. You'll notice that the storytellers are often surprised, even insulted, that life had proven to be difficult. It is as if they had been operating under the assumption that life should be easy and smooth. They often tell their stories with great resentment and anger as if life had chosen only them on which to inflict misery. In a very real sense, they have not come to grips with the great truth that life is difficult. Instead, they are still living in a childlike world where life is all peaches and cream and every challenge is easily navigated.

A number of years ago, I started to realize that I was one of those people. My realization began when I read Dr. M. Scott Peck's book *The Road Less Traveled*. He opens the book with the simple statement, "Life is difficult," and proceeds to call it one of the greatest truths and one that few people come to grips with. I remember thinking I had wasted my money on the book if that was all it had to say to me. "Tell me something new!" was my initial (and arrogant) thought.

As I thought more about it, though, I could see I hadn't really come to grips with this truth. I saw more deeply than ever before that I had spent all of my life believing that life should be easy and that something was horribly wrong when difficulty dared to rear its ugly head. I saw how much I resented problems coming my way and how I responded to them with a "How dare you do this to me!" attitude. I often found myself whining and moaning whenever difficulty happened to me.

Essentially, I had not grown up! I was looking at life much as a child does—through rose-colored glasses that made life look prettier and easier than it really is. When life wasn't pretty or easy, I would throw an internal, and sometimes external, temper tantrum that would match any five-year-old's best. Sound familiar? Maybe you can identify with my struggle to accept that life is, indeed, difficult. Maybe you also want to keep seeing life in rosier shades than it really is. Maybe you, like me, do your fair share of whining and moaning when life is tough. If so, I don't think we are alone.

Life Shouldn't Be Difficult?

With the evidence all around us that life is difficult, I am amazed at how many of us still refuse to accept it. I guess what we know intellectually and what we really believe down in our guts are two different things. We all intellectually know that problems are part of life, but many of us believe that they shouldn't be. From my twenty years of clinical experience, the typical client in counseling seems to think that life should be fairly easy and often blows a gasket when life proves otherwise. Let me give you an example.

Becky came to counseling with enough anger to fill an ocean. Because she often lost her temper, her boss told her that either she go to counseling or she go out the company door. She wasn't exactly what you might call a "happy camper" kind of client. The following exchange took place during one of our sessions:

"I don't know why I'm here," Becky said glumly. "My boss pretty much forced me to come because I lost my cool a few times with some customers at work."

"So you don't think you need to be here?"

"I'm sure I *don't* need to be here!" she adamantly replied. "I may lose my temper every so often, but the people I get angry at usually deserve it. They put me through so much unnecessary hassle, I just can't help getting furious with them!"

"You don't feel you have much control over your anger at those times."

"It feels like a wave coming over me. I can't stop it. I speak before I think and end up getting myself in trouble," she stated, as if she were confessing to a priest.

"Becky, I believe it's just the opposite. I believe you think *before* you speak. Play along with that thought for a minute. Let's assume you think before you speak. What do you think you might be telling yourself prior to getting angry at these people?"

"Your guess is as good as mine," she answered, as if I were one of her customers hassling her, not wanting to be much help.

"Come on, give it a try. What do you think is going through your mind about these people who put you through so much unnecessary hassle?"

"That they are jerks and shouldn't be making my life so difficult!"

"You think they are making your life more difficult than it should be, is that it?"

"Yes. I don't need them to make my life any more difficult than it already is."

"Becky, let me ask you what may seem to be an insane question. How difficult do you think your life should be?"

"What do you mean?"

"Well, you said that these customers make your life more difficult than it should be. That seems to imply that you have some sense of how difficult life ought to be. So let me ask you again, how difficult should your life be?"

"I don't think my life ought to be *that* difficult! I shouldn't have to put up with people who have nothing better to do than irritate me!"

"Let me ask you an equally insane question. Why not?"

"What do you mean, 'Why not'? Why should anyone have to put up with people like that?"

"Because life is full of people like that."

"You gotta be kidding me. I'm supposed to accept that life is full of jerks?"

"Yes."

"Dr. Thurman, with all due respect, I can't believe you're saying that to me. Why would I want to accept that?"

"Look at the price you are paying for not accepting it! You walk around ready to explode at a moment's notice, and you are close to losing a job you told me you like pretty much. The price you are paying for thinking life ought to be easy and 'jerk-free' is already pretty high and could go even higher if you lose your job."

"I just can't accept that my job should have hassles in it like that!" she fought back, refusing to budge.

"Becky, let me play a little rougher with you. Why do you think your life should be any different from anyone else's? Why should you have the only job on the planet where you don't have to deal with less-than-wonderful people? Are you royalty? Do you deserve a hassle-free life and the rest of us don't?"

"No, I don't think anyone should have to put up with difficulties that aren't necessary."

"Well, that doesn't really solve the problem, does it? Whether any of us *should* have to put up with irritating people and unnecessary problems or not, they show up on our doorstep anyway. There are lots of difficulties in life. You seem to be saying that rather than face that and accept it, you are just going to stay mad at it, no matter how much you lose in the process."

"When you put it that way, it doesn't really sound too good," she sheepishly responded.

"Maybe the truth of the matter is, that attitude *isn't* too good. Maybe that attitude is keeping you from handling life more maturely than you do."

"I don't know. Maybe you're right," she conceded, without really sounding convinced.

"Becky, let me be bold with you. I *am* right on this. You are telling yourself that your life ought to be free from certain kinds of difficulties, and you get furious when it isn't. The truth is that your life is just like mine and everyone else's—it has problems in it that aren't a lot of fun to deal with. And these problems are, in a sense, testing how mature you are. Your boss is trying to tell you that you are not doing too well on the 'maturity test' at work and that you need to do better or you will lose your job. For you to do better, you are going to need to come more fully to grips with the truth that life is difficult, both in tolerable and in not so tolerable ways, whether you like it or not. You can choose to squeal like a stuck pig when life is difficult or do the mature thing and accept the difficulty and handle it to the best of your ability."

"I think I'm getting your point. You're saying my anger toward the customers is tied to wrongly believing that they shouldn't be making my life difficult when the truth of the matter is that life *is* difficult and they are just proving that to me. I'm at odds with the fact that life is difficult rather than accepting it and dealing with it."

"That is exactly what I am trying to get across."

"I gotta tell you that your being right about this isn't much comfort. I still don't think I will be able to handle jerks at work any better. I will still tend to speak before I think."

"Isn't that why you are in counseling? Aren't you here to work on that problem? Don't you think your boss will keep you as long as you work on the problem and show some improvement over time?"

"Yes, she will keep me if I get better. She likes my work in general, and she seems pretty invested in helping me improve myself as an employee. And now that you mention it, maybe I am in counseling because I need to handle people better than I do. And not just at work but in my personal life as well. I get pretty angry there also."

"Becky, a lot of different issues figure into your anger outbursts at work, and we can use our sessions to explore what they are. So far, I am just suggesting that one of the more core issues is a basic unwillingness to accept the truth that life is difficult. Your work life was just pointing that out to you through the 'jerks' you were being asked to help. Life is a pretty good teacher at times if we will let it be. In this case, it was trying to teach you that you hadn't learned an important truth that you need to know in order to have a successful life. I'm confident you can learn to accept that life is difficult and not be so at odds with it."

"I sure hope so. I don't want to spend the rest of my life blowing up at people and things that bother me."

My sessions with Becky often came back to the "life is difficult" truth. Time and time again, she would bring into my office complaints about this hassle and that hassle, angry and resentful that life had dared to be difficult again. We kept trying to look at what life was telling her and kept trying to break past her unwillingness to listen. She did make progress, though it was slow at times. Bit by bit, she started to accept that life is full of problems and that staying at odds with that truth was only hurting her.

When I began writing this chapter, I was tempted to take the "life is difficult" truth and give you some more dramatic versions of it to prove the point. I was tempted to tell you stories like that of a client who was chased around her house as a child by her father with a knife in his hand threatening to kill her, or that of a client who was forced by her father to have sex when the mother was out of the house, or that of my client who lost all of his hard-earned money and a business he had devoted his life to because his business partner swindled him and put the business in bankruptcy. These are the stories that break your heart. Instead, I opted for one that involved a patient facing the difficulty of dealing with "jerks" at work.

The point is this: whether in small ways, large ways, or in-between ways, life is difficult. That is a vitally important truth. Stepping out on the planet thinking otherwise is inviting emotional trouble on a scale that none of us can ultimately survive. Becky came to see that. I hope you already have. If not, I hope this chapter has reminded you of it.

Before I send you into the next section, I want to bring some needed balance to what I am saying here. The truth that "life is difficult" doesn't mean that "life stinks" or that "everything in life is awful" or the like. The fact that all of us will face difficulty in life is not a reason for cynicism or pessimism. Either extreme in thinking—that life should be nothing but roses or that life is nothing but thorns—will lead you to emotional ruin. Life has its thorns and it has its roses and everything in between. That is the proper balance of thinking we need to have here.

Growthwork

I hope that you are a little more clear-minded about the fact that as long as you draw breath, you are going to have problems and they will make your life difficult. Knowing you are going to have problems and truly accepting that are two different things, though.

In light of that fact, I want you to do the following assignment. I want you to make a list of the problems you have had in your life so far that have made your life difficult. Don't worry if some of them sound small or petty; just write them down. Your list can encompass problems others caused you, problems you caused yourself, or problems no one caused (or all three). I'll lead the way and give you a few items from my list.

Problems I Have Had That Made My Life More Difficult

1. Moved around a lot as an Air Force "brat." Made relationships with friends less stable and long-lasting.

2. Seriously injured my knee as a college freshman. Has kept me from playing certain sports that I love since then.

3. Had acne as a high school and college student. Felt like I was a "walking zit" most of the time and felt a lot of shame and embarrassment. Didn't date much as a consequence.

4. Mom suddenly passed away at the age of fifty-seven from a brain aneurysm. Didn't get to share with her the joy of receiving my Ph.D., getting married, or having kids.

5. Didn't get accepted into the doctoral program I graduated from the first time I applied. Delayed getting my career started and meant laying out a year.

The problems I have had in my life are not likely to be turned into a big-budget motion picture. *Chris's Big Zit* starring Robert Redford (of course) isn't going to be coming to your neighborhood theaters anytime soon. My problems so far have been relatively minor compared to what some people have faced. Many of my clients, for example, have had much worse problems than mine. Yet they are still some of the problems that made my life difficult to some degree.

How about your list? Lots of major problems? Mostly minor ones with a big one or two thrown in for good measure? No major problems at all yet? How has life been to you so far?

More important, have you accepted the problems you have had yet? Have you come to grips with the fact that they happened and you have been able to move on from them, or are you still struggling with bitterness and resentment that these problems came along at all?

Now, the hard part. For each problem on your list, ask yourself, *Have I accepted that I had this problem yet?* For any problem that the answer is no, I want you to write in your journal why you think that is the case.

A quick word of caution before you do the assignment. Accepting a problem doesn't mean liking that it happened or that it doesn't still hurt. You can accept that something happened in your life and not be glad it did and still hurt over it when you think about it. Accepting it means that you have faced the fact that it happened (versus refusing to), understand why it occurred (versus being in the dark about why it did), have let it hurt (versus feel numb about it), and have come to a place of peace about it (versus still in turmoil over it).

Once you have written in your journal about the problems that you haven't accepted yet, I want to encourage you to let yourself finally do so. Along these lines, I want to give you a script:

I accept that _____ happened to me. First, I admit that it did happen. I am no longer going to say that it didn't or it shouldn't have. The fact of the matter is, it took place.

Second, I admit that I don't like that it happened—that it made my life difficult to some degree. Specifically, the problem made my life difficult in the following way: _____

_____

Third, I acknowledge that the problem was painful emotionally in that I felt _____, _____, and _____ during that time. It still hurts to this day in the following ways: _____, _____, _____.

Fourth, I acknowledge that having had the problem led to some growth in my life as a result. Specifically, I have grown in the following ways as result of this problem: _____

_____

Fifth, I understand why this problem occurred. It occurred because

_____

_____

Finally, I am committed to working on more deeply accepting that this problem happened—to allow this to be a process that will take time. I accept that this problem occurred as much as I can today, and I will try to accept it a little bit more tomorrow. I hope someday that I will have come to accept this problem completely, but I will be content to take small steps to get there.

By working to accept that life is difficult, you have become more realistic. In becoming more realistic, you have become more emotionally and spiritually healthy. As a former coach of mine used to say, "Ya done good!"

14

■

YOU REAP WHAT YOU SOW

Who is man's chief enemy?
Each man is his own.
—Anacharsis

More than a few of us hope that this truth, "you reap what you sow," isn't true. But true it is.

We eat a large bowl of our favorite ice cream each night for a week while watching television and then hope the scales won't reflect it. We spend money as if there is no tomorrow and hope the charge card people will forget to bill us at the end of the month. We don't exercise, yet we expect our bodies to remain healthy and firm throughout our lives. We ignore our kids and hope they will grow up to be healthy adults. We race down the highway at breakneck speed and hope there will be no police officers around.

In dozens of different ways we hope that we can avoid the consequences that accompany our actions.

The sad truth is that sometimes we *seem* to get away with certain actions and it doesn't appear that we are reaping in accordance to what we have sown. People often speed without getting caught by the police. People sometimes cheat on their taxes and don't get audited by the IRS. Some people even commit murder and do not end up in prison.

It appears that people can violate the reap/sow principle at times, that they can beat their fate, that they can fool themselves and others if they are just crafty enough. Yes, it *seems* that way. But I believe we *always* reap what we sow, even if it doesn't appear that way.

I believe everything we do contributes, for better or for worse, to who we are. Every action adds another stitch to the fabric of our character. We never actually get away with anything because whatever we do leaves its impression on our memories, our consciences, and our souls.

167

Take the highway speeder. He may speed down the interstate at ninety miles per hour and not get a ticket. Yet he has sown something into who he is. His "self"—his personality, his value system, his innate sense of right and wrong—has been affected in a negative and self-degrading way. He has added another stitch into the part of his being that disrespects rules, that rebels against authority, that treats other people's safety with indifference, and that shows a callous hostility toward society. He may reach his destination that day in record time, much to his delight, but he will have done so at the expense of his soul. Most regrettably of all, he will probably have done all this without even realizing it.

The sowing we do each day in small ways shows up sooner or later in several significant ways. Years may go by before the more public signs show up, but they ultimately appear. We may be shocked when we see the final fruits of what we have sown, but that just reflects how naive we have been. Most of us assume that the small, seemingly unimportant things we do each day aren't shaping us. But shape us they do.

When you stop to think about real-life incidents such as the demise of Bill Clinton's presidency, Pete Rose's baseball career, Donald Trump's financial empire, Leona Helmsley's hotel wealth, Rock Hudson's movie legacy, Jessica Savitch's news career, Elvis Presley's entertainment impact, and Jim Bakker's religious ministry, I think you can start to understand the point I am making. Those people seemed to be doing fine—even fantastic—on the surface. But in retrospect, we can see clearly the seeds of their downfall were sown all along the way to reach fruition in the banner headlines that shocked us all. Each downfall began with a small, seemingly innocuous action here, an apparently unimportant behavior there. Small seeds of moral carelessness sown along life's way turned into weeds of destruction later on.

I see the "you reap what you sow" truth all the time in the lives of my patients. Let me take you into my counseling office to illustrate the point.

As the Twig Is Bent

Hank came to see me because of a problem with pornography. He frequently rented videos with strong sexual content and bought "adult" magazines. He would often do this when his wife was going to be gone from the house all day or for a weekend. Hank's compulsion to rent pornographic videos and to buy lewd magazines was strong, and he felt that he couldn't stop himself from turning to pornography whenever an opportunity arose.

Because of strong religious values, Hank felt a tremendous amount of guilt and shame about his problem with pornography. He kept it hidden from his wife and friends. He experienced a great deal of anxiety about being seen renting or buying pornography. Even when that went "smoothly," Hank felt "like a scumbag" about doing it. He had lost self-respect because of the problem. He came to counseling, hoping to find a way out of the struggle. During one of our early sessions, Hank and I traced the origins of his problem.

"Hank, tell me if you can how far back your struggle with pornography goes."

"Well, I remember when I was really young that some of the older kids in our neighborhood had some adult magazines they were showing to everyone," Hank recalled. "I didn't really know what was going on, so I just looked at the pictures too."

"About how old were you at the time?" I asked.

"Somewhere about seven or eight, not any older I'm sure."

"What else do you remember?" I prodded.

Hank's eyes narrowed and he rubbed his chin. "Uh, we had a neighborhood drugstore that had a magazine rack. A lot of the magazines had provocative pictures on the covers of scantily clad women. I'd go in there and pretend I was checking out the sports magazines, but really I was looking at the adult magazines. Sometimes when the clerk was busy with a customer, I'd grab one of the magazines and quickly leaf through the pages and look at all the pictures."

"Anything else?"

"Well, yeah," said Hank, "there was temptation at home. My father kept a stack of men's magazines in his closet. Whenever my folks would be out of the house for any reason, I'd sneak into their room and look at those magazines. I'd always make sure I put them back exactly the way they were when I found them. I was scared to death that my dad might suspect I'd been looking at them. He never mentioned it, however, so I just figured I had gotten away with something."

"Did this go on a long time?" I asked.

"Oh, sure, for years," Hank admitted. "I'd think about those magazines pretty often. When I got older and my folks would go out for a night together, it meant I would be home alone for hours with those magazines. I was pretty obsessed with them even then."

"What age were you?"

"I discovered the magazines when I was about eleven or twelve," said Hank, "and I kept sneaking into the closet to look at them into my teenage years. When I hit puberty, it felt like I had lost my mind over sex. I couldn't seem to think about *anything* except sex. I was involved in sports and that helped a little bit, but once practice or a game was over, my mind would often revert to thoughts about sex."

"Did you ever consider talking to your father about this problem you were having?"

Hank flinched. "My dad? Are you kidding? My dad never once had a man-to-man talk with me about sex or girls or dating or anything like that. No, neither one of us ever brought up the subject."

"It appears that you and your father had a similar problem with pornography but never disclosed it openly," I replied. "You became a chip off the old block in a sense."

"Since getting older, I have come to see that about me and my dad, but not when I was still a kid," Hank answered. "In those days, the guys at school would talk about girls. You know, we'd say things in the locker room to make other guys think we knew a lot about sex. After we got our drivers' licenses, we'd go to R-rated movies. It seemed like we talked about sex all the time. Most of us had steady girlfriends by then, and we were all into heavy petting. We'd brag a lot, but the fact was, we didn't know as much as we pretended we did."

"What about after high school? Did it continue?"

"Definitely," said Hank. "I went to college, and I was in a dorm with guys who would buy porno magazines and pass them around. I bought some too. This was back in the days before videos."

"You were of legal age by then, right?"

"Yeah. I could buy anything I wanted. My buddies and I would sometimes go to X-rated films at a sleazy theater in a town thirty miles from the college campus. Back then they still had drive-ins, too, and some of them would run double-feature R-rated movies on the weekends. I knew I was hooked on this stuff when I couldn't find anyone to go with me one weekend and I drove out to the drive-in by myself."

"That must have been pretty lonely," I suggested.

"Yes, it was," said Hank. "But the sad part about it was, I liked to be by myself whenever I looked at pornography. I would fantasize that I was the guy that all those girls wanted. It was exciting, an escape of sorts. It actually helped me feel less lonely at times. At least for a couple of hours."

"Did these fantasies ever spill over into real life?"

"Little by little, they did," Hank admitted. "I'd find myself looking at the girls who were in class with me or who were walking across campus, and I'd carry this secret lust for them. Sometimes when I was on a date with a nice girl, I'd let a suggestive remark come out. It usually didn't go over very well. I even got my face slapped one time. You know, as I look back on that now, I can see how some women get the notion that the only thing men ever think about is sex. With a guy like me, that isn't too far from the truth."

"Once college was over, what was the struggle like?"

"I got a job that brought me here to Texas," Hank explained, "but I didn't know a single person other than the people at work. My nights were lonely, and my weekends were pure torture. So I fell back on the one cure for loneliness and boredom that had always seemed to help before. I bought adult magazines. Also, there were X-rated home videos available by then. I'd sometimes spend my whole day at work just marking time until I could go to the video store and rent some more porno movies. The anticipation was always really strong, but later that night, after I watched the videos, the sense of loneliness would come over me again. I felt empty."

"What about after you met some new people here?" I asked. "Did getting closer to people help you with your struggle with pornography?"

"Somewhat. Especially after I met some girls and started going out on dates. That gave me something other than videos and magazines to think about. But it wasn't a cure-all. There still were times when no dates were available, so I'd turn again to the pornography. It became a compulsion I couldn't seem to control, much less overcome."

"Eventually, you got married, though. How much did being married help?"

Hank lowered his head slightly. "I thought it would help a lot, but maybe I expected too much. I mean, my wife and I have an okay sex life and all, but my mind seems filled with pictures of other women I've looked at in magazines or on videos. That's distracting to me, and it's unfair to her. I find myself wanting variety, but one woman can't possibly be as versatile as a store filled with sexually explicit videos. So I find myself turning to pornography whenever I want variety, and that only compounds the problem. It makes sex with my wife less desirable. I know she must feel that I don't love her and that I don't find her sexually attractive. She tries to talk to me, but I just can't bring myself to tell her what's been going on behind her back."

"You're afraid that she'll be hurt and angry," I said.

"No doubt about it," Hank insisted. "It would shock her and break her heart. She wouldn't be able to understand. I can't imagine ever being able to tell her about my 'secret' life."

"You're afraid of losing her respect, aren't you? You want to protect the positive image she has of you."

"Sure. Every husband wants his wife to respect him. She thinks of me as a moral man. I don't want to shatter that view. But it's all a false front. And that's one reason why I've come to you. This is more than I can handle alone. I need some help. Big-time help."

"You've taken a positive step," I reassured Hank. "I know your struggle with pornography has been a tough one. But if your love for your wife was strong enough to motivate you to come here for help, you may be a lot closer to fitting the image she has of you than you think."

Hank's face lifted. I could tell he felt encouraged and he was glad he had come for counseling.

"The origin of your struggle goes back to when you were very young," I told Hank. "By looking at the pictures in the magazines, you became part of the group of onlookers. You weren't alone. It felt good to be part of the gang.

"Later, when you became old enough to derive sexual stimulation from such pictures, that added a powerful dimension to your desire to make pornography part of your life. You found pleasure and relief in pornography so often that the habit became very strongly rooted in you. Today, the habit is controlling you rather than your controlling it. In the process, your self-respect has taken a real beating."

Hank weighed my words, then nodded his agreement. "I think that pretty much hits the nail on the head. So what am I going to do about it?"

"I won't kid you," I said forthrightly. "You have spent so many years entrenched in this problem, it will be a tough one to overcome. I know that isn't exactly what you want to hear, but it's true nevertheless. We all reap what we sow, for better or for worse. In your situation, the sowing of all those thoughts and actions over the years has led to being addicted to sex."

Hank contemplated that a moment, then said, "I hadn't thought about my struggle with pornography as the result of reaping what I had sown, but I guess you're right. Every time I purchased a magazine or rented one of those videos, I was sowing more of the problem. Now I'm reaping all the negative results of that. I really wasn't getting away with anything all those years I thought people weren't 'catching' me at the porn shops. If I had really wanted to conquer this problem, I should have been *catching myself*."

"Well," I said, "before you beat yourself up too much, I want to point out that you didn't exactly get a lot of help along the way. Your father, by keeping adult magazines in his closet, was giving approval to pornography. Also, you grew up in a culture that is sex drenched and often treats women as sexual playthings, which was another message to you that it was all right to think of women as pornographic objects."

I let that sink in, then added, "A number of other elements figure into the equation here, but you understand what I'm getting at. I agree that you made your own choices along the way and that you are responsible for those choices. But you didn't get much help, either."

I spent a few minutes trying to explain the fine line between personal responsibility and impressionability—young boys being influenced by externals, such as male role models and cultural attitudes, for example.

"I appreciate what you're trying to say," Hank told me. "I know my dad's attitude toward pornography didn't help my situation. And growing up in a country that seems as sex-obsessed as America is probably only fanned the fire. Still, I can't get away from the fact that my choices were really bad."

"You're suffering now from the consequences of your previous choices. I hope that you can let that be enough punishment and that you will channel your energy into understanding the problem and fighting it."

Breaking Free

That is just what Hank has done with some success. He is fighting his problem as best he knows how. We have continued to explore his background and how it has affected his views of women, sex, and love. We also have spent time examining how he used and still uses pornography to run from intimacy. We have further examined how pornography fed his need to be in control, to be powerful, and to be the center of attention.

These efforts have helped Hank see his struggle in a more honest light and have helped him develop more self-control when it comes to buying magazines and renting videos. Hank opened up about his problem to a close friend who was also struggling in this area. Hank and his friend have agreed to discuss their mutual problem regularly and to encourage each other to keep fighting it. Hank made the very wise decision to join a counseling group for sex addicts and to tell his wife about his struggle. The revelation was very upsetting to her, but she has supported him and his efforts to overcome his addiction to sex.

Hank's story is similar to ones that most of us could tell. Although his struggle was with pornography, it could have been with any number of other things. We are all addicted to something—food, drugs, money, approval, recreation, work, whatever. The point I have been making in this chapter is that most of our current problems are simply the long-term reaping of years of sowing the wrong thoughts and actions. As the quotation opening for this chapter suggests, we are often our own worst enemies in that we sow some unhealthy thoughts and actions in our lives, causing us to reap some pretty painful and destructive results.

The examples of the truth "you reap what you sow" in this chapter have focused on negative reaping and sowing, yet the flip side of this truth is also available to us: each of us can sow positive thoughts and actions and reap the healthy consequences of having done so. For example, a person can sow healthy exercise and nutrition habits for a long enough time that he will reap physical health throughout his adult life. In this light, we can also be our own best friend when it comes to reaping and sowing.

"You reap what you sow" is central to the theme of this book. If you "sow" lies in your mind long enough, you will reap all the emotional and spiritual problems that lies cause. On the other hand, if you "sow" truth in your mind long enough, you will reap all the healthy benefits that the truth can lead to. We are, to a large degree, what we think. If you want to know what you will be like in ten years, it will pretty much come down to what you spent those years telling yourself. If you spend the next ten years sowing lies in your mind, you will be a mess in ten years. If you spend the next ten years sowing truth in your mind, you will be the kind of person you always dreamed of being.

What kind of sower are you?

Growthwork

"You reap what you sow" is a psychological/spiritual law you can't violate. It applies to you whether you want it to or not.

You do have a choice concerning which version of reaping and sowing you make your own. If you sow unhealthy thoughts and actions, you will experience painful, destructive reaping. If you sow healthy thoughts and actions, you will experience life in full.

Take a minute to apply the sow/reap principle to your life. What are some of the ways that you have experienced the up and down side of this truth? Write them in your journal. Let me lead the way for you by sharing some of my own:

Positive Sowing

1. Have paid off monthly debts every month for years.

2. Have exercised regularly for years.

Positive Reaping

1. Debt free (except for our house).

2. Physically fit, at appropriate weight.

Negative Sowing

1. Have stayed up late working and watching television for years.

Negative Reaping

1. Find it difficult to go to bed before 1:00 or 2:00 A.M.

2. Have been work and productivity
   oriented most of my adult life.

2. Have a hard time relaxing
   and being able to have fun.

I think you get the point. My life has seen both the positive and the negative sides of sowing and reaping, and I am sure yours has too. In your journal, try to write down as many examples of each as you can think of.

Once you have done that, I want you to take another step. On the negative side of reaping what you have sown, choose one that you are willing to do something about. Ask a friend or group of friends to hold you accountable for making some changes in this area.

For example, you may have chosen to face a problem with too many years of not exercising or dieting properly, or you may have chosen to face being in debt because you have allowed your spending to go beyond what you make. Whatever you chose, get some help to turn it around.

A quick thought. There is an expression that says, "Nature abhors a vacuum." The personal growth implication of this statement is this: you can't just stop doing something; you have to put something in its place. If you are trying to stop watching so much television, you have to replace that behavior with something healthier—reading good books, taking walks, playing board games with the family, or getting some extra sleep. In your efforts to move from negative sowing/reaping to positive sowing/reaping, think not only about what you want to stop sowing but also about what you want to start sowing.

Again, make sure you have someone in your life who knows what you are trying to do and can hold you accountable for doing it. Efforts to make changes by yourself are almost always doomed to fail. Find a Tonto so that the journey to making needed personal changes isn't a lonely one.

15

■

YOU ARE NOT ENTITLED TO ANYTHING

*This is the true joy in life, the being used for a purpose recognized by yourself as a mighty
one; the being thoroughly worn out before you are thrown on the scrap heap; the being a
force of nature instead of a feverish, selfish little clod of ailments and grievances complaining
that the world will not devote itself to making you happy.*
—George Bernard Shaw

One of the most difficult attitude problems any counselor faces is that of entitlement. Entitlement is an attitude of "I'm owed . . ." or "I deserve . . ." based
on who one is or what one has done. It is apparent in statements such as:

"I'm a college graduate, so I deserve a high-paying job."

"I've been good to my friends, so they should be good to me too."

"I'm a senior citizen, so I deserve younger people's respect."

"I have had a lot of negative experiences, so life owes me something better."

"I took good care of my kids when they were young, so I am entitled to
their help when I grow old."

Our culture loves to foster entitlement notions in us. During the 1970s,
McDonald's restaurants built an entire ad campaign around this slogan: "You
deserve a break today." Notice that McDonald's didn't say, "You need a break
today" or "You probably want a break today" or "Wouldn't a break today be
nice!" No, McDonald's wanted to convince you that you deserve a break—
you're entitled to one because you are such a wonderful person or you do so
much hard work! In the 1990s, it was, "You *owe* it to yourself to buy a
Mercedes-Benz." Again, the idea isn't that you need a car or want a car, but
that you owe it to yourself. And not just any car, but a Mercedes-Benz—that's
how awesome you are! Society continues to bombard us with the message that
we are deserving people who are entitled to wonderful things.

Nothing could be farther from the truth. As hard as it may be for you to
hear this, I want to tell you something loud and clear: *you are not entitled to*

anything while you are on the planet! You do not deserve a break today! You do not owe it to yourself to get a Mercedes-Benz! You are not entitled to "life, liberty, and the pursuit of happiness"!

Demanding Versus Desiring

There, I'm glad I got that off my chest! Now, before you throw this book in the trash, I want you to look at the other side of the coin. Although you are not entitled to anything, you have all the freedom in the world to "want" things in life. Wanting something (within reason) is fine, but feeling entitled to it is pathological. There is a *huge* difference between wanting something and feeling entitled to it.

What is the difference between wanting and thinking you are entitled to something? Let me walk you through a scenario to help you see just how big the difference is.

Let's say I am the world's greatest husband (a real stretch, granted). Let's say that I love my wife, Holly, unconditionally, and that I meet all of her needs 100 percent of the time. Let's say, though, that there are two versions of me as this perfect husband. Perfect Husband Version A feels *entitled* to getting the same thing in return from Holly, and Perfect Husband Version B *wants* the same thing in return. Now, let's see how different they are in life.

Let's say I come home from work after a long day, and I am Version A. I'm thinking, *Holly owes me love (kindness, support, attention), given that I am loving to her all the time.* Well, one of two things can happen at this point. First, let's say Holly is loving. That's great, but the problem is, I was *expecting* that from her. All I'm thinking is, *She is just giving me what I deserved, what she owed me.* Consequently, I don't really, truly appreciate her offering of love. The second thing that can happen is that Holly isn't loving. I become pretty upset and resentful, thinking, *After all the love I have given her, how dare she not love me in return?*

Before we move on to Version B of me, I want you to notice that the *best* that can come out of feeling entitled to my wife's love is that I don't appreciate it when she gives it. The *worst* that comes out of thinking I am owed her love is a great deal of anger, resentment, and bitterness toward her that she failed to give me what I felt I was entitled to. The emotional ceiling in the relationship is set very low here and can't get any higher as long as I think I'm entitled to Holly's love.

Now, compare this to me as Version B. I come home from a long day at work *wanting* Holly's love but not feeling entitled to it. One of two things can happen at this point. First, Holly acts lovingly. If she does, my thoughts would be like these: *Wow, I really appreciate the fact that she is loving toward me. I know she doesn't have to love me, and it means a lot to me that she does.* Yet it is also possible that Holly does not act lovingly that day, but wanting her love and not getting it lead to thoughts like these: *It hurts that she isn't being loving. I was hoping she would be. She doesn't have to love me, so I am not bitter. But wanting her love is fine, and I feel hurt and disappointed that it didn't come.*

Notice the difference in the possible results of wanting Holly's love. If I get it, I am thankful, appreciative, and happy. If I don't get it, I feel hurt and disappointed. Do you see how high the ceiling in the marriage is raised when I want (versus feel entitled to) love from my wife? The highest I get with entitlement is a lack of appreciation when love comes. The highest with wanting her love is appreciation when it comes. The lowest I get with feeling entitled to Holly's love is pretty low—resentment, bitterness, even rage. The lowest I get with wanting her love is hurt and disappointment.

I believe bitterness and resentment are poisonous emotional toxins to the human soul that we were not meant to be able to handle. The only way you can end up with these two is to stomp around the planet feeling entitled to things. That is how bitterness and resentment are created. On the other hand, not getting what you want in life doesn't create toxins. Hurt and disappointment don't destroy you—they are painful feelings and not easy to carry, but you can handle them.

The point is this: there is a huge emotional difference between what entitlement produces in us and what wanting something produces in us. We need to see that entitlement thinking is the kiss of death to emotional well-being and healthy relationships with others. If you want a sure prescription for being miserable, think you are entitled to something.

You Owe Me!

To some degree, we all have entitlement feelings. We all carry around some degree of feeling owed for something we have done or for some wonderful thing we are. When we feel entitled, we focus on what we are owed, not what we might need to do for others. It is a "one-way street" mind-set. Unfortunately, the one-way street of entitlement has a horrible collision waiting for us down the road.

Such was the case of Stan and Julie, a couple who came to see me because their marriage was in serious trouble. They had been married for just a year and were already contemplating a divorce. They were extremely angry and bitter toward each other, and each felt that the other person was to blame for how bad their marriage had turned out (the "all our marital problems are your fault" lie). As I explored their feelings with them, I began to see just how strongly both felt entitled to certain things from the marriage.

"Julie never listens to what I have to say," Stan complained. "She wants to be heard, but she never wants to listen."

"That's not true," Julie replied defensively. "I'm more than happy to listen. It's Stan who's never willing to listen to what I have to say."

"Why *should* I listen to you?" snapped Stan. "All you ever do is attack me for not meeting your needs . . . as if anyone could! You take and take and take, but you never want to give back."

"Boy, this is the pot calling the kettle black. All you ever do is think about what you want and how you are going to get it," Julie fired back.

I lifted my hands.

"Time out for just a second. Both of you sound pretty angry. You both seem to feel that something isn't being offered that you deserve."

"Well, I know I don't get what I deserve from Julie," Stan acknowledged. "I work hard all day, take care of the upkeep on both of our cars, mow the lawn, pay the bills . . . I do everything and she's not grateful."

"He's far worse," Julie countered. "I work all day, too, but I still do the laundry and most of the cooking. But does he show any gratitude? Never!"

They glared at each other, unblinking.

"I think I see one of the main problems in your marriage," I said as referee. "Both of you seem to have a pretty strong case of it."

"What are you talking about?" Julie asked.

"It seems to me that each of you feels entitled to the other's love," I explained. "Each of you seems to believe that the other person is indebted to you for what you do. You *expect* special treatment as appropriate payment. Indirectly, you both are saying to each other, 'Because I did this for you, I am entitled to something from you.'"

"So? What's wrong with that?" Stan asked, exasperated. "The whole world is based on 'I do this for you and you do that for me.' Give and take. You scratch my back and I'll scratch yours. Why shouldn't marriage be the same way?"

"Stan, a 50-50 approach to marriage doesn't work," I answered. "Feeling you deserve or are owed something from each other only fosters rebellion in each of you."

"Dr. Thurman, I'm not sure what you mean. Are you saying that if I love Julie, I don't deserve to be loved back?" Stan responded in his typical defensive manner.

"Yes, Stan, I am. It isn't your birthright to get something back just because you offer it in your marriage."

"Then why would anybody in his right mind want to give anything in marriage?" Stan demanded.

"Because it's the right thing to do."

"What!" Stan said, nearly gasping. "You're joking, right?"

"No joke," I assured him. "I'm suggesting you need to do things like listen to each other, help each other, and work for each other with no strings attached because it is the mature and healthy thing to do. Look what happens when the two of you don't: you both become bitter and vindictive.

"It is human nature to rebel when we feel that people think they are entitled to our doing things for them. We don't appreciate the lack of respect that conveys. You rebel toward each other to show that you don't have to do what the other expects. The response is childish, but it's typical.

"You both throw your personal versions of a temper tantrum, and everyone loses. Demand or feel entitled to 'something for something' from each other, and you will continue to see the relationship suffer. The only relationships that really work are 100-100 relationships—those where both partners do what is loving and right, whether they get anything back or not."

"What if the other person doesn't do the same thing?" Stan kept pressing. "Wouldn't the marriage get out of balance fast?"

"Yes, it could, but would that be any worse than the situation you're already in? Marriages based on nonentitlement don't typically get out of balance. When both people are doing what needs to be done without feeling entitled to payback, the marriage usually stays on pretty solid ground. Taking a nonentitlement stance with each other usually fosters emotional health, cooperation, and mutual respect. Marriages based on 'something for something' (entitlement) are doomed from the start. They never work!" I stated adamantly, knowing how cut and dried it sounded.

"So you're saying that a lot of our marital problems come from feeling that we are owed each other's attention, love, help, and so on," Julie summarized. "Our marriage is troubled because we feel entitled to things from each other when we really aren't. And because we approach each other that way, we end up rebelling toward each other."

"I'm saying that is one of the more critical elements in why your marriage has been so troubled, yes," I replied.

That was the first time Stan and Julie had been asked to look at the issue of entitlement in their marriage. It was a new concept for them and one that was hard to see at first. They continued in their old patterns of "I did this for you, so you should do this for me" for a while, but small changes did occur as time went on. They eventually came to see the truth that they were not entitled to each other's love, respect, loyalty, and help. This truth helped them appreciate what the other person did in the marriage, and they started to sense that their marriage could be saved and enriched. They rebelled less toward each other. Entitlement thinking came close to destroying their marriage; nonentitlement thinking helped to heal it.

Entitlement and You

How much entitlement do you walk around with in your life? I can see a fair amount of it in mine. I feel those "I deserve" feelings more often than I want to admit. Even in small things, I can see the problem. When I hold a door open for someone, I feel he owes me a "thank you," and I get miffed when I don't get one. In my marriage, I sometimes catch myself thinking, *Holly owes me* _____ *because I did* _____ *for her*. Even with my kids, I run into it. If I go to a lot of trouble to make a day special for them, I can sometimes find myself thinking, *Okay, you kids owe me some good behavior, as well as your lifelong appreciation for what a great dad I am.* (Unfortunately, they are thinking, *We are so doggone cute, it must be a real privilege for Dad to get to spend a day with such adorable kids as we are. We are responsible for most of the old boy's joy in life. He really owes us a lot.*)

The painful truth is that we are not entitled to anything on this planet. We aren't entitled to education, housing, health care, crime-free cities, an unpolluted world, love, kindness, fairness, or support. We are not even guaranteed a place in heaven. We aren't owed a high-paying job, healthy kids, or a "thank you" for a job well done. Wanting each of these things is great. Getting off our duffs and pursuing them is even greater. If they come our way, we are truly blessed and need to be appreciative. If they don't, we feel (deeply) disappointed and should.

Entitlement is a self-serving, arrogant attitude that creates bitterness and resentment in those of us who think this way and drives away people around us who don't like being treated in such a manner. Before you move on to the next chapter, take a minute to examine your entitlement assumptions. Have you fallen into this way of thinking? Toward whom or what do you harbor feelings of entitlement? How has it affected you emotionally? How has it affected your relationships?

Are you willing to try to let go of entitlement attitudes and feelings wherever they may be directed? My hope is that this chapter has helped you recognize your need for change in this area and that you will decide to change.

Growthwork

I have devised an Entitlement Quiz for you to take (it is a nonscientific quiz, meaning I came up with it just a few minutes ago and haven't done anything to verify that it measures what it is supposed to measure). For each of the fifteen statements, mark a number from 1 to 7, which gauges your personal feelings about the statement. Answer as honestly as you can, not how you think you should answer. Avoid using 4 as your answer if at all possible.

Entitlement Quiz

Please respond to the statements using the following scale:

1	2	3	4	5	6	7
Strongly Disagree			Neutral			Strongly Agree

_____ 1. I deserve respect from others.

_____ 2. I demand good service in a restaurant.

_____ 3. My closest friends owe me loyalty.

_____ 4. I expect fairness from others.

_____ 5. I'm owed a good-paying job given my education/abilities.

_____ 6. People should treat me the way I treat them.

_____ 7. When I do something nice for someone, I find that I secretly expect him to do something nice for me.

_____ 8. I deserve a "thank you" when I hold a door open for someone or let someone ahead of me in traffic.

_____ 9. People should listen to what I have to say.

_____ 10. I often feel "owed" for things I have done.

_____ 11. Other people have told me I demand too much.

_____ 12. All in all, I deserve a good life.

_____ 13. I am entitled to "life, liberty, and the pursuit of happiness."

_____ 14. I find myself getting angry inside when others don't do things for me they should.

_____ 15. My children owe me cooperation and obedience for all the sacrifices I have made for them.

Add up all of your answers to get a grand total. If you scored from 15 to 44, you are low in entitlement thinking. This means you don't tend to feel entitled to or owed things from people or life, and as such, you probably don't tend to feel bitter or resentful when what you want doesn't come through. If you scored from 45 to 74, you are moderate in entitlement thinking. This means you have a tendency to feel owed or entitled to things and probably carry around a fair amount of bitterness and resentment when things don't go your way. If you scored from 75 to 105, you are high in entitlement thinking. This means you frequently feel owed certain things from people and life and are probably carrying around a great deal of bitterness and resentment in your soul. It means you need help.

In your journal, I want you to take what you think you are entitled to and make an entry acknowledging that you are not entitled to it but that it is fine to want it. Let me show you what I mean:

"I am not entitled to my spouse's love, but it is fine to want it."
"I am not entitled to a good-paying job, but it is fine to want one."
"I am not entitled to physical health, but it is okay to want it."
"I am not owed appreciation when I do something nice for someone, but it is fine to want it."
"I am not entitled to obedient kids, but it is okay to want them to be obedient."
"I am not entitled to being happy, but it is fine to want to be happy."

McDonald's was wrong—you don't *deserve* a break today. You don't *deserve* a break the rest of your life. But I hope you *want* a break and take one when you need one. Knowing the difference is critically important in achieving emotional and spiritual health.

16

■

EMOTIONAL PAIN IS GOOD

One often learns more from ten days of agony than
from ten years of contentment.
—Merle Shain

Back in Chapter 12 we spent time looking at the value of facing our problems directly, whether they involve difficult relationships, finances, or self-destructive habits. We learned that it was getting involved in the struggle—making the effort—that really counted, not the reward.

Now that you've had time to let that become part of your new way of thinking, I want to take that line of thought to another level. I want to try to convince you that emotional pain is good.

No one wants to be in emotional pain, and we often bemoan the times we are. We sometimes bitterly complain when we feel depressed or anxious or angry or guilty about something. Rarely, if ever, do we see the beneficial side of emotional pain. Most of us seem certain there isn't a "good" side to it. But I want to try to convince you that emotional pain serves a very important function in our lives. To get you to agree with me, I want to take you into my home.

We have smoke detectors installed in several places throughout our house. I don't know all the ins and outs of how they actually detect smoke; I just know that they do. If a fire started in our home while we were asleep, the smoke detectors would sense it and would sound an alarm to let us know. By hearing the alarm, we would have a chance either to put out the fire or get out of the house. Without the smoke detectors, a fire could start undetected in our home while we were sleeping and spread so that by the time we were aware of it, it would be too late for us to get out of our home alive.

Now, I very seriously doubt that anyone in his right mind would wake up to the sound of a smoke detector going off at 2:00 A.M. and say, "Dang that smoke alarm. I wish it hadn't gone off!" No, that would be the height of stupidity.

Instead, we would be saying, "Thank the Lord for that smoke alarm. We saved ourselves and the house because it went off!" Although we wouldn't be happy about the fact that our house was on fire, we would be delighted that the smoke alarm let us know.

The Soul's "Smoke Alarm"

We humans have a similar alarm system wired into our souls. When the soul has a psychological/spiritual problem, the "smoke detector" goes off in the form of painful emotions such as guilt, hurt, anger, depression, and anxiety. In a very real sense, our painful emotions are warning signals—alarms!—telling us that something is not right inside us. They seek to warn us that something needs attention. If the underlying psychological/spiritual "fire" causing the emotions to "sound off" is not attended to, the soul incurs more serious damage. Sometimes, our souls become damaged to the point that we lose who we are.

As such, emotional pain is good. It is the warning signal we need to become aware we have an internal problem and to make us motivated to face it now so that it won't develop into a more serious problem later.

Unfortunately, too many of us hear our emotional smoke alarms go off and ignore them. We may feel depressed for days, months, even years, and yet ignore it and act as if everything is fine. We may explode with rage at the smallest frustration, yet ignore it, even though we know it's a warning signal that all is not well. We may feel chronically anxious, yet act as if it means nothing. The whole time our emotions are trying to tell us something, we may refuse to heed them. Many of us suffer much more damage to our souls than was necessary if we had just listened more attentively to what our emotions were saying.

Sometimes we don't just ignore our emotional pain; we make it go away through self-medication. Sometimes we react to being in emotional pain by doing things that create immediate pleasure, so we won't feel our pain. For example, take a person who is anxious. Instead of looking at the personal issue that is causing him to feel anxious, he may choose to drink alcohol, overeat, or use drugs to make the pain go away. The truth of the matter is that turning to these pleasurable substances "works": we feel better immediately, but we haven't really dealt with what was making us anxious in the first place. Ultimately, we may end up with two serious problems—the original one that was causing us to be anxious and an addiction to something.

Back to our analogy, seeking immediate relief from emotional pain via instant gratification/self-medication is like going up to the smoke detector in your home after it has gone off and clipping the wires. Then there is no noise to hear. I wonder if the function of addictions isn't just that—a way to make sure we don't feel our pain. But again, avoiding pain this way makes our pain ten times worse down the road when the addiction overtakes and cannibalizes our lives.

I find it rather amazing that an inanimate object such as an automobile can sometimes appear to have more common sense than a human being. If you purchase a brand-new car, it will have several computerized check systems built into it. If your car's oil level gets too low, a red warning light will flash on the dashboard. The same happens when the antifreeze, gasoline, and brake and transmission fluids get low. The car senses a problem approaching, so it sends a warning signal for something to be done. If the warning is heeded, the car's life is extended many extra miles. If not heeded, the car breaks down prematurely.

Emotional pain functions in a similar way. It signals us that maintenance is needed: a reduction of work-related stress, more physical exercise, improvement in our way of thinking, more sleep, dealing with hurt, and so on. If we would heed these warnings and care for ourselves as well as we do our cars, we would enjoy life more and live a lot longer.

When the Alarm Goes Off

Keith fit the profile of a man who was ignoring his emotional warning signs. He had struggled with overwhelming feelings of anger and shame his whole life, yet he refused to let these feelings warn him that he needed help. So, Keith avoided facing the painful internal issues that were crying out for help, and in the process, he destroyed his marriage and lost a loving wife. His anger had become so uncontrollable, his wife felt threatened by his outbursts. For her safety, she finally chose to leave him.

Keith felt quite broken by what happened. He came for counseling to sort things out.

"I know my anger drove her away, but I just couldn't handle her way of doing things," Keith confessed to me. "It aggravated me to no end!"

"Like what?" I asked.

"I guess the biggest irritation was just how much of a pack rat she was. There were things all over the house all the time. It drove me nuts to come home and see all the piles of clutter everywhere. Sometimes I would just explode at her."

"Did you ever stop long enough to think about what your anger was telling you?" I asked.

"Telling me? What do you mean?"

"Well, it seems to me that painful emotions are signals to us that something isn't right inside. Your anger kept trying to signal you, but you ignored it," I explained.

"I've never thought of it that way. My anger didn't seem like a signal, though. It was more like a reaction to something that frustrated me."

"Our natural tendency is to see our emotions as a statement about someone else rather than as a statement about ourselves. Does that make sense to you?"

Keith pondered that a moment.

"Sure, it makes sense in a way," he said. "I know that when I'm angry, I feel that it's a statement about what a jerk the other person is who I'm angry at. Is that what you mean?"

He looked surprised when I nodded my agreement.

"Yes. You thought your anger was a statement about your wife, for example, when it really was a statement about you," I said. "Your anger was trying to alert you to some problems inside you. You appear not to have used it that way, so this just created bigger problems in your life."

"You know, I used to be in the military, and I worked with radar. What you're saying kind of relates to how we used a rotating beam to spot enemy planes before they got too close," said Keith. "Without the radar, we would have been destroyed. With it, we could react appropriately and lessen the damage."

"That's a good analogy," I said. "Emotions—even the smallest versions of them—are often trying to warn us that something inside us is in trouble and needs to be attended to. In that sense, they are extremely helpful—even good—for us."

"I never thought I would call my anger good, but I can see your point. If I can just use it as a cue rather than always spew it all over the place, I might save myself a lot of trouble," he decided.

"Using your emotions this way is something that can be learned," I encouraged him. "You can get much better at it with practice. Right now, you're just learning to view your emotions this way. Getting better at it will come with time and effort."

Keith began to see his emotions in a new light, and not just anger but also fear, joy, depression, and hurt. He had an especially tough time acknowledging his hurt and using it as a cue that something important was happening inside him. Keith had been raised to believe that hurt was a sign of weakness and that he shouldn't feel it at all. Yet he did learn to see that even hurt was a feeling that was trying to cue him to some important issues that needed to be faced in his life.

Keith learned to pay attention to the type of emotions he was feeling as a way of gauging the stresses and challenges he was dealing with in his life. He learned to recognize the signs.

Detecting the Signals

Maury Wills of the Los Angeles Dodgers was one of baseball's greatest players. His specialty was stealing bases. One evening, after Maury had stolen his hundredth base of the season, a television sports commentator interviewed him. The interviewer noted that Maury had great physical strength, great agility, and great speed. The interviewer asked Maury if these were the secrets of being a great base stealer.

"They help," said Maury, "but the real secret is in mastering the art of telegraph detection."

"What's that?" asked the broadcaster.

"I make it a point to study the players on the other team," said Maury. "Every person has a set of special quirks and habits, and I try to pick up on them. Usually, these physical signs will telegraph a message to me about what a player is about to do."

"Telegraph?" asked the announcer.

"Right," said Maury. "For example, there's one pitcher who has the habit of pulling the visor of his cap before he tries to pick me off base. There's a second baseman who takes two steps sideways as the pitcher goes into his windup if it's going to be a pitchout and a throw down to second base. Dozens of these motions and gestures telegraph messages to me about when it's safe or risky to try to steal a base. If I watch the signs closely enough, I never get tagged out when I try to steal a base."

Just as Maury Wills was alert to "messages telegraphed" to him by his opponents, so, too, people like my client Keith have learned to recognize the emotional warnings telegraphed to them. When a client can go from viewing emotional pain as a problem to viewing it as a plus, he is on his way to health and maturity that will make his life much better.

Pain Motivates

Another reason emotional problems are good has to do with the simple fact that the pain involved in them often motivates us to change. Change is painful, and most of us would rather not change unless we have to. Painful emotions often serve as the "have to." You know what I'm talking about if you have ever been so miserable that you would do almost anything to stop hurting. The two great motivators seem to be misery and desire. Emotional pain is often the "misery" that motivates us to try to move beyond the status quo.

I see evidence of this truth all the time in the counseling I do. The majority of my clients come for help because their pain level got so bad that they "either had to come in or not make it." This tendency to wait until things are so bad that it becomes "do or die" is unfortunate because much misery could have been avoided with a more preventative outlook. It is like the person who gains a few pounds but refuses to exercise until those few pounds have turned into twenty or thirty. A small molehill of a problem turns into a huge mountain of one because people do not use the early, smaller levels of pain as the motivation to do something.

There is an important medical parallel to what I'm suggesting in this chapter. We have all run into it. We will on occasion develop a physical symptom, such as a fever, and we'll go to a physician to find out what is causing it. The misery the fever causes not only alerts us to the fact that something is wrong physically, but it also motivates us to find out what it is.

Recently, for example, I developed a severe sore throat, one of those kinds where each time you swallow your whole body yells, "Ouch!" I usually ignore such painful symptoms, choosing instead to be macho and just tough it out. But in this instance, the pain only became worse. The sore throat was both a cue and a motivation to do something. I went to our family physician and found out I had bronchitis and pharyngitis. He put me on antibiotics, and in a few days I was feeling better.

But what if my throat had never become sore or the pain become severe? I would never have known something was "ill" inside me. The disease could have become much worse. As much as I moaned and complained about the sore throat, it was actually a blessing. It "blessed" me by saying, "Hey, Thurman, you have a problem, and it's going to keep hurting you until you fix it."

In a perfect world you would never have any medical symptoms because there would be no viruses or bacteria. In the real world there are both. Similarly, in an ideal world you would never see depression, anxiety, anger, sadness, or hurt because there would be no problems to cause them. But in the real world we suffer emotional pain. As strange as it may sound, I am convinced that this pain is a blessing.

A final example of what I am talking about in this chapter can be found in the life of Kate Jackson, the dark-haired actress who has starred in such TV shows as *The Rookies*, *Charlie's Angels*, and *Scarecrow and Mrs. King*.

To look at Kate Jackson, you would have always assumed that she had the world on a string. She was successful (three hit TV series); she was pretty (her face had appeared on the covers of dozens of national magazines); she was wealthy (her Beverly Hills mansion cost $2.4 million); and she was famous (her fan mail arrived by the truckloads). Internally, however, she was a bundle of nerves. Emotional and physical signals began to telegraph messages to her, but Kate ignored them. She had flashes of anger; she had days of listlessness; she had bouts with self-doubt.

Although the signals were warning her that she was in a "danger" mode, she continued to work and drive and push herself beyond her limits. Then one night she had a bizarre experience. Kate had a nightmare in which she dreamed that something was terribly wrong with her physically. The nightmare was even specific enough to make her think that the problem was breast cancer.

"I know it sounds weird," Kate told a *Redbook* magazine reporter (April 1991), "but that's exactly what happened. I believe your body talks to you, and you *have* to listen to it!"

Kate went to a clinic and had a mammogram. Sure enough, there was a malignant growth in her left breast. The growth was removed by surgery in 1987. The series of events caused Kate to reevaluate her life. She began to try to get more sleep and to work less, but the demands of a hit TV show continued to pull at her. Soon, she was back into the same ultrastressful lifestyle she had been in prior to the surgery. Then in September 1989, the cancer appeared again in her left breast. To correct it, Kate had to undergo a partial mastectomy and reconstructive plastic surgery.

"I was scared," she said of that time. "I was petrified. I thought, *Why me?* I was angry."

It took the second bout with cancer to convince Kate Jackson that ignoring her emotional and physical symptoms had been a bad decision. She set about immediately to correct matters. She sold her posh California home and moved to a serene 125-acre farm in Virginia. She began a daily program of physical exercise. She changed her diet to fruits, grains, fish, and cereal—no fats, no junk food, no cigarettes. She also started getting plenty of sleep at night.

"I don't want the anxiety I used to live with," said Kate. "That's why I moved to Virginia. I don't want the stress. I don't need all that."

We all can't afford to care for ourselves the way Kate Jackson did, but we can afford to learn her lesson. The next time you are tempted to view your emotional (or physical) pain as bad, you might think about seeing it as your mind's way of telling you that it wants to keep you healthy. It's warning you that something inside you is working against that. To think otherwise is to miss the signal.

Don't ignore your smoke alarm going off!

Growthwork

I want you to use the truth you learned in this chapter to initiate a new self-examination exercise. The procedure is simple to follow, yet its results can be profound.

I want you to find a time and place when you can be alone with your journal. Across the top of the paper, I want you to write "Emotional Pain Is Good." Then make two columns. At the top of the left-hand column, write "Emotionally Painful Event." At the top of the right-hand column, write "What My Pain Was Telling Me."

Now, think about situations from your life that were/are emotionally painful (past or present). Put them in the left-hand column. For each situation, write in the right-hand column what the emotional pain was trying to say to you. Let me give you some examples from my life to get you started:

Emotional Pain Is Good

Emotionally Painful Event	What My Pain Was Telling Me
1. Felt very lonely while working at the University of Tennessee for a year as the head resident of a dorm.	1. "It is not good that man should be alone." I was "alone" as far as having close male friends and also did not have a girlfriend for companionship. Not having close, intimate relationships shows itself in the emotion of feeling lonely.
2. Felt anxious about moving my family to Austin after living comfortably in Dallas for six years.	2. Lots of uncertainty about making a good enough income in my new job and deciding on purchasing a new home. My anxiety was trying to tell me I was feeling

threatened about the possibility that the move would not turn out well and that I had unnecessarily put my family in a bad situation.

3. Felt very sad over the death of my mom. She passed away suddenly at age fifty-seven.

3. I was close to Mom, and her death left a relationship "void" in my life. When we experience a loss of any kind, we often feel sad and blue as a result.

4. Felt angry when someone rode my bumper and "flipped me off" before he sped away.

4. People acting that way is disrespectful. Anger can be a sign that disrespect of some kind has been shown to us. In this case, my anger was trying to tell me that I don't like to be treated rudely (who does?).

These examples from my life should give you a better understanding of what I want you to do. The main purpose of this assignment is to help you start paying attention to painful emotions as signals that something important has just taken place in your life rather than see them as unpleasant irritations. Use this assignment to think through previous situations that were painful for you, and try to figure out the "message" of the emotional pain.

A second assignment is to look at your life right now from this perspective. What painful emotions have you been feeling, and what are they trying to signal you about? Take time to think through whether or not you are currently depressed, angry, hurt, or anxious, and see if you can't link these emotions to what the internal issue might be.

The bottom line is this: I want you to begin to appreciate, even be thankful for, the fact that when you have trouble in your soul, emotional pain will let you know. It will alert you to it and motivate you to figure out what the problem is and solve it.

Emotional pain is good! Believe it!

17

■

You Are Going to Die

Pale death with impartial tread beats at the poor man's
cottage door and at the palaces of kings.
—Horace

Few truths have the potential to affect our lives as strongly as the one that warns, "You *are* going to *die*." Death waits around the corner for us all. As Dr. Irvin Yalom expressed in his book *Existential Psychotherapy*, "The most obvious, the most easily apprehended ultimate concern is death. We exist now, but one day shall cease to be. Death will come, and there is no escape from it. It is a terrible truth, and we respond to it with mortal terror."[1]

Death may be "a terrible truth," but it is a truth that can prompt us to live life more fully if we allow it to. I'm not trying to use positive thinking on you here and make you view death as a categorically great and wonderful thing. However, I do hope to strongly impress upon you that seeing death for what it is can beneficially change your way of living.

Death is the ultimate limitation placed on life. Dr. Dennis Hensley explained in his book *How to Manage Your Time* how mankind has sought for centuries, in a variety of ways, to extend the time we have on earth; yet death always wins and in an amazingly predictable way:

> We are all destined for a guaranteed termination. No one has ever beaten the system. In fact, the Bible even tells us about how long we have before our termination: three score and ten (Psalm 90:10). It's interesting to note that even though that calculation was recorded three millennia ago, it hasn't changed. After thirty centuries of medical, educational, social and scientific advances, research conducted annually by insurance companies reveals that the average person lives to be from seventy to seventy-five years old (three score and ten). Every moment of life is valuable. Once time is gone, it's gone

forever. You can't buy it back, borrow it back, bribe it back, or even pray it back. A wasted moment is irretrievable.[2]

We are headed toward a "guaranteed termination" whether we like it or not, an end point past which our time here on earth will be over. The limitation death places on our lives makes our time precious. If we will let it, the fact that our time on earth is finite can be used to motivate us to lead quality lives. Because of the reality of death, we are pushed to see life as something valuable and, thus, to live accordingly.

Now, before you get too self-assured that you are already time-conscious and leading a quality-filled life, let me share some statistics with you. If you get eight hours of sleep a night, you will spend approximately 122 days a year sleeping. If you spend one hour each for breakfast, lunch, and dinner every day, you will spend 46 days a year in these activities alone. Sleeping and eating combined cost you half of each year you are alive. Add to that all the time spent in personal grooming, traveling to and from work, bill paying, shopping, and taking care of other life maintenance requirements, and you can see how much time "slips away" virtually undetected.

With what little time we have left for making life meaningful, too many of us find ourselves going through the motions and achieving very little of lasting value. We live as if we have all the time in the world, when the truth of the matter is that our time on earth is short. We truly are "here today, gone tomorrow," making every second precious.

I once heard a story of a man who was driving by an apple orchard when he happened to see a farmer lifting his pigs, one at a time, up to the tree branches so that the pigs could eat the apples. The man stopped his car, got out, and approached the farmer. "Excuse me," he said, "but isn't that an awfully time-consuming practice?" The farmer looked at the man, shrugged his shoulders, and said, "So what? What's time to a pig?" I sometimes wonder if a lot of people are just as blind as the farmer when it comes to recognizing areas in their lives where they are squandering time.

Having the Time of Your Life

The fact that placing a time limitation on something often makes it more valuable came through loud and clear to me during a vacation. My wife, Holly, and I took a trip to Jamaica prior to the birth of Kelly, our third child. (It was one of those "we'd better go have some fun *now* while we still can" kind of vacations.) While there, I decided to rent a jet ski, which was something I had never done. The hotel charged thirty dollars per half hour of riding time. That struck me as pretty expensive, but I paid it anyway.

Given the time limitation of just thirty minutes hanging over my head, I got as much enjoyment out of that ride as I could. I went 347 miles an hour on that jet ski (okay, I am exaggerating a bit), sprayed tourists on the beach with my wake, knocked other jet skiers off their jet skis, and even purposely fell off a few dozen times just to increase the excitement. I was determined to make sure I got my money's worth.

Yet throughout the ride I kept an eye on my watch, knowing that my time would be up relatively soon. I knew the rental guys would start to wave me in to the beach as soon as my thirty minutes were over. This time constraint motivated me to try to squeeze every second of enjoyment possible from that ride.

Suppose when I registered at the hotel, I had been told that I was the one millionth customer to have booked a reservation, and as a prize for this, I was going to be given unlimited time on a jet ski during all the days I was in Jamaica. Do you think I would have found it as meaningful to ride a jet ski under those circumstances? Would having use of the jet ski with no time limitations have made riding more valuable? No, not hardly. If the hotel had let me ride a jet ski whenever I wanted to, as long as I wanted to, I would not have enjoyed or valued it as much.

I'm convinced the same reality applies to life. You have a limited amount of time to live. Someday, and you don't know when, your time will be up, and you will be "waved to the beach." Your ride is over. If you understand that, even appreciate it, you will live life with vigor, with passion. You won't waste a second of the time you have here.

Think about the alternative for a moment. Can you imagine how you would live your life if you were going to live here on earth forever? Let's say that you woke up tomorrow knowing that you would spend eternity as a human being here on earth. How would you live? Would that trigger excitement and enthusiasm for life in you? Most of us, I think, would be pretty lethargic about the whole thing. Shoot, most of us are already lethargic about living life when all we have is seventy years!

Those of us who truly recognize and respect that life has a time limit will make an effort to get the best "ride" we can. We will do everything possible to experience life fully and will appreciate all the wonderful things about life that are available to us while we are here. If seeing death for what it really is can motivate us to make maximum use of our time while we are here, it is a *very* positive thing that we are going to die.

Why Do We Live Such Boring Lives?

All right then, we will accept death as an important motivator for living life well. But that raises a serious question: Why aren't people more motivated to have a fuller life given that they know their days are numbered? More specifically, why do so many people mope along at a mediocre, unexciting pace or fill their lives with meaningless activities when they know that their time is running out? Hey, let's face it. Life is not a dress rehearsal—this is the real thing. Lights, camera, action! You're *on*, friend! This is your life. You have the starring role. It's either an Oscar or obscurity. The choice is yours.

So why isn't everybody shooting for an Oscar? I'm sure there are numerous reasons, but one reason may be that people are so terrified by death that they will do anything to avoid facing it. Like children who put their hands over their ears and say over and over, "I'm not listening, I'm not listening, I'm not listening," some of us put our hands over our eyes and say, "I'm not going to face death, I'm not going to face death, I'm not going to face death." The more terrified we are by the reality of death, the more we will stay focused on "doing things" so that we don't have to think about it.

Woody Allen once remarked, "I'm not afraid of death. I just don't want to be there when it happens." Too many of us feel that same way. But death awaits us all. As I've said, rather than face the reality of death, many of us numb ourselves to it in one way or another. Some of us try to ignore it through busyness; others try to run from it via instant gratification. Some try to postpone it; others try to outsmart it. Nothing works, however. Death always comes.

For a long time my version of avoiding the reality of death (and trying to improve a shaky sense of self-esteem) was to be a workaholic. I guess I thought that death wouldn't have a way to invade my conscious thoughts if I just kept myself constantly busy. So, constantly busy I stayed. You may have done something similar, or you may have used some other way of running from this "terrible truth." I can tell you this, however: your way of running is no more successful than mine was. Death still waits. Refusing to face it as something real often results in a less-than-fulfilling life.

When Death Becomes Real

Sometimes it takes a major wake-up call like almost losing your life or loved ones losing theirs to realize how precious life is. How many times have you heard about a person who came close to death and used that experience as a springboard to a more purposeful and enjoyable life? A man may almost be killed in an airplane crash and, by facing death so squarely, come to appreciate and savor life more fully. A woman may be told she has a life-threatening cancer but, thanks to a successful operation, survives. Afterward, she quits her job as a salesclerk and becomes a teacher because she finds it more rewarding. A rebellious teenager may be involved in a near fatal car accident, yet walks away; afterward, he has a new sense of the value of life and he becomes more meaningfully involved in high school activities and community service.

It could be that our unwillingness to accept death under normal circumstances makes near-death experiences and even times of personal crisis so potentially life-changing. These moments often provoke us to examine what life is really all about. We see the "big picture" a little more clearly at these times and do some major reevaluations about how we are living.

American author Jack London went through an experience like that. Hoping to make a gold strike and come home a rich man, he traveled to the Yukon. He staked one claim, but it held no gold. When winter came, London was unable to leave because of the heavy snows. He spent four months in a cabin, often by himself, waiting for the spring thaw. He had a lot of time to reflect on his random style of living. He had been an oyster pirate in San Francisco, a seal hunter off the coasts of Japan and Russia, a factory worker, a hobo, a high-school dropout. It began to bother him greatly that he had been busy but had done nothing significant with his life.

That spring Jack London left Canada, came home, finished his high school work, spent a semester at the University of California, then turned all his energies toward becoming a writer. During the next eighteen years, London wrote 190 short stories, 22 novels, 5 plays, 28 poems, and more than 200 newspaper articles. He became the first person in history to earn more than a million dollars strictly from writing.

When asked to summarize what motivated him to his huge success as a writer, Jack London said that while he was trapped in the Yukon, he developed a credo that he swore would guide him for the rest of his life. His credo was as follows: "I would rather be a superb meteor, every atom of me in magnificent glow, than a sleepy and permanent planet. The proper function of man is to live, not just exist. I shall not waste my days in trying to prolong them. I shall use my time." Jack London knew the reality of death, so he used each day to its fullest.

Pretty amazing, isn't it? Jack London went from being a high school dropout with no money to becoming the most successful author the world had known to that time because he was forced to acknowledge that his days on earth were limited and that he had been wasting them. And he did it all in just eighteen years. That's not a bad trade-off: four lonely months of snowbound "death" stuck in a cabin in exchange for eighteen years of unbridled success.

Your Personal Awakening

A motion picture starring Robert De Niro and Robin Williams called *Awakenings* tells the story of a physician who uses a drug to bring people out of a physical disorder referred to as "sleeping sickness." De Niro plays the part of a man who went into a comalike sleep when he was in his twenties and is brought back to consciousness in his late forties. When De Niro fully realizes what has happened to his life, he frantically seeks to make up for lost time. He reads books, goes dancing, plays sports, and even finds a girlfriend.

People who have seen the movie may experience conflicting emotions: on the one hand, they are delighted that this man is well again and so excited about life; on the other hand, they surely have to be uneasy about the fact that their own lives are just as far behind in truly being lived as his—*only they haven't been in a coma!*

I wonder sometimes if it would not be good for most of us to have a near-death or a Rip Van Winkle experience so that we could have a personal awakening. Consider this: Russel Noyes reported in *Psychiatry* magazine that after studying the lives of two hundred people who had near-death experiences, 23 percent felt the ordeal had helped them discover more of what life was all about.[3] They said they learned that life was brief and precious, and this realization gave greater zest to their lives. They also said they had heightened perceptions of their immediate surroundings and, hence, had greater emotional responsiveness to all living things. They learned to live in the moment and to savor time. They developed an urge to enjoy as much as possible before it was too late.

These findings coincide with work psychiatrist Irvin Yalom did with people who had terminal cancer. Yalom reported that once his patients accepted the fact that their lives were rapidly drawing to an end, significant changes in priorities and behavior became evident along the following lines:

- A rearrangement of life's priorities, a trivializing of the trivial.

- A sense of liberation; being able to choose not to do those things they did not wish to do.

- An enhanced sense of living in the immediate present, rather than postponing good times until after retirement or some other point in the future.

- A vivid appreciation of the elemental facts of life: the changing seasons, a fresh breeze, autumn leaves turning colors, and holiday joyousness.

- Deeper communication with loved ones.

- Fewer interpersonal fears, less concern about rejection, and greater willingness to take risks.[4]

It's sad to admit, isn't it, that most of us would have to almost die or be dying before we would begin to appreciate life. We really don't know what we have until we almost lose it. Norman Cousins aptly stated, "Death is not the greatest loss in life. The greatest loss in life is what dies inside of us while we live."

Tolstoy's short story "The Death of Ivan Ilyich" brings out this point about the difference between going through life and actually living life to the fullest. Ivan Ilyich is a sour and evil fellow. He develops cancer and begins to suffer greatly. As he endures his agony, he comes to a life-changing realization: *he is dying badly because he has lived badly*. The recognition of this truth alters Ivan Ilyich's whole perspective on life, and he makes radical changes in his personality and his way of living. He starts to see life as valuable, and he attempts to make the maximum use of whatever time he has left.

The inevitability of death can motivate us to live life more passionately. Knowing death is waiting on us can actually push us to spend our days well. If we spend our lives well, death loses its sting. Leonardo da Vinci put it this way: "As a well-spent day brings happy sleep, so life well-used brings happy death."

You are going to die. That is a given. The more important issue is this: How are you living?

Growthwork

As we draw this chapter to an end, I'm going to walk you through an activity that can motivate you to make the most of the time you have left to live. Let me preface the explanation by reminding you of Charles Dickens's classic story *A Christmas Carol*. You will recall that Ebenezer Scrooge spent his life in a miserly, selfish, lonely existence. All he cared about was accumulating and hoarding money.

Then one Christmas Eve a supernatural thing occurred: three ghosts visited Scrooge. One ghost made him recall his past and forced him to confront the fact that he had once had good friends and the love of a beautiful young lady, but his greed had driven them all away.

The second ghost made Scrooge take a revealing look at the present. He saw starving children, overworked laborers, and destitute beggars whom he passed without seeing every day on his way to work. He saw the family of his employee Bob Cratchit. Bob's youngest son, Tiny Tim, was dying because the family lacked money for proper medical care for the boy. If Scrooge had ever had an ounce of concern, he would have known of the situation, but he was always too occupied counting his gold and reviewing the ledgers.

The third ghost showed Scrooge the immediate future. Not only was Tiny Tim going to die, but so was Scrooge. After his death, people were going to ransack his house and mock his memory. Everyone would rejoice over his death. No one would put flowers on his grave.

Naturally, all this terrified old Ebenezer. He recognized that he had wasted his life in petty, lonely, small-minded activities.

As you know, the story has a happy ending. Scrooge was given a second chance. Instead of dying, he was allowed to go on living for several more years. Scrooge set to work immediately to make up for lost time. He bought food for the poor; he donated money to the needy; he paid a visit to his nephew's home; and he gave Bob Cratchit a raise that doubled his salary. All this change in his character made him "as giddy as a school boy." We are left with the feeling that Scrooge probably did more *living* during the last years of his life than he did in all the previous sixty years.

Now, I want you to have the same experience. In your journal, write in today's date. Then jot down some of the accomplishments of your life, such as "graduated from college," "spent two years in U.S. Army," "married for eleven years," "raised two terrific children," "elected church deacon," "won four tennis trophies," "completely rebuilt a 1965 Mustang," "became store manager in 1992." Make a note of whatever you are proud of having achieved in life thus far.

Then, skip a line, and write in what the date will be exactly one year from today. Underneath that date, write down three or four things that would greatly enrich your life if you were to accomplish them within that time frame. You might jot down "attend a seminar on money management" or "read the whole Bible" or "start a sideline business in antique jewelry" or "take a class in real estate" or "develop a closer relationship with my best friend." Consider these to be your goals for the coming year.

Continuing in this manner, write in the dates five, ten, and twenty years from today. Stretch your imagination. What would you like to do, like to be, like to experience, like to learn, like to share, like to see, and like to try by those dates?

Finally, like Scrooge, try to leap (via your imagination) to the end of your life. What will people remember about you after you die? What will your obituary say? How would a *Who's Who* entry about you read at the end of your life? Put these dreams and goals into a list, for example, "was a loving spouse" or "became a millionaire" or "won a seat in Congress" or "wrote a best-selling novel" or "discovered a cure for AIDS" or "was named Teacher of the Year" or "visited twenty countries" or "discovered a rare archeological dig." Put down on paper your greatest ambitions.

Now, here is a gift more valuable than you may have ever stopped to appreciate: you get to go on living. You have something more valuable than gold—life! You have time—time to pursue your goals and to fulfill your dreams. Yes, one day you are going to die. That painful truth can't be escaped by any of us. But today, it really is lights, camera, action! You are being asked to step out on stage and give your best effort. You have the gift of life to use as meaningfully and abundantly as possible. With all that you have in you, give life your best shot.

Remember, pale death beats at your door. *Live!*

18

■

Is There an Ultimate Source of Truth?

Keep one thing in view forever—the truth; and if you do this,
though it may seem to lead you away from the opinion of men,
it will assuredly conduct you to the throne of God.
—Horace Mann

I hope by this point in the book you are convinced that believing lies destroys your emotional health, intimate relationships with others, and closeness with God and that believing the truth enables you to have all three.

Yet a critically important question remains to be answered: Is there an ultimate source of truth? Carl Jung, one of the founders of modern psychology, got to the heart of the matter when he asked, "Are we related to something infinite or not? That is the telling question of life."

I agree with Carl Jung—the most important question we can ask concerns whether or not an infinite being exists. If the answer is yes, then we have found our authority on truth, and we can stop looking. If the answer is no, then the field is wide open, and everyone's version of "truth" needs to be considered.

Is there an infinite being who is the ultimate authority on truth? I'd like to give you my answer to that question by taking you back into my counseling office.

Where Does Truth Come From?

Do you remember my client Bill from Chapter 7? When I first introduced you to him, he was struggling with a major job setback, guilt over how he had handled a situation involving his son, and frustration toward his wife concerning pressure she was putting on him to buy a new home. I attempted to help Bill with his problems by encouraging him to discover and apply the truth to each situation that was bothering him.

Bill worked pretty hard in counseling to dedicate himself to the truth. Certain truths were especially important in helping him face his problems. We talked frequently about the truth "to err is human" in an effort to help him accept that making mistakes as a worker, a spouse, and a parent is unavoidable and no cause for self-condemnation. We spent a number of sessions on the truth "you don't *have to*" to help Bill overcome the erroneous notion that he *had to* do what people wanted him to do, such as buy a new home when he knew it wasn't the right thing to do at that time. We also explored the truth "you can't please everyone" to enable him to defeat his self-destructive style of trying to keep everyone in his life happy. Finally, we worked pretty hard on facing the fact that "no pain, no gain," to help Bill tackle problems head-on, whatever the cost may be, rather than run from them, hoping they will go away. He had put a lot of time and energy into counseling, and the dividends were showing. He was more peaceful, content, and confident, and his relationships with people at work, his wife, and his son had noticeably improved.

As our work together neared completion, Bill and I turned our attention to the focus of this chapter. Here is how it went: "Dr. Thurman, I feel that I've made a lot of progress in counseling. All my problems haven't disappeared, but I'm a lot less driven to please everyone, more realistic about making mistakes, and freer from feeling that I have to do things just because people want me to. I've also come to appreciate that for good things to happen, I need to face problems head-on and be willing to go through some pain in the process."

"You've worked hard to face the truth and apply it to your life, Bill. Your efforts have paid off nicely. I couldn't be happier about the progress you've made."

"There is something bothering me, though."

"What's that?"

"Well, you and I have worked diligently on the truth, and there is no doubt that it has helped. But outside of just using common sense or relying on people like yourself to help me, how can I really know what the truth is?"

"That's a good question. I struggled with that same issue in my life at one point."

"How did you resolve it?"

"I know psychologists are supposed to keep their personal convictions out of the counseling office, but I would like to answer your question honestly and directly."

"Good. I'd like to hear what you think."

"I realized somewhere along the way that neither my intellectual abilities nor anyone else's are enough to reliably know what the truth is. What people have called 'truth' throughout history changes too much, as have my own notions of truth. Five hundred years ago, the greatest thinkers of the day thought the earth was flat. So, as smart as people are, they aren't perfectly smart. In fact, people are pretty imperfectly smart."

"You don't trust people's ability to know what's true?"

"No, certainly not completely. People have not proven to be very good at getting the truth figured out. As much as we might want to trust human intelligence and reason as a way to know what's true, it often falls short. Sometimes it fails miserably. Some of the worst evils ever committed by mankind have been done in the name of what people thought the 'truth' was. So, no, I don't totally trust myself or others to know the truth."

"Who do you trust?"

"God."

"That simple, huh?"

"That simple."

Is There Any Proof God Exists?

"Why? I mean, how do you know He even exists, much less that He can help you with truth?"

"There are three main reasons I think He exists. The most basic is the universe itself and those of us who live in it. I don't think the universe created itself, and I don't believe we human beings came out of some primordial chemical swamp."

"You have a hard time believing what scientists have to say about the origin of life and how the universe came about."

"Yes, Bill, I do. Scientists change their minds a lot and don't even agree with one another on these matters. I sometimes wonder if they even believe their own theories. It is almost as if they just can't bring themselves to admit there is a God, so they have to come up with some way of explaining things without Him. As far as I'm concerned, some of their explanations for why the universe exists and how we humans came about require more faith than what is needed for believing in the existence of God."

"You don't trust their motives," Bill replied, starting to sound a lot like a counselor.

"No, I don't. The bottom line is that I believe the universe and those of us in it testify to the existence of a supremely intelligent being who brought everything into being. Let me give you an analogy for this. If I walk up to a golf course, I know somebody had to create it. It didn't just magically show up there as a result of some 'big bang' or whatever. Its beauty and its design tell me someone very smart and creative was behind it. Same thing with humans. The beauty of how we are made, the design that went into us, the way all of our parts work together suggest an incredibly brilliant, creative designer. On that basis alone, I believe there is a God."

"You said there were 'reasons' you believe in the existence of God. What is another?"

"He made an appearance."

"What do you mean?"

"I mean God came here. He showed up on the planet."

"Christ, right?"

"Right. Not only did God make our universe, but He decided to show up in the person of Jesus Christ in order to prove His existence."

"How do you know Christ was God and not just some great person?"

"Well, while there have been a number of 'great' people throughout history who had a lot of valuable things to say about life, Christ was different."

"How?"

"He didn't just claim to know a lot of truth. He claimed to *be* truth."

"He equated Himself with truth?" Bill asked.

"Yes. He made no distinction between Himself and truth. That claim made Him either the greatest lunatic of all time or who He said He was—God in human form."

"Why didn't it mean He was a lunatic? After all, that is one grandiose claim."

"Not if it is true, and in Christ's case I believe it was true. I think He proved His claim a number of ways."

"How?"

"First, He lived a morally perfect life. That alone made Him different. No one had ever done that before, nor has anyone done it since. Second, He performed many miracles during His time on earth, thirty-five of which were recorded in the Bible. No human being could have done the things He did."

"Like walk on water, turn water into wine, and give sight to the blind?"

"Exactly. Performing miracles also made Him different and substantiated His claim as far as I'm concerned. But He did something even more miraculous than perform miracles. He came back from the dead, which He predicted He would do. I have never seen anyone pull that off, either."

"Neither have I. So you are saying that not only did He make the claim to be God, but He backed it up?"

"Yes. To me, all that He did is a pretty impressive résumé for the title of God that He claimed."

"You said there were three main reasons you believe God exists. What's the third reason?"

"Changed lives."

"What do you mean?"

"I've seen people significantly changed because of their belief in Christ. That is the modern-day miracle that Christ keeps performing, even though He is no longer here in a physical body. Christ brings about change in people's lives that is truly miraculous. I have seen alcoholics quit drinking, rageaholics quit raging, selfish people learn to have concern for others, and fearful people become bold because of their commitment to Christ. My life has been changed because of my belief in Christ in ways that I cannot attribute to my efforts or power or understanding."

"Isn't that a lot of religious hocus-pocus? How do you know people who believe in Christ don't change for some other reason? How do you know they changed because of their relationship with Christ?"

"I can't categorically prove to you that these changes weren't due to the power of believing or other factors, but the view I have had of these changes in my life and the lives of others tells me a supernatural force was at work bringing about the changes, not human effort alone."

"So you put a lot of stock in Christ and what He had to say about the truth?"

"No, I haven't put a 'lot of stock' in Christ. I've put all of my stock in Him. Christ is the centerpiece of my life. In fact, my faith in Christ dictates how I counsel people. It dictated the way I worked with you. My work with you has been based on truths straight from God, right out of the Bible."

Applied Theology

"You mean to tell me that our work together has been based on what the Bible says?"

"Yes."

"Give me some examples."

"Okay. One of the basic principles we worked on together is the idea that what you think dictates how healthy you are and how well you handle life. The Bible is full of statements about how important it is to have the same attitude as Christ, to renew our minds, to take thoughts captive, and to set our minds on the truth and not lies. You were telling yourself a number of lies about things going on in your life, and you were paying a high price emotionally for having done so. When you started seeing the truth and using it to deal with your problems, you became much more emotionally healthy. The Bible teaches that the truth sets people free, and you have proved that to a certain degree in your life."

"So the Bible teaches that what we believe basically determines who we are and how well we handle things?"

"Yes, and it emphasizes truth as the 'eyewear' through which we need to view life."

"What else about our work together came out of the Bible?"

"The specific truths I taught you all come from the Bible."

"You're kidding!"

"No, not at all. For example, we worked on 'to err is human,' didn't we?"

"Yes."

"That is the human way of saying what the Bible is talking about in passages such as Romans 3:23 (NIV), where it says, 'For all have sinned and fall short of the glory of God,' and 1 John 1:8 (NIV), where it says, 'If we claim to be without sin, we deceive ourselves and the truth is not in us.' The Bible teaches that it is our natural bent to sin, to miss the moral mark."

"So the Bible teaches that everyone messes up and that making mistakes is an inherent part of being a human being."

"Yes, it does."

"What other truths that we worked on came out of the Bible?"

"Well, we also worked on 'you don't have to.' That truth is taught in the Bible as free will. The Bible teaches that God gave us free will and that we are free to do what we want to do, for better or for worse. We don't have to do anything we don't want to do. That is why I pushed you to see that you were free not to buy a new home if you didn't feel it was right, even though your wife might not like it. You came in acting as if you had no free will, and I just tried to remind you that you do."

"I assume there is another truth we worked on that came out of the Bible," Bill said.

"Sure. We worked on the idea that you can't please everyone. The Bible makes it clear that we are not here for people's approval when it says in the books of Colossians and Galatians that we are to do things for God's approval, not people's, and that we can't really serve God if we want the approval of people."

"What else do you have up your sleeve about all this?"

"Well, I do have a final curveball that I want to throw your way."

"I figured you did. Give me your best pitch."

Human Effort Is Vain Effort

"Human effort alone to know the truth in any complete way is doomed to fail. We bring our finiteness and fallenness into the effort, and it ends up costing us a clear view of reality. God, on the other hand, brings neither finiteness nor fallenness into the issue of truth. He is the ultimate Source of all truth, and we need Him in our lives for help to know truth. He wants to help us figure out the truth. If we try to understand truth apart from God helping us, I think we labor in vain."

"You're saying that I need to take a very serious look at God and that if I am trying to make sense out of my life apart from Him, I am being foolish."

"Yes, that's right. Without God, there is no ultimate truth, no lasting power to live the truth, and no eternal life. That isn't me talking. That is God talking."

"Well, if God is truth, why do Christians who claim to believe in God seem as messed up as anyone else? I would think that with God on their side to help them know and do the truth, Christians would be the healthiest, most mature group of all."

"That is the way it is supposed to work, Bill, but Christians can fall into just as many distorted ideas and beliefs as anybody else if they don't dedicate themselves on a consistent basis to truth. Saying you believe in God and actually listening to Him and doing things His way, day by day, are two completely different things. Too many Christians are in the former group, and seemingly too few in the latter."

"So the bottom line to the whole truth issue is God."

"Yes, God is the bottom line. What He inspired people to write in the Bible was His way of telling us the truths we need to know for how to live meaningful, abundant lives. God owns the truth, and the Bible is His Owner's Manual that He wants us to study so we can know how we are supposed to live."

"There's the answer to my question. You can know truth by pursuing God and studying the Book He wrote on truth."

"Yes. How does all that sound to you?"

"Like a lot to think seriously about."

What About You?

I want to make the same challenge to you that I made to Bill. I want to challenge you to take a serious look at who or what your source of truth is. Are you relying on human reason and understanding to know the truth, or are you relying on the ultimate Source of truth—God? If you are looking for the truth, God is it. Don't keep looking for truth in places that can't ultimately satisfy you. Don't listen to your common sense. Don't listen to the "experts." Listen to the Expert.

If you already believe in God, let me challenge you by suggesting that you may not be listening much better than the nonbeliever to what God is trying to say to you. You may know God is truth but still be listening to your thoughts or somebody else's as your real source of truth. God's thoughts have to become your own, or you will not be any healthier or more mature than those who don't believe in God.

The psalmist wrote, "I have chosen the way of truth" (Ps. 119:30 NKJV). That is what I want for you—to choose the way of truth as the basis for your life. The way of truth pays huge dividends, that is certain. But more importantly, the way of truth takes you to God, the Source of all truth and eternal life. The way of truth provides it all—peace and contentment here on earth that go beyond our circumstances and eternal life in heaven that will be more wonderful than we can ever begin to grasp. Choose the way of truth and have it all.

Growthwork

The assignment for this chapter may well be the most important assignment of all. I want you to grab your journal and answer the following question: *Who is my source of truth?*

If your answer is God, then I want you to take the next step by answering the following question in your journal: *Do I really believe what God says?* Be completely honest in answering. Be willing to acknowledge areas of your life where you are living in ways that indicate you don't truly believe what God says (being anxious about whether or not you will find a job when God promises to meet "all your needs," or feeling worthless when God says you are "fearfully and wonderfully made," or accumulating things here on earth when God says that we are to "lay up treasures in heaven").

If your source of truth is *not* God, then I want you to take the next step by answering the following question: *Why do I trust myself or other people as my authority on truth?* Be honest in answering. If you are relying on yourself as the ultimate authority for discerning truth, why do you think you can trust yourself? If it is another person or a collection of people, why do you turn to them? What makes you or others smart enough, discerning enough, or wise enough to depend upon for knowing truth?

Whether you realize it or not, choosing your authority on truth is the single biggest decision you will ever make. Choose wisely—your *life* hangs in the balance.

19
■

THE TRUTH ABOUT GOD AND
THE TRUTH ABOUT YOU

Christian truth, then is redemption truth because it requires not simply
knowledge about something, but knowledge of someone. It is personal.
—Harold Cooke Phillips

I have a friend named Gary who likes to tell me about his men's Bible study group that meets for breakfast on Wednesday mornings. On any given Wednesday, five to eight guys meet with Gary to discuss how God and the teachings of the Bible relate to their personal lives.

One Wednesday, Gary began the study with a question that was both simple and profound: *Who is God?*

The answers were fascinating.

"I think of God as a good guy," Art answered. "He does anything He can to help us, bails us out of trouble when we mess up, makes everything right."

"No, I see God very differently," Jack chimed in. "God is very just. He wants me to live a pure life." Then he added, "And if I don't live up to that standard, He'll punish me!"

"I don't think of God that way," Bart confessed. "I really see Him as more of an old-fashioned, uncool kind of grandpa. Don't get me wrong, I believe He really loves me, but He's just a little behind the times."

Frank was next to speak. "I hate to admit this, but I've never viewed God as the kind and gentle type." He paused and stated in a whisper, "Actually, I see God as more of a mean old man whose only purpose is to keep me from having any fun in life."

Everyone had offered an opinion except Dave. Gary prompted him, "Dave, what's your view on God?"

Dave sat in silence for another few seconds and then confessed, "God is real . . . I know that . . . but He feels very far away from me right now. Sometimes I feel as if He just doesn't care about what we are doing or what is going on in our everyday lives. I wish He were closer."

As Gary retold the story to me, he made an astute observation: "Each one of the guys had a certain degree of distorted thinking in his view of God that was negatively impacting his life."

I agreed with Gary. Each man in his Bible study seemed to think about God in a way that missed who He really is. According to those in Gary's group, God rescues people from their problems, loves to punish, is out of touch with the modern world, likes to be a party pooper, and is aloof.

What was true about Gary's Bible study group is also true about all of us. We all have some distorted perceptions of God. Thus, we don't know who God really is. J. I. Packer, in his classic book *Knowing God*, makes clear the cost of not knowing God:

> The world becomes a strange, mad, painful place, and life in it a disappointing and unpleasant business, for those who do not know God. Disregard the study of God, and you sentence yourself to stumble and blunder through life blindfolded, as it were, with no sense of direction and no understanding of what surrounds you. This way you can waste your life and lose your soul.[1]

I believe that knowing God is central to mental and spiritual health. And knowing who God is, is central to knowing who we are. In this chapter, I want to address both issues. First, who is God? What is He *really* like? Second, who are we? What are we *really* like? Knowing who God is and who we are is non-negotiable if we want to live an abundant life. So, let's put aside our biases, prejudices, stereotypes, and blind spots and see the truth about God and ourselves.

The Truth About God

We live in a world where there is a heightened interest in God. However, a popular belief is that God can be anything you want Him to be. Talk to fifty different people about God, and you will probably get fifty different descriptions of who He is. In the marketplace of views about God, you can choose from among a seemingly infinite number of versions.

We need the real God to stand up and be recognized, and He has. God stood up when He made the world and everything in it. God stood up for people to see when He chose the Jews as His people and did miraculous things for them and through them. God stood up in the human form of Christ when He came to earth to die for people's sins. God stands up today through changed lives. Throughout it all, God inspired people to write about Him. Those writings are collected for us in the Bible and are available for our study.

We can have a picture of God relatively free from distortion if we want one. By relying on what God says about Himself in the Bible, we can know, however incompletely, who He really is. Understanding the attributes of God can be a tremendous source of comfort as we face problems. God is an awesome God. Let's look at some of His attributes, each of which warrants a whole book by itself.

God Is Self-Existent

Have you ever stopped to consider the fact that God has no beginning? He wasn't created—He has always existed. This prayer of Moses was recorded in the book of Psalms:

> Before the mountains were born
> or you brought forth the earth and the world,
> from everlasting to everlasting you are God.[2]

John began his Gospel account by emphasizing that Jesus (the Word) was with God and was God from the beginning. He wrote,

> In the beginning was the Word, and the Word was with God, and the Word was God. He was in the beginning with God. All things were made through Him, and without Him nothing was made that was made. In Him was life, and the life was the light of men. And the light shines in the darkness, and the darkness did not comprehend it.[3]

We are God's creation, but nothing created Him. God has always existed, "from everlasting to everlasting." He had no beginning, and He will have no end.

God Is All-Powerful

God can do anything He wants to do. When the Bible refers to God as "Almighty," it isn't kidding around or being loose with words—He is *all mighty*. Theologians refer to this as His *omnipotence*. Job, after his time of struggle with God, came to this conclusion about God: "I know that You can do everything, and that no purpose of Yours can be withheld from You."[4]

If God wants to do something, He can do it. If He wants to turn water into wine, raise the dead, or move mountains, it is within His power to do so.

God Is Everywhere at Once

Have you ever felt that God was too busy for you? Sometimes we conjure up the mental picture of a long line of people, each waiting his turn to have a moment to speak with God, and God being able to give His attention to only one at a time while having to put the rest of the universe on hold.

But that's not the way it is. God is everywhere at once, and all of Him is there. Theologians call that His *omnipresence*. You don't have to wait for Him to finish with someone else before He can turn His attention to you. David wrote,

> Where can I go from Your Spirit?
> Or where can I flee from Your presence?
> If I ascend into heaven, You are there;
> If I make my bed in hell, behold, You are there.
> If I take the wings of the morning,
> And dwell in the uttermost parts of the sea,
> Even there Your hand shall lead me,
> And Your right hand shall hold me.[5]

God has time for you. He fills up the whole universe and can be found any-time, anyplace.

God Is All-Knowing

God knows everything there is to know. Unlike us finite human beings who know but an infinitesimally small percentage of what can be known, God knows all 100 percent. Nothing that can be known has escaped Him. The psalmist acknowledged this in Psalm 147:5 (NKJV), saying, "Great is our Lord, and mighty in power; His understanding is infinite."

God knows so much more than we do, it isn't even fair to compare. The apostle Paul spoke of God's wisdom in this way:

> Oh, the depth of the riches both of the wisdom and knowledge of God!
> How unsearchable are His judgments and His ways past finding out!
> "For who has known the mind of the LORD?
> Or who has become His counselor?"
> "Or who has first given to Him
> And it shall be repaid to him?"
> For of Him and through Him and to Him are all things, to whom be glory
> forever. Amen.[6]

Isn't it comforting to know that the God of the universe isn't ever going to be surprised by some new piece of information? God can't be beaten in a debate because He knows all facts. It is stupid to argue with God because He is a couple of zillion times smarter than we are.

God Is Holy

God is *holy* in two senses of the word. First, there is no one like God. He is unique, one of a kind. Second, God is perfectly perfect. There are no impurities in Him.

> No one is holy like the LORD,
> For there is none besides You,
> Nor is there any rock like our God.[7]

God is distinct from anything else, completely pure and righteous. He does only what is right. There is no one else like Him and no one who does right all the time as He does.

God Is Good

This attribute is one of my favorites because of its sheer simplicity. Among all the glowing terms used to describe God's character, it's nice to know He is just plain good.

> Good and upright is the LORD;
> Therefore He teaches sinners in the way.[8]

Everything God does is good. There is not a mean "bone" in God's make-up. He is always about the business of doing things that are for our good. I find that incredibly encouraging. Also, God can take anything that happens to us and ultimately bring good out of it. Remember Romans 8:28? "We know that in all things God works for the good of those who love him, who have been called according to his purpose." (NIV)

Isn't it comforting to know that in a world where people are sometimes out to harm you, God is always out to do you good?

God Is Just

If you're like me, you feel bothered when you see people get away with doing wrong. We want to see people "get their due" (except for ourselves, of course!). Well, another attribute of God that ought to comfort us (and scare us as well) is that He is just. When He metes out punishment, it is warranted and proportional to the wrong action: "Far be it from You to do such a thing as this, to slay the righteous with the wicked, so that the righteous should be as the wicked; far be it from You! Shall not the Judge of all the earth do right?"[9]

God punishes the guilty and rewards the righteous. People may get away with things here on earth, but there will be ultimate justice where all people will get their due someday.

God Is Merciful

God is also merciful. The justice of God means that He never punishes people who don't deserve it or gives people *more* punishment than they deserve. The mercy of God means that He sometimes gives *less* punishment to wrongdoers than they deserve and *more* reward to "right doers" than they deserve. Paul wrote of this truth in Romans:

> For he says to Moses,
> "I will have mercy on whom I have mercy,
> and I will have compassion on whom I have compassion."[10]

Christianity is about God's mercy—God offering us salvation and eternity in heaven when we deserved condemnation and eternity in hell. Peter wrote of God's mercy in his first letter: "Blessed be the God and Father of our Lord Jesus Christ, who according to His abundant mercy has begotten us again to a living hope through the resurrection of Jesus Christ from the dead."[11]

Thank God (literally) that He is merciful. Our situation would be worse than bleak for all of us if He wasn't.

God Is Sovereign

Nothing is out of God's control. The fact that He controls the universe is called *sovereignty*. It's the same term one uses to describe a king over his dominion. God is in control and going to bring about His will regardless of what any of us do to get in His way. Consider these verses from a psalm:

> Whatever the LORD pleases He does,
> In heaven and in earth,
> In the seas and in all deep places.[12]

Nothing can thwart God's plans. The die has been cast, and God was the One who cast it. God is in control, and everything is headed toward an incredible ending that He scripted. He's got the whole world in His hands.

God Is Unchanging
Have you ever attended a high school reunion? Isn't it an eye-opening experience? It's interesting to go back after ten, fifteen, or twenty years to see how people have changed. It's rather shocking to see the star athlete or head cheerleader at middle age carrying a few extra pounds around and looking a bit worse for wear. And, of course, who could have known back then that the quiet little guy or gal in the back of the room would become the highly respected medical doctor or chief executive officer of a major company? People do change!

But God stays the same. He doesn't change. Theologians call this His *immutability.* God is the same all the time in that He is never inconsistent or growing or developing. His words are recorded in the Old Testament:

> For I am the LORD, I do not change;
> Therefore you are not consumed, O sons of Jacob.[13]

In the New Testament, James wrote about God's immutability when he said, "Every good and perfect gift is from above, coming down from the Father of the heavenly lights, who does not change like shifting shadows."[14]

Isn't it comforting to know that in a world that seems to change minute by minute, God is the same from age to age? We need that kind of stability.

God Is Love
I saved the best for last. God loves us. He is incapable of not loving us. Everything He does is for our best and is completely unselfish. Because of His love, He is greatly concerned about us and acts to help us. John put it this way: "Whoever does not love does not know God, because God is love."[15]

The best we get here on earth from other people is imperfect love. God loves us perfectly. His love is unconditional. It is constantly aimed at helping us become mature and free. We can count on it. We can't do a single thing to earn it. His love opens the door to a relationship with Him:

> God, who is rich in mercy, because of His great love with which He loved us, even when we were dead in trespasses, made us alive together with Christ (by grace you have been saved), and raised us up together, and made

us sit together in the heavenly places in Christ Jesus. . . . For by grace you have been saved through faith, and that not of yourselves; it is the gift of God, not of works, lest anyone should boast.[16]

I have presented these attributes of God to assist you in seeing God more clearly. Distortions about God cause real damage to emotional health and spiritual life. It's critically important to know who God really is and how that relates to us as human beings.

Now, let's turn our attention to what the Bible says about who we are.

The Truth About You

Patty is a hard-driving, anxiety-prone woman in her late thirties. On the outside, she appears to have it all together. She is a smart dresser, carries herself with an air of confidence, and is friendly and helpful to others. But deep down inside Patty is very different from her outward appearance. She is full of self-doubt and insecurity.

"I'm sure it goes back to my childhood," she started. "I was overweight, and kids made fun of me unmercifully."

"What sorts of memories do you have of growing up?" I asked.

"Bad memories—painful ones," she recalled. "I remember being called 'Fatty Patty' by the kids. I remember when they chose sides for playground games, I was always last to be picked. I can still see myself asking to be chosen, totally humiliating myself, just to be picked."

"Were your parents supportive of you at this time?" I inquired.

"Yes and no," Patty responded. "I know Mom and Dad loved me, but they tended to downplay what I was going through. I don't think they really understood the pain I was experiencing." She laughed and added, "I can still recall my mom telling me that everything would be all right. Then she would bring me a piece of pie or some cookies and say, 'Here, eat this. It'll help make things better.'" Patty began to softly sob into a tissue.

"It sounds to me like one of the only ways your mom knew how to comfort you was to give you sweets," I suggested.

"That's exactly how it was, Dr. Thurman. She said 'I love you' by giving me desserts. She would say how she never had dessert growing up during the Great Depression. She was so proud that she could do that for me. And of course, I would eat every bite."

"Please go on with your story."

"Well, the main issue is that I still feel the same way today as I did back then. When I went off to college, I lost a lot of weight and began to take real pride in my appearance. I've been real disciplined in my diet and exercise. A lot of good things have happened to me in my adult life. But I'm still the little fat girl deep down inside. I feel that I don't have anything to offer."

"Do you really believe that?"

She paused. "Yes, I'm afraid I really do. I just feel like a big zero—a loser."

I can't begin to estimate how many people I've spoken with whose story is similar to Patty's. The details vary, but the bottom-line self-perception is still the same: I'm a zero. It may be tied to appearance issues, such as being overweight, having crooked teeth, being short, or having too many freckles. It may be tied to achievement issues, such as not getting a college degree, being on the lower rung of the climb to success, or not making enough money. It may be tied to relationship issues, such as being lonely, being rejected by someone, or experiencing inconsistent love from others. Whatever the issue, too many of us have ended up with a distorted perception of who we really are that must be corrected if we hope to enjoy a fuller, healthier life.

Seeing yourself as you really are is essential to mental and spiritual health. The only way you can see yourself accurately is through the teachings of the Bible. Let me warn you—some of the news is bad. What the Bible says about us sometimes stings badly. Yet for those who turn their lives over to God, the news couldn't be better. Let's go into both the good and the bad news about ourselves.

You Are a Special Creation of God

One of the "good news" passages concerning who we are is found in Psalm 139. Here King David stated some important truths:

> For you created my inmost being;
>   you knit me together in my mother's womb.
> I praise you because I am fearfully and
>   wonderfully made;
>   your works are wonderful,
>   I know that full well.
> My frame was not hidden from you
>   when I was made in the secret place.
> When I was woven together in the depths of the earth,
>   your eyes saw my unformed body.
> All the days ordained for me
>   were written in your book
>   before one of them came to be.[17]

God doesn't make junk! We have all heard that before, but it is really true. His works are wonderful, and we are the apex of all His works! No one needs to walk around thinking he is "a zero" because God doesn't make "zeros."

Not only are we "fearfully and wonderfully made," but I believe this passage teaches that God made each of us a unique individual. Though we human beings are alike in many ways, no one else is exactly like us, either. As trite as it sounds, when God made you, He broke the mold.

You may be thinking, *Thank goodness no one else is like me—I'm such a loser,* but the truth of the matter is that you are a very special creation of God and there is no duplicate. In a world where too many things have a look of sameness, it is worth feeling good about the fact that God created you to be the only *you* on the planet.

You Are Adam's Offspring

Now, for some *really* bad news. According to the Bible, each person is born corrupt. When Adam and Eve committed the original (first) sin, it devastated everything and has negatively impacted all mankind since then. We are all born with a sinful nature. David put it this way: "Surely I was sinful at birth, sinful from the time my mother conceived me."[18]

So, the horrible truth of it is that we are not basically "good." We are basically "bad" in that we are bent in the direction of sin from birth. Adam and Eve messed it up for all of us, and things have been a fractured mess here on earth ever since. The Westminster Confession says it so much more articulately than I can:

> By this sin they fell from their original righteousness and communion with God, and so became dead in sin, and wholly defiled in all the parts and faculties of soul and body. They being the root of all mankind, the guilt of this sin was imputed, and the same death in sin, and corrupted nature, conveyed to all their posterity descending from them by ordinary generation. From this original corruption, whereby we are utterly indisposed, disabled, and made opposite to all good, and wholly inclined to all evil, do proceed to all actual transgressions.[19]

All this is worse news than most of us realize. The Bible teaches that every one of us is born "in Adam," spiritually dead and an enemy of God. We are sinners, not people who happen to sin. Our nature is morally corrupt, not good. Everything about us—mind, will, emotions, and body—has been horribly disfigured by the original sin of Adam and Eve. While we do not act as immorally as we could (no one is totally depraved), we all act badly. In Romans 3:10–12 (NKJV), Paul said straightforwardly,

> There is none righteous, no, not one;
> There is none who understands;
> There is none who seeks after God.
> They have all turned aside;
> They have together become unprofitable;
> There is none who does good, no, not one.

Because of all of this, Christ's coming was good news (actually, it was incredible, awesome, unbelievable news). If we are spiritually dead sinners at birth, we need something to bring us back to life, or we go to hell forever. Christ's atoning death on the cross is the "something" that was necessary to allow us new life and heaven for eternity.

You Are of Infinite Value to God

I want to ask you a question that isn't easy to answer. It will require some thought, but I want you to be as honest as possible. What do you think you're worth? Don't answer in dollar-and-cents terms, but in broader terms.

The value of an object is often reflected by the price we are willing to pay for it. Have you ever considered what God was willing to "pay" for you? Look at Paul's words: "There is one God and one mediator between God and men, the man Christ Jesus, who gave himself as a ransom for all men—the testimony given in its proper time."[20]

God "ransomed" you with the most valuable thing He had, His Son, to die for our sins. God paid the highest price possible to redeem our souls. That ought to tell us something. I sure wouldn't offer the life of one of my children as a ransom unless it was for something of utmost value. Even then, it would kill me to do so. It had to have been torturous for God the Father to send His Son to die for our sins, yet God doing that tells us how much we must be worth to Him.

From here on, the things I go into are true only about people who have put their faith in Christ and have become Christians. I am not trying to be mean-spirited here. It's just that the Bible is exclusionary. It excludes people from heaven on the basis of whether or not they have put their faith in Jesus Christ. If you put your faith in Christ, you're in. If you didn't, you're out. If you did, there are things that are true about you now that are not true about the non-Christian. Not my idea—God's.

You Are God's Child

Have you ever been at a party where people play games that are made up of fantasy questions? They'll ask questions such as, "If you could be any person in history, who would you be?" or "If you were a type of car, what kind would you be?" Here's one I want you to answer: If you could choose any person from history to be your father, who would you choose?

I have no idea who you chose as your fantasy father. Maybe you chose a king or a president or a movie star or a sports hero or a minister. But let's leave fantasyland and look at the truth. Besides your earthly father, there is another Father who adopted you when you became a Christian. Paul wrote about this in his letter to the Ephesians: "In love he predestined us to be adopted as his sons through Jesus Christ, in accordance with his pleasure and will—to the praise of his glorious grace, which he has freely given us in the One he loves."[21]

One of Jesus' disciples, John, wrote about this great truth as well. From his words, you can tell how astonished John was about this: "How great is the love the Father has lavished on us, that we should be called children of God! And that is what we are!"[22]

So, if you are a Christian, you now have God for your Father. You now have an all-knowing, all-powerful, everywhere at once, just, merciful, good, in control, unchanging, and perfectly loving Dad. How does that compare to the one you chose when I posed the question to you?

You Are a Brother or Sister to Christ

Many times people who are down on themselves walk around carrying a lot of shame. They dwell on bad things they've done or bad things that have happened to them. This issue of shame becomes particularly potent when we think of our relationship with God. We convince ourselves that God is so upset with us over what we've done that He is actually ashamed of us! Read the words of the writer to the Hebrews:

> Both the one who makes men holy and those who are made holy are of the same family. So Jesus is not ashamed to call them brothers. He says,
> "I will declare your name to my brothers; in the presence of the congregation I will sing your praises."[23]

That's a passage loaded with powerful truth! Jesus Christ, God the Son, is not ashamed to call you His brother or sister. You are in the family of God, have God the Father as your Dad, and Christ as your Brother. That would make a pretty incredible family portrait, wouldn't you say?

You Are a Joint Heir with Christ

Have you ever been jealous of someone who appeared to have it all? You know the kind of person I'm talking about. He wears all the right clothes, drives the right car, lives in the right neighborhood, eats at the right restaurants, hangs out with all the right people. I remember seeing someone like this and later found out that this person had inherited all his money. Just think of it. All he did to have it all was to be born into the right family, and then he simply inherited all that he had!

That's what it means to be an heir. You inherit what is legally or naturally a part of your parents' estate. Think of the spiritual implications of this concept. With God as your Father, you inherit everything from Him. Paul wrote of this in his letter to the Galatians: "Because you are sons, God sent the Spirit of his Son into our hearts, the Spirit who calls out, 'Abba, Father.' So you are no longer a slave, but a son; and since you are a son, God has made you also an heir."[24]

You are a joint heir with Christ, which means that everything He has is yours as well, and He has it all. Man, are you loaded!

You Have the Holy Spirit As a Guarantee That You Belong to God

When you became a Christian, the Holy Spirit of God took up residence in your heart. God isn't just up in heaven on His throne. He is now inside you sitting on the throne of your heart. The Holy Spirit living inside you means that you have a constant companion who is there whenever you need Him. Isn't that a comforting truth? The key passage about this truth is in Ephesians:

> You also were included in Christ when you heard the word of truth, the gospel of your salvation. Having believed, you were marked in him with a seal, the promised Holy Spirit, who is a deposit guaranteeing our inheritance until the redemption of those who are God's possession—to the praise of his glory.[25]

We hear a lot about guarantees in commercials and advertisements. It's the sponsor's way of saying he stands behind his product. Isn't it great that God stands behind our salvation by giving us the Holy Spirit as His guarantee?

You Have Christ's Life within You

Another life-changing truth out of the Bible is that when we became Christians, we were made "new creatures" in Christ and have the life of Christ in us. The important passage in Paul's letter to the Colossians on this point states, "Set your minds on things above, not on earthly things. For you died, and your life is now hidden with Christ in God. When Christ, who is your life, appears, then you also will appear with him in glory."[26]

As Jesus lives in you, He will change you. You aren't hopelessly bound to your past or your weaknesses. Ask God to help you believe that Jesus lives in you and that you can change. Thank Him that Jesus not only showed us how to live when He was on the earth, but by living within us, Christ enables us to live like Him today. In that sense, we imitate Him and are to live with the question, "What would Jesus do?" hanging over every action.

You Have Christ's Righteousness

Part of seeing yourself in an emotionally and spiritually healthy way is seeing yourself realistically. Too many of us tend to dwell on the shortcomings in our lives. This sort of distorted thinking is damaging and defeating.

According to the Bible, those who are in Christ now have His righteousness credited to them. According to the apostle Paul, "God made him who had no sin to be sin for us, so that in him we might become the righteousness of God."[27]

When Jesus, as your substitute, took your sin, you received His perfect righteousness. This is the core of the Bible's teaching—your acceptance by God is because of Christ, not because of your performance.

You Will Never Be Condemned by God

We don't like to have stones thrown our way. The pain of making a mistake is bad enough without somebody rubbing our faces in it. Another incredible truth for us as Christians is that no matter how badly we act, there are no stones coming our way from God. God will discipline us when we do wrong, but He will not condemn us. Paul stated in clear terms to the Romans: "Therefore, there is now no condemnation for those who are in Christ Jesus, because through Christ Jesus the law of the Spirit of life set me free from the law of sin and death."[28]

Isn't it good to know that condemnation is now a thing of the past and that we won't experience it anymore unless we do it to ourselves or others choose to do it to us? God is not a stone thrower.

You Are a Foreigner in This World
Earlier in this book we talked about the need some of us have to be loved and accepted by *everybody*. Having the love and approval of everyone is quite an unrealistic expectation and a self-destructive thing to do to ourselves. Read this important truth: "Dear friends, I urge you, as aliens and strangers in the world, to abstain from sinful desires, which war against your soul."[29]

Once, as part of the world, you were a stranger and foreigner to God. Now, as a Christian, you are a stranger and foreigner in this world. Because you are a Christian, you are now a displaced person or a migrant because your citizenship is in heaven! Because you are in God's family, you now live under different values and priorities. As a result, you will be misunderstood, even persecuted and rejected, by those in the world who are not Christians.

You Have Special God-Given Abilities
You have a very special role in the family of God. God has equipped you with certain gifts that enable you to fulfill your special role. Although no individual has all of God's spiritual endowments, your gifts have been especially designed by God to benefit the family of God in some way:

> Just as each of us has one body with many members, and these members do not all have the same function, so in Christ we who are many form one body, and each member belongs to all the others. We have different gifts, according to the grace given us.[30]

No member of God's family is useless or unnecessary. You were created by God to make a valuable contribution to the body of Christ. You may have been gifted to teach, serve, administrate, give of your resources, or encourage, but you have something special to offer as a Christian to other Christians.

You Are an Ambassador
Have you ever visited Washington, D.C.? It's quite an experience to be in our nation's capital and see government in action. I think part of the excitement is getting to see the pomp and pageantry that so often occur in governmental events. Whether it's a military parade, a long limousine with tiny American flags waving on the hood, or a stirring version of the National Anthem, it is a privilege to be an American.

If you're reading this right now in your house or apartment, do you realize you are in an embassy? That's right—for you, as a Christian, are an ambassador.

Paul told the Corinthians, "We are therefore Christ's ambassadors, as though God were making his appeal through us. We implore you on Christ's behalf: Be reconciled to God."[31]

If you have ever wondered why you are here on this planet, it is to be an ambassador for Christ. That is your calling. It is your most important task. Sure, you may be a teacher, lawyer, nurse, or accountant in your job, but your main position in life is that of ambassador. Let the pomp and circumstance begin.

You Can Confidently Ask God for Help

Some of us live our lives as if we are burdens and we should never let our needs be known because we might inconvenience somebody. "I don't want to trouble anyone" is a comment you may have said on occasion.

These feelings of being a burden can surface in the spiritual life as well. We may find ourselves saying, "I don't want to bother God with my problems." But the truth is, God desires to hear from us—about everything. We learn from the writer to the Hebrews: "Let us then approach the throne of grace with confidence, so that we may receive mercy and find grace to help us in our time of need."[32]

God's throne is a throne of help. God wants you to approach and present your needs to Him. The last thing God wants us, as His children, to think is that we will be irritations or burdens to Him. God wants to help us in our time of need.

Let's take a minute to review all that we have learned about who God is and who you are.

God is	self-existent
	all-powerful
	everywhere at once
	all-knowing
	holy
	good
	just
	merciful
	sovereign
	unchanging
	love
You	are a special creation of God
	are Adam's offspring

are of infinite value
(*Christians Only*)
are a child of God
are a brother or sister to Jesus
are a joint heir with Christ
have the Holy Spirit as a guarantee that
    you belong to God
have Christ's life within you
have Christ's righteousness
will never be condemned by God
are a foreigner in this world
have special God-given abilities
are an ambassador
can confidently ask God for help

Quite an impressive list, wouldn't you say? Now, ask yourself the following questions: *Do I really believe any of this? Do I really believe God is all-powerful? Do I really believe God is good? Do I really believe God is in control? Do I really believe that I am a wonderfully made, unique creation of God? Do I really believe I am worth more than riches to Him? As I Christian, do I really believe I have the Holy Spirit in me as a guarantee that I am God's child and am going to heaven someday? As a Christian, do I really believe there is no condemnation for me anymore?*

If the answer to any of the questions is no, you may want to take some time and think about why. Why don't you believe these truths? Is God a liar? Is the Bible untrue? Grapple with this at the deepest level of your soul. If anything taught about God or yourself in this chapter is something you don't believe, you are living your life as if God is a liar. Do you really want to live that way?

Growthwork

Look back over the list of God's attributes that we covered and select the one you have the most trouble believing. In your journal, write down your thoughts about why you find it hard to believe that about God. How would your life be different if you really believed that about God?

Now, do the same thing with the list we covered concerning you. What on that list do you have the hardest time believing? Why is it hard to believe? How would your life be different if you really believed it?

A final assignment I would also like you to do is to memorize the Bible verse I gave for the attribute of God you have the most trouble with and the Bible verse that goes with the truth about you that you have the most difficult time accepting. After you memorize these verses, meditate on them. Chew on each verse for five minutes each (longer if you would like). Try to get everything you can out of each verse. Allow God to use these verses to turn on the light in your mind about who He is and who you are. Run these verses through your mind as often as you can each day, like playing a favorite tape in your car stereo every chance you get.

Knowing God for who He really is, is the one assignment in life we cannot afford to skip. In knowing God, we come to know who we are. You can't really know yourself apart from knowing God. Distorted thinking in one area means distorted thinking in another. If you misperceive who God is, you won't see yourself for who you are. If you misperceive who you are, you won't be able to see God for who He is.

Know God! Know Yourself!

PART 3

LIVING THE TRUTH

20

■

DOING THE TRUTH

Do not merely listen to the word, and so deceive yourselves.
Do what it says.
—James 1:22 (NIV)

We have come a long way on our journey together. You have done well to have traveled this far. Before we go any farther, I want to ask you to turn around and take a look at where you have been.

The road we have traveled has had numerous "landmarks" in the form of principles and teachings that must be understood if we hope to achieve psychological and spiritual health. During our journey, you have learned that

- what we tell ourselves (our self-talk) significantly impacts how emotionally healthy we are, how intimate our relationships with others are, and how mature our spiritual lives are.

- telling ourselves lies causes emotional, relational, and spiritual damage.

- certain lies we tell ourselves, such as those covered in this book, are among the most destructive of all.

- truth sets people free—free from unnecessary pain, free to experience life in full.

- there are "truths about the truth" that are essential to understand before trying to live a life based on truth.

- ten significantly important truths must be believed if we want to achieve mental and spiritual health.

- God is the owner of and ultimate authority on truth.

- knowing God is required for mental and spiritual health.

- certain truths about God provide encouragement, comfort, and stability as we go through life.

- knowing who we are is necessary in order to live healthy and meaningful lives.

- specific truths about who we are as Christians provide a clear sense of identity, worth, and purpose while we live our lives.

- following Christ and developing His "mind" is the ultimate requirement for having a healthy, intimate, and meaningful life.

I think you can see that you have learned a great deal to this point, and I hope you can allow yourself to feel a sense of accomplishment concerning how much you have learned. As Munger said, "All truth is an achievement."

Looking forward now, let me set the stage for you concerning what lies ahead in your efforts to develop "the mind of Christ" and grow as a person.

The Battle for Our Minds

Whether you realize it or not, a "civil war" is being waged in your mind every day. God, who is Truth, wants you to believe the truth because He knows it is best for you. Satan, who is the "father of lies" (John 8:44 NIV), wants you to believe lies because he knows they destroy you. All of us, non-Christian and Christian alike, make moment-by-moment decisions to think God's truth or Satan's lies. All those decisions come together over time to determine who we are and how well we live our lives.

When the United States fought its own Civil War, the North's victory was crucial to the country's future. If the South had won, slavery would have continued, and slavery destroys human beings. We are created by God to be free, not slaves. The same is true about the war going on in our minds between truth and lies. When lies win, we become slaves—slaves to depraved thinking, slaves to emotional misery, slaves to troubled relationships, and slaves to spiritual turmoil. When truth wins, we are free—free to be emotionally healthy, free to be intimately involved with others, free to enjoy God and bring glory to Him.

The battle for control of your mind is the most important battle of all. All other battles pale in comparison. The stakes couldn't be higher. And it is winner take all. You cannot afford for lies to control one single second of your life. Truth has to rule the day every day. Your freedom and maturity as a human being hang in the balance.

We live in a time when "truth is fallen in the street" (Isa. 59:14 NKJV). Everywhere we turn, we are bombarded by lies. Advertisers sometimes lie to us. Politicians sometimes lie to us. Corporations sometimes lie to us. Religious leaders sometimes lie to us. Even loved ones sometimes lie to us. My own field, psychology, has contributed greatly to this problem. Far too many times psychologists offer us their "expertise" when what they are saying is actually untrue and damages those of us who buy into it (for example, "You can trust your feelings—they are your best guide"; "You should think 'positively'" [as opposed to truthfully]; "You can do anything you set your mind to"; and "People are basically good"). We frequently believe what we are told, only to realize, often too late, that we have been led down the garden path to our own destruction.

Hear this and hear it well: there are no true "experts" here on earth for what it takes to live life properly! There is only one Expert on the matter—God. God proved His expertise when He came to earth and lived a perfect life. Anyone who can pull that off is certainly worth listening to. Anything we come up with that happens to be true and useful for living life well is really God's truth, not ours. The best we human "experts" can hope for when we write our books is that we serve as God's "pens." If we are anything else, we have become part of the problem, not part of the solution.

As we embark on the final part of our journey, I want to ask you to commit yourself not only to know the truth but to experience it and live it as well. Truth cannot set us free until we do so. It isn't enough to know the truth. The Bible says that even demons (fallen angels) know there is one God (James 2:19). *Knowing* the truth obviously hasn't done the demons much good. They're still demons! We must live the truth for it to make a genuine difference in our lives.

This is the most important chapter of the book because if you quit here, you will simply know more than you did when you read the first chapter. Knowledge only puffs us up (1 Cor. 8:1) in that we arrogantly think knowing something makes us wise. It doesn't. Truth is of zero value if it is not incorporated into our lives. Doing the truth makes us wise.

So, let's get on with it. Let's put the truth to use. Let's allow the truth to set us free.

The Truth Workout

The Truth Workout is an intensive, twelve-week program designed to help you take what you have learned in this book and "exercise" it into your life. Just as it takes effort to get in physical shape, the Truth Workout will take hard work on your part for you to get in psychological and spiritual shape.

Keep in mind that the Truth Workout is not a "cure" but ongoing "treatment" that can help you become healthier over time. There are no cures on the road to emotional and spiritual health. Fighting the lies you tell yourself with the truth will be an ongoing battle that will require your dedication throughout the rest of your life. The Truth Workout is aimed at helping you turn more and more of your mind over to truth so that you can have a fuller, more meaningful life.

The best approach to the Truth Workout is to do each week consecutively. Don't get discouraged and quit if you miss a week or two, though. Push yourself to start "working out" again where you left off. The key to successfully completing the Truth Workout is to not "grow weary" and stop altogether. Taking small steps over time is the way to success here.

The bottom line to the Truth Workout is this: you have to do the workouts if you want the results. Remember, "no pain, no gain!"

Week One:
Identifying the Lies You Tell Yourself

To identify the lies you need to focus on during future workouts, I want you to complete the Lie Questionnaire once again. Since you have taken it before, you are already "test wise" in that you know how you "should" answer. So, make sure your response to each statement reflects how you *really* think, not how you think you should think. Try to avoid using the neutral (4) response.

1	2	3	4	5	6	7
Strongly Disagree			Neutral			Strongly Agree

Self-Lies:

_____ 1. I must be perfect.

_____ 2. I must have everyone's love and approval.

_____ 3. It is easier to avoid problems than to face them.

_____ 4. I can't be happy unless things go my way.

_____ 5. My unhappiness is somebody else's fault.

Worldly Lies:

_____ 6. You can have it all.

_____ 7. My worth is determined by my performance.

_____ 8. Life should be easy.

_____ 9. Life should be fair.

_____ 10. You shouldn't have to wait for what you want.

_____ 11. People are basically good.

Marital Lies:

_____ 12. All my marital problems are my spouse's fault.

_____ 13. If my marriage takes hard work, my spouse and I must not be right for each other.

_____ 14. My spouse can and should meet all of my emotional needs.

_____ 15. My spouse owes me for what I have done for him/her.

_____ 16. I shouldn't have to change who I am in order to make my marriage better.

_____ 17. My spouse should be like me.

Distortion Lies:

_____ 18. I often make mountains out of molehills.

_____ 19. I often take things personally.

_____ 20. Things are black and white to me.

_____ 21. I often miss the forest for the trees.

_____ 22. The past predicts the future.

_____ 23. I often reason things out with my feelings rather than the facts.

Religious Lies:

_____ 24. God's love must be earned.

_____ 25. God hates the sin and the sinner.

_____ 26. Because I'm a Christian, God will protect me from pain and suffering.

_____ 27. All of my problems are caused by my sins.

_____ 28. It is my Christian duty to meet all the needs of others.

_____ 29. A good Christian doesn't feel anxious, angry, or depressed.

_____ 30. God can't use me unless I'm spiritually strong.

Look back through your responses, and circle any marked 5, 6, or 7. Add up the number of circled answers. Write down your responses to each statement from the first time you took the questionnaire to the left of your responses this time. Compare the two. Overall, did you have as many 5s, 6s, and 7s this time? Were there any lies you no longer believe as strongly? What were the most significant changes from this time to last as far as your answers to each specific lie?

Now, look back through your responses this time, and identify the three lies you still believe the most strongly. In the spaces provided, write each lie, write a short statement on why it is a lie, and then write a Bible verse that opposes this lie.

Lie #1:_____

This is a lie because _____

_____

The Bible verse that opposes this lie is _____

_____

Lie #2:_____

This is a lie because _____

_____

The Bible verse that opposes this lie is _____

_____

Lie #3:_____

_____

This is a lie because _____
_____

The Bible verse that opposes this lie is _____
_____

If you have a computer, I want you to type these three lies in large, bold-faced print and put "My Top Three Lies" at the top of the page (do this by hand if you don't have a computer). Then, print numerous copies, and post them in various places (on the bathroom mirror, on the refrigerator, on your car dashboard, on your office wall). Make sure you post these lies wherever you can so that you are reminded of them frequently. These three lies are destroying you, and you have to stay aware of them.

Finally, I want you to get a close friend involved in this effort. Let someone you trust know about these three destructive lies, and ask him to check with you once a week on how your effort to fight them is going.

Week Two:
Knowing Your A-B-Cs

Track the lies you tell yourself for the next seven days using the A-B-C model. Use the space provided to keep a record of the A-B-Cs you experience. Make as many entries as you can that involve any of the lies we covered in this book.

Dedicate yourself to this task for seven days. Write down the trigger events that happen ("A"), the lie or lies you tell yourself ("B"), and the unhealthy reactions that result ("C"). If you can't write the A-B-Cs at the moment they happen, try to write them down as soon as possible, so you don't forget them.

As you make each journal entry, assess how big the trigger event ("A") was and how big your reaction ("C") was, using the 5¢ (really small and unimportant) to $500 (really big and extremely important) scale you learned earlier in the book.

In writing down your A-B-Cs, your entries need to look something like this:

"A" (Event)	"B" (Self-Talk)	"C" (Response)
Waited for fifteen minutes in a long line,	*Why don't things ever go my way? I*	Muscles tensed; felt angry and

only to be told they were out of what I wanted. ($2.00)

can't believe this! Life should be a lot easier than this! I shouldn't have to put up with this nonsense.

resentful; let the guy at the counter "have it" and stormed out. ($100.00)

Let me challenge you once again to be diligent about doing this assignment. To truly change, you are going to have to stay on top of what you are telling yourself from day to day and how it is impacting your reactions. Don't let a single day go by without writing down at least a couple of A-B-C's from your life.

"A" (Event)	"B" (Self-Talk)	"C" (Response)
#1: _____	_____	_____
_____	_____	_____
_____	_____	_____
_____	_____	_____
#2: _____	_____	_____
_____	_____	_____
_____	_____	_____
_____	_____	_____
#3: _____	_____	_____
_____	_____	_____
_____	_____	_____
_____	_____	_____
#4: _____	_____	_____
_____	_____	_____
_____	_____	_____
_____	_____	_____
#5: _____	_____	_____
_____	_____	_____
_____	_____	_____
_____	_____	_____

#6: _____ _____ _____
_____ _____ _____
_____ _____ _____
_____ _____ _____

#7: _____ _____ _____
_____ _____ _____
_____ _____ _____
_____ _____ _____

#8: _____ _____ _____
_____ _____ _____
_____ _____ _____
_____ _____ _____

#9: _____ _____ _____
_____ _____ _____
_____ _____ _____
_____ _____ _____

#10: _____ _____ _____
_____ _____ _____
_____ _____ _____
_____ _____ _____

#11: _____ _____ _____
_____ _____ _____
_____ _____ _____
_____ _____ _____

#12: _____ _____ _____
_____ _____ _____
_____ _____ _____
_____ _____ _____

#13: _____ _____ _____
_____ _____ _____
_____ _____ _____
_____ _____ _____

#14: _____ _____ _____
_____ _____ _____
_____ _____ _____
_____ _____ _____

#15: _____ _____ _____
_____ _____ _____
_____ _____ _____
_____ _____ _____

#16: _____ _____ _____
_____ _____ _____
_____ _____ _____
_____ _____ _____

#17: _____ _____ _____
_____ _____ _____
_____ _____ _____
_____ _____ _____

#18: _____ _____ _____
_____ _____ _____
_____ _____ _____
_____ _____ _____

#19: _____ _____ _____
_____ _____ _____
_____ _____ _____
_____ _____ _____

#20: _____ _____ _____
_____ _____ _____
_____ _____ _____
_____ _____ _____

After keeping up with your A-B-Cs for seven days, complete the following statements:

1. The three events that I became the most upset over were:

Event #1:_____

Event #2:_____

Event #3:_____

2. The three lies that I told myself the most often at "B" were:

Lie #1:_____

Lie #2:_____

Lie #3:_____

3. The three emotions that I felt most often at "C" were:

Emotion #1:_____

Emotion #2:_____

Emotion #3:_____

4. The single worst behavioral reaction I had at "C" all week was:

_____

5. The A-B-C that involved the biggest overreaction from "A" to "C" was:

Event ("A"):_____

Self-Talk ("B"):_____

Response ("C"):_____

6. What did you learn from doing this assignment?

_____

_____

_____

Week Three:
Challenging Your Lies with the Truth

For the next seven days, I want you to take the next step and challenge your lies with the truth using the A-B-C-D-E model. To complete this assignment, take one specific situation from each day that was upsetting or bothersome to you, and analyze it using the A-B-C-D-E model.

To help you with this assignment, I have provided an example of a situation analyzed along these lines:

"A" (Event): A close friend starts spending a lot of time with a new friend he has made. The close friend hardly calls anymore as his new friend becomes a "best" friend.

"B" (Faulty Self-Talk/Lies): You can't trust anybody to be a true friend. He never really cared about me in the first place. I will never find another person to be a close friend. I'll never get over this. Life really stinks.

"C" (Response): Physically tense; shallow breathing; felt hurt, depressed, and angry; started avoiding my friend; began eating too much; didn't return his phone calls.

"D" (New Self-Talk/Truth): My friend being less available hurts, but the fact that he is spending more time with someone else doesn't mean I'm not a worthwhile person or a good friend. I know that friendships can change, even end, but that doesn't mean that my life has to be miserable. I don't have to spend the rest of my days bemoaning what happened. Maybe the friendship can still go on in some enjoyable manner. I'll do what I can to find out. If he doesn't want to be my friend any longer, it will have been worth the effort to find out rather than just let the friendship die without any effort on my part. If I've lost a friend, it will hurt. Yet there are other friendships to be found and enjoyed.

"E" (New Response): Less physical tension; breathing a little easier; some decrease in feelings of hurt and depression; less anger; still somewhat isolated from him; still overeating.

As you use the A-B-C-D-E model for the next seven days, you may notice that the truth ("D") helps some but doesn't eliminate all the unhealthy feelings and responses ("C") you had toward the trigger event ("A") initially. The truth about the truth is that it needs a lot of "watering" before it produces its "crop." Don't give up on telling yourself the truth just because the emotional and behavioral dividends aren't immediate.

Day #1

"A" (Event):_____

_____

"B" (Faulty Self-Talk/Lies):_____

_____

"C" (Response):_____

_____

"D" (New Self-Talk/Truth):_____

_____

"E" (New Response):_____

_____

Day #2

"A" (Event):_____

_____

"B" (Faulty Self-Talk/Lies):_____

_____

"C" (Response):_____

_____

"D" (New Self-Talk/Truth):_____

_____

"E" (New Response):_____

_____

Day #3

"A" (Event):_____

_____

"B" (Faulty Self-Talk/Lies):_____

_____

"C" (Response):_____

_____

"D" (New Self-Talk/Truth):_____

_____

"E" (New Response):_____

_____

Day #4

"A" (Event):_____

_____

"B" (Faulty Self-Talk/Lies):_____

_____

"C" (Response):_____

_____

"D" (New Self-Talk/Truth):_____

_____

"E" (New Response):_____

_____

Day #5

"A" (Event):_____

_____

"B" (Faulty Self-Talk/Lies):_____

_____

"C" (Response):_____

_____

"D" (New Self-Talk/Truth):_____

_____

"E" (New Response):_____

_____

Day #6

"A" (Event):_____

_____

"B" (Faulty Self-Talk/Lies):_____

_____

"C" (Response):_____

_____

"D" (New Self-Talk/Truth):_____

_____

"E" (New Response):_____

_____

Day #7

"A" (Event):_____

_____

"B" (Faulty Self-Talk/Lies):_____

_____

"C" (Response):_____

_____

"D" *(New Self-Talk/Truth):*_____

_____

"E" *(New Response):*_____

_____

Once again, go back through all your entries and use the 5¢ to $500 rating scale to assess the original event ("A"), your initial response ("C"), and your final response ("E"). Are there any instances where your reactions improved from "C" to "E"? Put a star by those entries—truth helped you there!

Finally, look back through your seven entries and see if you notice any themes. Were there certain trigger events ("A") that showed up more often than not? Were certain lies ("B") more of a problem than others? Did certain emotions occur more frequently than others? What truths ("D") did you find yourself relying on the most? Did telling yourself the truth actually help you have a healthier response ("E") to the original situation?

Week Four:
Dealing with Past Events

I want you to do another A-B-C-D-E workout, but this time I want you to do it related to events from early childhood through adolescence. Looking back through those years, what five events ("A") were the most painful and upsetting? What lie or lies ("B") did you tell yourself at the time? What emotions did you feel at the time, and how did you cope ("C")? What truthful self-talk ("D") do you know now that counters the lie or lies you told yourself when the event first occurred? What change, if any, has occurred in how you feel and cope as a result of telling yourself the truth ("E")?

A journal entry might look this:

"A" *(What Happened)*: Teacher screamed at me in front of other students when I talked during class in the fifth grade.

"B" *(What I Told Myself Then [Lies])*: *It is all my fault my teacher yelled at me. I made him mad. I am a horrible person for causing all this. My friends all think I'm a stupid idiot. I'll never be able to show my face around school again.*

"C" *(How I Felt/Coped Then)*: Face became flushed; started breathing shallowly; heart started racing; felt embarrassed, humiliated, ashamed, and anxious; sat down at my desk and didn't say another word the rest of class; went straight to my room and hid from my parents when I got home.

"D" (What I Tell Myself Now [Truth]): It was wrong for me to talk dur-ing class, but that didn't make my teacher yell at me. He was wrong to react that way. Being caught talking didn't mean I was a stupid idiot or a horrible person. I made a mistake then, and my teacher compounded it by losing his cool. I forgive him for what he did and won't hold it against him anymore.

"E" (How I Feel/Cope Now): No longer feel humiliated or ashamed; have forgiven the teacher who yelled at me; learned from the situation to be more sen-sitive about not talking when others are trying to conduct a class or meeting.

As you approach this assignment, take a few minutes to think through the most painful situations from your past that still bother you. My intent here is not to unnecessarily stir up unpleasant feelings. I do intend, however, to get you to examine your formative years more closely. I agree to some extent with Alice Miller, in her book *The Drama of the Gifted Child*, when she writes, "Experience has taught us that we have only one enduring weapon in our struggle against mental illness: the emotional discovery and the emotional acceptance of the truth in the individual and unique history of our childhood."[1] The truth about our early years—what happened to us, how we interpreted it, how it felt, how we coped—is critically important to understand if we are to make progress in the here and now as adults.

Use the space provided to make your A-B-C-D-E entries concerning those events from your past that you feel were the most emotionally significant.

Event #1

*"A" (What Happened):*_____

_____

*"B" (What I Told Myself Then [Lies]):*_____

_____

*"C" (How I Felt/Coped Then):*_____

_____

*"D" (What I Tell Myself Now [Truth]):*_____

_____

*"E" (How I Feel/Cope Now):*_____

_____

Event #2

"A" *(What Happened):*_____

_____

"B" *(What I Told Myself Then [Lies]):*_____

_____

"C" *(How I Felt/Coped Then):*_____

_____

"D" *(What I Tell Myself Now [Truth]):*_____

_____

"E" *(How I Feel/Cope Now):*_____

_____

Event #3

"A" *(What Happened):*_____

_____

"B" *(What I Told Myself Then [Lies]):*_____

_____

"C" *(How I Felt/Coped Then):*_____

_____

"D" *(What I Tell Myself Now [Truth]):*_____

_____

"E" *(How I Feel/Cope Now):*_____

_____

Event #4

"A" *(What Happened):*_____

_____

"B" *(What I Told Myself Then [Lies]):*_____

_____

"C" *(How I Felt/Coped Then):*_____

_____

"D" *(What I Tell Myself Now [Truth]):*_____

_____

"E" *(How I Feel/Cope Now):*_____

_____

Event #5

"A" *(What Happened):*_____

_____

"B" *(What I Told Myself Then [Lies]):*_____

_____

"C" *(How I Felt/Coped Then):*_____

_____

"D" *(What I Tell Myself Now [Truth]):*_____

_____

"E" *(How I Feel/Cope Now):*_____

_____

Look back through your five entries, and answer the following questions:

1. Was a certain person involved more than once? If so, who?

_____

2. In terms of the lies you may have told yourself at the time, did you tell yourself one or more of these?

_____ What happened was all my fault.

_____ I must be a rotten person to have caused this.

_____ If I had acted differently, this wouldn't have happened.

_____ I deserve to be treated this way.

_____ There is something wrong with me that is causing all this.

_____ I deserve to be treated this way from now on.

_____ I'm not worth loving.

_____ The future will just be more of the same.

3. What emotions were the most common across the five events?

Hurt _____

Anger _____

Shame _____

Humiliation _____

Anxiety _____

Depression _____

Other: _____

4. How did you cope with what happened?

Isolated _____

Self-medicated _____

Attacked _____

Tried harder _____

Other: _____

5. What truths do you tell yourself now that help you better understand what happened to you?

Truth: _____

_____

Truth: _____

_____

Truth: _____

_____

6. Have you been able to forgive people for what they did to you? If so, how were you able to forgive them? If not, why not?

_____

_____

_____

A balance must be struck concerning the past. One extreme is to ignore it and act as if what happened back then had no impact on shaping you as a person. The other extreme is to obsess about it and use what happened as a scapegoat for who you are today. The balance is to examine the truth about your past and to use it to walk wisely today. Easier said than done? Sure it is. Worth doing? Absolutely.

The ultimate bottom line to painful events from the past is facing the truth about them and being able to forgive and move on. Not being willing to forgive is the kiss of death. Unforgiveness, as one writer described it, is like gnawing on your own bone. It is a self-destructive act to refuse to forgive another person. I hope by doing this exercise that you are a little closer to seeing the truth about your past and its impact on you. I also hope that you, as an act of your will, will choose to forgive the person or people who hurt you. Do it for your own sake if for no other reason.

One final request before you move on to next week's workout. Read Matthew 18:21–35, and use this space to summarize what it says:

_____

_____

_____

_____

Week Five:
Overcoming Perfectionism

During the next few weeks, we will focus on a specific lie that we tell ourselves. This week is Perfectionism Week. Most of us, to some degree or another, struggle with perfectionistic thinking, and this week I want you to deal with yours.

I want you to write down three examples of how your perfectionistic tendencies show up. An example from my life is that I don't like things to be out of place. In my home growing up, I was taught "there is a place for everything and everything has its place." Boy, did I learn that lesson well because that is exactly how I am around my own home (much to the chagrin of my family!).

As you list each example, I want you to write down how you would act differently if you weren't so perfectionistic. In other words, if you were more balanced in this area (more realistic, more laid-back, less obsessive), how would you handle the situation? Concerning my perfectionistic "everything must be in its place" approach to life, I have learned to simply let things be out of place longer, not immediately put them away, or get someone else to do so. I have learned to accept a certain amount of clutter and not to let it bother me as much. I am a little "saner" because of this, and I am not driving my family as crazy (which they appreciate greatly!).

What about you? What are some of the ways you are perfectionistic? And how would you be different?

I'm perfectionistic in that I _____

_____

_____

If I were not so perfectionistic, I would _____

_____

_____

I'm perfectionistic in that I _____

_____

_____

If I were not so perfectionistic, I would _____

_____

_____

I'm perfectionistic in that I _____

_____

_____

If I were not so perfectionistic, I would _____

_____

_____

Looking back through what you wrote, which specific example of your perfectionism would you like to do something about? Choose the one that bothers you (or others) the most. Now, for the rest of the week, do exactly what you said you would do about it if you were not so perfectionistic. Make the change—be "antiperfectionistic" in this area of your life for a week.

After you have practiced this new behavior for a week, respond to the following questions:

1. How did you feel when you were not being perfectionistic?

_____

_____

2. How were things better for you and those around you because you were not being perfectionistic?

_____

_____

3. How were things worse?

_____

_____

4. How hard was it for you to do the new behavior (did you feel uptight, get frustrated, lapse into the old way of doing things)?

_____

_____

Changing our focus some, I want you to write down examples of imperfections in others that you have a hard time accepting. Perfectionism shows itself not only in the idealistic expectations we have of ourselves but also in the unrealistic standards we set for others. An example from my life is other people's driving. People never drive perfectly enough for me. They don't always signal, they go too slow, they go too fast, they don't totally stop at stop signs—well, you get the point. Rather than accept that, I let it bother me that people are imperfect drivers. I keep going out on the highway, expecting people to drive perfectly, and I am always disappointed.

What about you? What imperfections in others drive you up the proverbial wall? List them here:

1. _____

_____

2. _____

_____

3. _____

_____

4. _____

_____

5. _____

_____

Choose one of the five you listed, and make a commitment to quit expecting people to be any different. Let them off the hook for being that way, and just accept that as how they are, whether you like it or not.

Shifting gears a little, I want to further challenge your perfectionism by asking you to consider doing something imperfect on purpose. Go out and do something that you know isn't perfect. Let me give you some ideas to choose from, but I want you to feel free to come up with one on your own:

- Wear socks of a different color.

- Spill something on purpose and don't clean it up.

- Move things around on your work desk until they are out of place and leave them there for a few days.

- Wear your watch on your other wrist.

- Eat with your fingers.

- Put your underwear in the sock drawer.

- Go out in public looking like a wreck.

- Tilt all the paintings in your home.

- Don't shave for a few days.

Your idea:_____

The purpose of this assignment is to get you to do the very thing you don't want to do—be imperfect—so that you can accept it and *let it be*! Instead of fighting to be perfect when you can't be, let yourself enjoy the freedom you have to be an imperfect human being.

Please don't misinterpret what I'm saying. There are some areas of life where we can't be perfect but need to keep trying to improve ourselves and strive for excellence every day (our faith, our marriages, our parenting, our friendships, our work abilities). To not do so would be wrong. But I want you to quit trying to be perfect about all "the small stuff" that we aren't supposed to "sweat." So many things in life really don't matter, and to be perfectionistic about them is crazy.

One final assignment. Read the following passages of the Bible, and summarize what they are trying to say:

Philippians 3:12:_____

_____

1 John 1:8:_____

_____

Psalm 18:30:_____

_____

What is God trying to tell you through these passages? What is God saying that He wants from you? Far too many Christians are caught up in a legalistic approach to Christianity that simply isn't biblical, a kind of "If I just dot all the right moral 'i's' and cross all the right moral 't's,' then God will love me and I might make it into heaven." Nothing you do can make God love you more, and nothing you do can get you into heaven. The balance for us as Christians is to keep "pressing on to the mark" of being more like Christ every day, knowing we will never be exactly like Him while simultaneously avoiding continuing to sin so that grace may "abound."

Bottom line: do your very best, apologize when you fall short, and learn from your mistakes. That is what is asked of you.

Week Six:
Defeating the Need for Approval

This is Approval Week. During this workout, I want you to examine how much of a need for approval you have and take some steps to overcome unhealthy approval needs.

Before we get started, though, I want to say that I believe that we all come prewired with a need for approval and that there is nothing wrong with that. What little kid doesn't want his mom, dad, teacher, coach, or friend to approve of something he is or has done? What adult doesn't want the approval of other adults? It is human to want approval.

This week I want you to focus on whether or not your need for approval is too strong and leads you into being something you are not in order to get someone to approve of you. Do you put on a "mask" or "false self" to get the approval of others? Do you do things that violate your morals just to get people to like you? That is the issue here.

I certainly have done that very thing. One tendency I have is to be "polite" in conversations with others at the expense of saying what I really think sometimes. I nod my head and say "uh-huh" fifty times as if I agree when I really don't and am afraid to say so because the person may not like me if I do. Sound familiar?

Now, take a few minutes to respond to some questions. First, whose approval do you feel that you want and how strongly do you want it (0 = don't want it at all; 100 = will die if I don't get it)?

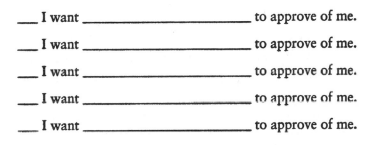

___ I want _____ to approve of me.

___ I want _____ to approve of me.

___ I want _____ to approve of me.

___ I want _____ to approve of me.

___ I want _____ to approve of me.

Thinking about your need for the approval of those you listed, what have you done to get it that you would agree was inappropriate? In other words, how did you violate your sense of right/wrong, ethics, or common sense to get these people to accept you?

1. _____
_____

2. _____
_____

3. _____
_____

4. _____
_____

5. _____
_____

Now, I want you to focus on a certain person whose approval you currently need too much, inappropriate ways you go about getting the approval, and what you are willing to do to change.

The person in my day-to-day life whose approval I need too much is

_____

What I do to get the approval that I know is wrong or inappropriate is

_____

_____

In order to change, I am willing to _____

_____

Implement the change(s) to quit seeking this person's approval in unhealthy ways. Be willing for your relationship with him or her to change, maybe get worse. People often grow accustomed to our needing their approval, and they don't always take too kindly to our stopping what we do to get it. Be prepared for a "jolt" to your relationship with this person, maybe even for the relationship to end. Just remember this: if you have to violate your conscience to get or keep somebody's approval, the approval isn't worth having.

Another thing I would like you to do this week is to purposely do something that you know will lead to people disapproving of you. No, I am not asking you to do something immoral such as rob a bank or shoot a neighbor you don't like. I'm asking you to purposely trigger disapproval in an *amoral* way so that you can work on not needing approval so much. Here are some "fun" possibilities on how to do this:

- Yell out the time of day in the center of a large store. Walk backwards in a mall.

- Walk through a shopping mall while wearing Mickey Mouse ears. Wear a baseball cap with a goofy saying on it.

- Go up the "down" escalator (don't hurt anyone).

- Drive the speed limit in the fast lane.

- Sing (in a semi-low voice) in an elevator.

- Tell your kids no (that'll shock 'em)!

- Take the opposite point of view from what someone is saying.

Once you decide what to do, do it. Try to pay attention to how you feel before you do it, while you are doing it, and after you do it. If you need people's approval as badly as most of us do, you will feel pretty anxious throughout the whole event. I want you to realize in doing this assignment that five minutes after it is over, no one will really care (and if anyone does, he needs more help that you do!). I really want you to see that you can live with people's disapproval and that you get a certain amount of freedom back when you quit worrying so much about what people think.

Again, I am not trying to push you in the direction of being immoral or insensitive to others. We definitely need to act morally and respectfully toward others. To do something wrong for the purpose of hurting others just to prove we don't need people's approval would be way out of line with living our lives properly. The healthy person doesn't do things just for the sake of approval nor does he purposely do wrong things in order to elicit disapproval. He does what is right whether anyone approves or not and is able to enjoy whatever approval that does come his way.

Finally, I want you to look up the following verses in the Bible to see what it has to say about the issue of needing people's approval. Summarize what each verse says in the space provided:

Galatians 1:10:_____

_____

Romans 14:8:_____

_____

Is it okay to want approval? Yes. Is it healthy to want it from everyone? No. Is it appropriate to want it so badly from one person that you will violate God's laws to get it? No. What is the best kind of approval to have? The kind that comes from living morally.

Is that the kind of approval you are looking for?

Week Seven:
Facing Problems

Another lie explored in this book is the idea that "it is easier to avoid problems than to face them." Of course, we know that problems only get worse when they are avoided, but we avoid them anyway. This week I want to push you to confront this lie head-on.

First, look back in time to instances in your life where you avoided facing a problem. Write down three examples and the cost (emotional, spiritual, relational, financial) of avoiding them.

The problem I avoided was _____

_____

The price I paid for avoiding this problem was _____
_____

The problem I avoided was _____
_____

The price I paid for avoiding this problem was _____
_____

The problem I avoided was _____
_____

The price I paid for avoiding this problem was _____
_____

Review your responses. Did you end up suffering more because you avoided the problem than you would have if you had faced it? My guess is that the answer to that question is yes. It almost always is.

Now, I want you to think about current problems in your life. In the spaces provided, write down examples of problems you are currently avoiding and what, if any, price you have paid so far for having done so.

A problem I am currently avoiding is _____
_____

The price I have paid so far for avoiding this problem is _____
_____

A problem I am currently avoiding is _____
_____

The price I have paid so far for avoiding this problem is _____
_____

A problem I am currently avoiding is _____
_____

The price I have paid so far for avoiding this problem is _____
_____

Now, for the hard part. From among the problems you are currently avoiding, I want you to choose one and face it. Do it now if you can. Do it in the next twenty-four to forty-eight hours for sure. Don't put this problem off any longer. You are paying too high a price for avoiding this problem in your life, and it is time you did something about it.

An oil filter commercial from years ago had a popular slogan: "Pay me now, or pay me later." The idea behind the ad was that you could spend a few bucks now on a new oil filter or hundreds of dollars later on a new engine. The bottom line is that either way you go, you are going to have to pay, so why not pay the smaller amount up front? That ad had a lot of wisdom to it.

The same goes for our personal lives. The issue isn't, "Are we going to suffer?" Of course, we are. The issue is, "Which kind of suffering are we going to choose?" Are we going to be willing to suffer appropriately by facing our problems head-on when they occur, or are we going to put them off and suffer ten times as much down the road? The choice truly is ours. The route we choose makes or breaks us as we journey through life.

Before we wrap up this workout, I want you to take a moment and make as complete a list as possible of all the problems you are currently avoiding in your life.

Problem #1:_____

_____

Problem #2:_____

_____

Problem #3:_____

_____

Problem #4:_____

_____

Problem #5:_____

_____

Problem #6:_____

_____

Problem #7:_____

_____

Problem #8:_____

_____

Problem #9:_____

_____

Problem #10:_____

_____

The truth of the matter is that each problem you listed is an opportunity to protect yourself from worse problems down the road and thus keep your mental health in the process.

Maybe an analogy will help. I ask my kids to brush their teeth every day. They protest, "Oh, Dad, do I have to?" Well, the truth of the matter is, they don't. The truth of the matter is, they get to. They get to brush their teeth and thus protect themselves from painful cavities and related dental work down the road. Try to sell my kids on that idea, and you'll see eyes start to roll and lips start to complain. But it is no less true just because they don't buy it. They get to brush their teeth and thus have the blessing of healthy teeth down the road.

Do you see your problems in that light? Or are you still thinking like a child and whining and moaning every time a problem presents itself? I want you to go back to your list of problems and say each one out loud, beginning with "I get to . . ." Say each problem this way two or three times if necessary. Face each problem now—don't pay more later on. It isn't worth it.

To put a nice cherry on top of this cake, read James 1:2–4, and summarize in the space provided what you think it is saying:

_____

_____

_____

That's the right attitude toward problems, isn't it?

Week Eight:
Discovering Your Identity and Worth

Two things that all of us seem to need as we go through life are a sense of who we are and a sense of worth. If we fail to nail down either one, we are in bad shape. When we don't have a proper sense of these two things, we are more troubled, unhappy, and self-destructive. This week, I want to push you to honestly examine where you get your identity and worth from. I also want to help you see where they need to come from.

Far too many of us get both our identity and our worth from the various roles we play. Our identity may come from "I'm a parent" or "I'm a teacher." Our worth then comes from how well we perform in those roles. Letting our identity come from the roles we play and allowing our worth to come from how well we play those roles are two humongous mistakes.

Take a minute to look at this issue. What roles do you play in life, and how much does your sense of worth depend upon how well you perform in these roles (1 = very little; 7 = a great deal)?

How Much My Sense of Worth Depends on the Role I Play	How Well I Perform in This Role						
_____ Spouse	1	2	3	4	5	6	7
_____ Parent	1	2	3	4	5	6	7
_____ Worker (Job)	1	2	3	4	5	6	7
_____ Friend	1	2	3	4	5	6	7
_____ Neighbor	1	2	3	4	5	6	7
_____ Volunteer	1	2	3	4	5	6	7
_____ Other:_____	1	2	3	4	5	6	7
_____ Other:_____	1	2	3	4	5	6	7
_____ Other:_____	1	2	3	4	5	6	7

Take a minute to look at the roles you checked and how much your sense of worth depends on your performance in each role. I would like you to answer two questions. What specific role do you depend on the most for your sense of worth? What has it been like emotionally over the past few years of your life to have depended upon that role for your sense of worth? _____

_____

I want to help you understand something here that is critically important. Our self-esteem ought to come from how well we perform in the various roles we play, but not our identity and not our worth. Let me explain.

Every psychologist has a definition of what self-esteem is. The best one I have ever come across is from William James, considered by many to be the father of American psychology. William James defined *self-esteem* this way: Self-esteem = success/expectations. In other words, your self-esteem is a function of how well you perform (your "successes") compared to how well you thought you should perform (your "expectations").

Let's try an example using a 0 to 100 scale. Let's say I am somebody's best friend. Let's say I expect myself to be a perfect best friend, thus my "expectations" level is 100. But let's say over the past six months that I have been a pretty poor best friend (haven't talked to him very often, haven't shown a lot of interest in his problems), thus my "successes" level has been around 40. Using William James's definition, my self-esteem as a best friend would be 40/100 and thus would be pretty low.

But let's say that I am employed as a sales rep at a pharmaceutical company. I think I should do a fantastic job, so my "expectations" level is 100. It turns out I am the company's leading sales rep every year and I am constantly setting new sales records that no other sales rep comes even close to, so my "successes" level is 98. According to William James's definition, my self-esteem as a sales rep would be 98/100 and thus would be extremely high.

One final variation on the theme. Let's say I volunteer one hour a week at the concession stand at the baseball park where my son plays baseball. I don't expect myself to be a very good concessionaire, so my "expectations" level is 30. Let's say I do the bare minimum in my role (get customers what they want, smile nicely, don't spill drinks on anyone), so my "successes" level is 25. Well, according to good old William James, I still ought to have high self-esteem as a volunteer concessionaire because my self-esteem score is 25/30, which is pretty good.

If William James is right, our self-esteem in various areas of life ought to fluctuate as our performances and expectations in those areas go up and down. If I expect myself to perform well in a certain area and don't, then my self-esteem in that area ought to be low. If I expect myself to perform well in a certain role and do, then my self-esteem ought to be high.

Translate this into your children's lives for just a minute. If one child is capable of making As in math and is bringing home Fs due to laziness and indifference, you don't want him to have high self-esteem as a math student. If he is capable of making Bs in history and is bringing home B+s because he is working really hard to do well, you would want him to have high self-esteem as a history student.

With all this said and done, go back to the various roles you play, and rate your self-esteem in each role.

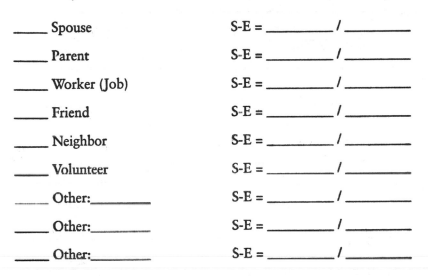

Role I Play	Self-Esteem = Successes/Expectations
_____ Spouse	S-E = _____ / _____
_____ Parent	S-E = _____ / _____
_____ Worker (Job)	S-E = _____ / _____
_____ Friend	S-E = _____ / _____
_____ Neighbor	S-E = _____ / _____
_____ Volunteer	S-E = _____ / _____
_____ Other:_____	S-E = _____ / _____
_____ Other:_____	S-E = _____ / _____
_____ Other:_____	S-E = _____ / _____

Before we leave this issue, the implications for how to raise self-esteem are fairly simple. First, you can improve your "successes" level. If your self-esteem is low because you are not performing well enough, you need to do whatever you can to perform better. Second, you can improve your self-esteem by lowering your expectations. Sometimes we struggle with low self-esteem because our expectations are unrealistic—we aim too high. Setting more realistic standards is the key. Third, we can do both—improve our performance while simultaneously making our expectations more realistic. This option is usually the best course of action for raising self-esteem.

Now, let's turn our attention to the issues of identity and worth. The most important thing for you to understand is that neither identity nor worth has anything to do with performance. Nothing! Let's look at each issue separately.

Identity has to do with who you are in your being. We explored this issue in Chapter 19, and we need to explore it again now. I want you to take the following "identities" you have as a Christian, read the biblical passages on them, and write a brief sentence or two on what each means to you:

Holy (1 Cor. 1:2):_____

_____

Blameless (Eph. 1:4):_____

_____

Complete (Col. 2:10):_____
_____

Child of God (John 1:12):_____
_____

Slave of Righteousness (Rom. 6:18):_____
_____

Temple of God (1 Cor. 3:16):_____
_____

New Creation (2 Cor. 5:17):_____
_____

Saint (Eph. 1:1):_____
_____

Christ's Friend (John 15:15):_____
_____

Conqueror Over Evil (Rom. 8:37):_____
_____

Citizen of Heaven (Phil. 3:20):_____
_____

Joint Heir with Christ (Rom. 8:17):_____
_____

Your identity is not "loser," "idiot," "failure," or "wimp." Your identity is "child of God," "saint," "heir," and "new creation." When you assume the wrong identity, you lose not only an accurate sense of who you are but all the emotional and spiritual health that goes with it. When you have the correct identity, you don't have to find one in a role you play (spouse, parent, worker, friend) or buy into false identities that may have been handed to you by somebody else.

Now, let's talk about worth. Worth has to do with your value. It is based not on what you do but on who made you. For example, the value of a painting is tied to the artist who created it. I am not a skilled artist (stick figures are the best I can do). Consequently, any paintings I might paint would be worth very little. Yet a Rembrandt is worth a substantial sum of money because of the artist who painted it.

The point I am trying to make here is that you have incredible worth because of who "painted" you. God, the greatest Painter of all, created you. You are His masterpiece. God may have made you, in human terms, with more or less intelligence, looks, or talent than His other masterpieces, but each person has God's "signature" on him as being made by God. Consequently, you are priceless. All the money, jewels, and precious metals in the world would not be enough to purchase you.

The Bible says very clearly what it took to purchase you (Rev. 5:9). It took the life of Christ. There is nothing and no one of greater value than that. The highest price possible was paid for you, something that ought to tell you what you are worth. What does it mean to you that you were bought with the life of Christ? _____

_____

Before I let you go, I want you to do three things. First, choose a role you play in life in which you have low self-esteem, and do what it takes to raise your self-esteem. That means both performing better and being realistic as far as what you expect of yourself. Second, choose one "identity" you have as a Christian from among those noted here, and memorize the Bible verse that went with it. Third, find a quiet place where you won't be disturbed, and meditate for five minutes on the following statement: *I am God's priceless masterpiece.*

Week Nine:
Rejecting Your "Have To's"

Earlier in this book I tried to sell you on the idea that we often victimize ourselves by thinking we *have to* do certain things when the truth of the matter is that we *choose to* do what we do. The *have to* mind-set leads to bitterness and resentment, while the *choose to* mind-set leads to peace and freedom.

The purpose of this week's workout is to take you back into *have to* versus *choose to* and get you to apply these notions to your life. First, list all the things you feel that you *have to* do.

I have to

1. _____;

2. _____;

3. _____;

4. _____;

5. _____;

6. _____;

7. _____;

8. _____;

9. _____;

10. _____;

11. _____;

12. _____;

13. _____;

14. _____;

15. _____.

Look back through the list, and choose five *have to*'s that bother you the most (make you feel angry, frustrated, resentful). For each one, write in the spaces provided that you *choose to* do it and give the reason(s) why. Let me give you an example to get you started.

I sometimes struggle with this: "I have to take the kids to school on Thursday morning." When I think this way, I find myself feeling resentful, and the trip to school is anything but enjoyable. The truth of the matter is, I don't have to take my kids to school on Thursday morning. I choose to. I choose to because it helps my wife, Holly, and it gives me time with the kids that morning that I wouldn't usually have. So, I am free to not take them to school, I choose to do it, and there are good reasons for making that choice.

Now, it is your turn. Take five "have to's" and turn them into "choose to's" and give reasons for your choice.

I choose to _____

because _____

_____

I choose to _____

because _____

_____

I choose to _____

because _____

_____

I choose to _____

because _____

_____

I choose to _____

because _____

_____

I hope you are able to see that there is nothing you have to do in life and that you choose to do the things you do. This is a critical fork in the road between mental/spiritual misery and mental/spiritual health.

A final step for you to take: pick a *have to* from among your list and choose *not* to do it. Yes, you heard me right. Prove to yourself that you don't have to do it by not doing it. A word of caution: choose a *have to* that won't hurt anyone if you don't do it. For example, you don't have to feed your kids today, but it will harm them if you don't. Pick something such as, "I have to clean out the garage this weekend," and *don't do it*!

There is a statement in the Bible that I want you to look up. It is Deuteronomy 30:19. Summarize what you think it is saying: _____

_____

_____

Our choices make or break us. We need to choose wisely each day so that we reap the positive consequences available to us. Do everything you can to switch from *have to* thinking to *choose to* thinking so that mental and spiritual health can be yours.

Week Ten:
Facing Your Own Death

We are all going to die someday. That is an inescapable reality. Have you truly faced that fact? In this workout, I am going to push you to do just that.

First, I want to ask you some questions.

1. Have you ever been close to someone who died? _____ Yes_____ No

2. If yes, who was it? _____

3. How old was the person at the time of death? _____

4. Had he or she prepared for his death? _____ Yes _____ No

5. If so, how was he or she prepared? _____
_____

6. How painful was his or her death for you? _____
_____

7. When you think about this person, what do you think? _____
_____

If you were suddenly informed that you were going to die in five years but that you have to keep working, how would you live differently? What would you do more, and what would you do less?

If I were going to die in five years, I would do more of the following:

1. _____

2. _____

3. _____

4. _____

5. _____

If I were going to die in five years, I would do less of the following:

1. _____

2. _____

3. _____

4. _____

5. _____

Now, I want you to write your obituary in the space provided as it would appear if you died today. You may want to read your local paper to see how obituaries are done, but I want you to write one the way you would like it to appear. _____

_____

_____

_____

_____

_____

_____

Unless Christ returns first, we are going to have a funeral in our honor someday. At your funeral, people are going to get up and say something about you. Who would you like to speak on your behalf, and what would you like them to say?

I would like _____ to speak at my funeral and

say _____

_____

_____

I would like _____ to speak at my funeral and

say _____

_____

_____

I would like _____ to speak at my funeral and

say _____

_____

_____

When you die, what truth would be the most painful or embarrassing that someone could say about you at your funeral?

_____

_____

_____

_____

Think about your tombstone. What one word or short phrase about you would you like to have engraved on it? _____

_____

Next, I want you to set aside a night to rent two movies, *A Christmas Carol* and *It's a Wonderful Life*. After you have watched both, grapple with the following question: *If I died today, would I have lived my life as a George Bailey, who influenced so many people for the good, or an Ebenezer Scrooge, who affected so many people for the bad?* Explain your answer.

_____

_____

_____

_____

_____

To wrap up this workout, I want to ask you to do one more thing. Earlier in the book we talked about how some people don't face the prospect of their death very well because they live so badly. Think about how you are living your life for a minute. What about your life are you willing to change right this very minute in order to live it more meaningfully? What specific change can you make in your life right now that would improve the quality of your life? The assignment: do it! Right now! No excuses!

Week Eleven:
Being Needy, Meeting Needs[2]

The next workout deals with the fact that we have needs. Simply put, we are all needy. We have physical needs for air, food, and water that must be met for us to survive. We also have spiritual needs, the most important of which is for an intimate relationship with God. I believe God created us with emotional needs as well. That is what I would like to focus on here.

First, a word of caution. There are two major mistakes you can make with regard to having emotional needs. One is to deny that you have them—to deny your neediness as a human being. The second is to demand that your emotional needs be the center of the universe and to care only about your needs being met while ignoring the needs of others. Either mistake will cost you psychological health and spiritual growth.

A list of emotional needs is provided. In the space next to each emotional need, write your personal definition of that need.

Acceptance:_____

_____

Affection:_____

_____

Affirmation:_____

_____

Appreciation:_____

_____

Attention:_____

_____

Comfort:_____

_____

Encouragement:_____

_____

Respect:_____

_____

Security:_____

_____

Support:_____

_____

Understanding:_____

_____

These emotional needs are "hard-wired" into us. We have them from the first day we draw breath until the last. Having these emotional needs makes us human, and we don't need to apologize for having them.

When our emotional needs go unmet, God has created us in such a way that we are going to experience two powerful emotions: hurt and anger. These are natural reactions. The challenge, which we will discuss in a minute, is how to feel hurt and angry without reacting badly.

Think for a minute about some of your current A-B-Cs that involve hurt and anger as your response at "C." Write down the event that triggered your hurt and anger, and then try to identify the emotional need or needs that went unmet when the event took place.

Let me help you along with a couple of examples. An event that triggers mild hurt and anger in me is holding a door open for someone and not hearing a "thank you." The emotional need underneath those feelings is the need for appreciation. Another event that triggers hurt and anger in me is someone talking rudely to me. Underneath that situation is the emotional need for respect

Now, write down five events from your life that you currently feel hurt and/or angry about, and identify the emotional need or needs underlying each event.

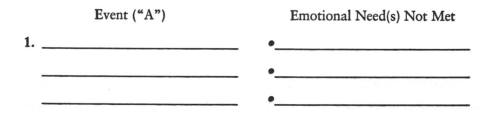

Event ("A")	Emotional Need(s) Not Met
1. _____	• _____
_____	• _____
_____	• _____

2. _____   • _____
   _____   • _____
   _____   • _____

3. _____   • _____
   _____   • _____
   _____   • _____

4. _____   • _____
   _____   • _____
   _____   • _____

5. _____   • _____
   _____   • _____
   _____   • _____

   Next, I would like you to identify two people from your life: the person you feel hurt you the most and the person you feel loved you the most. Write down the emotional needs that were unmet by the first person and the emotional needs that were met by the second person.

   The person who hurt me the most:_____

   The emotional needs that they didn't meet: _____
   _____
   _____
   _____
   _____

   The person who loved me the most:_____

   The emotional needs that they didn't meet: _____
   _____
   _____
   _____

Although we do not need to apologize for having emotional needs or for feeling hurt and angry when they go unmet, we often do need to apologize for how badly we handle those two feelings when we have them. There are five main ways we tend to mishandle hurt and anger related to unmet emotional needs. For each of the five, write down any examples of how you act this way when your emotional needs aren't met.

1. Isolate/Stuff (say/do nothing, hide feelings, act fine): _____

_____

_____

_____

2. Attack/Spew (yell, browbeat, hit, break things): _____

_____

_____

_____

3. Indirect Attack (cold shoulder, aloofness, cynicism, sarcasm): _____

_____

_____

_____

4. Self-Medicate (drugs, alcohol, food, sex, work, spending, TV): _____

_____

_____

_____

5. Perfectionism (try to be flawless):_____

_____

_____

_____

Not only are we wounded by others when they don't meet our emotional needs, but we tend to wound others by not meeting their emotional needs as well. Usually, we pay more attention to how others hurt us than how we hurt them. To fight that tendency, I want you to think for a minute or two about who you have hurt by failing to meet their emotional needs. Who are the people you have hurt, and which of their emotional needs did you fail to meet?

I hurt _____ when I failed to meet his/her
emotional need(s) for _____
by _____
_____

I hurt _____ when I failed to meet his/her
emotional need(s) for _____
by _____
_____

I hurt _____ when I failed to meet his/her
emotional need(s) for _____
by _____
_____

They say that confession is good for the soul. I want you to put that into practice by going to one of the people you mentioned here and confessing your failure to meet his or her emotional needs, asking for forgiveness, and committing yourself to meet his or her needs more consistently. Be careful—don't confess your "sins" unless you mean it and are ready to change.

Now, focus on your emotional needs for a minute. From the list that I gave you, what would you say are your top three (the three needs that are the most important to you)?

My top three emotional needs are

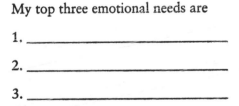

1. _____

2. _____

3. _____

Of the three emotional needs you identified, choose one that you would like a certain person to meet and ask him/her (nicely) if he/she would be willing to meet it. Yes, I know this sounds forward or brash or selfish, but it really is a way to practice humility and brokenness if you look at it from the right angle. Going to someone and saying, "Would you be willing to affirm me when you see me doing something good?" is admitting to a need and owning up to the fact that you are not self-sufficient in meeting all your own needs. You allow others in your life to feel needed, something that benefits them. Everyone wins when we appropriately let our needs be known and allow others to meet them.

The flip side of that assignment is something I want you to do as well. Show the list of emotional needs to someone to whom you are close, and ask him or her if there is any need you could meet for him in the weeks to come. Give him or her a chance to let you meet his needs.

More broadly, I want to challenge you to step out onto the planet each day and look for ways to meet the emotional needs of people—friends, coworkers, subordinates, strangers, you name it. Each and every day is an opportunity to make the world a better place in this way. You will be amazed at how much people will brighten up when you meet their emotional needs, and you will also be amazed at what they will do in return to meet yours.

There are a few Bible verses I want you to read and summarize before this workout is over. They drive home the point that God knows what we need, is committed to meeting all of our needs, and wants us to love others by being committed to meeting their needs as well.

Matthew 6:7–8:_____

_____

_____

Philippians 4:19:_____

_____

_____

1 John 3:17–18:_____

_____

_____

Enough said.

Week Twelve:
Developing the Mind of Christ

This final workout has the potential to be extremely powerful in helping to change your life for the better. I hope you will do this workout (and the other ones) time and time again.

I want you to choose one of the four Gospels (Matthew, Mark, Luke, and John) and read it from start to finish. As you read it, I want you to take the A-

B-C model and apply it to the life of Christ. Specifically, I want you to write down the events ("A") that happened to Him, what His self-talk about those events was ("B"), and how He reacted ("C").

The hardest part of the assignment will be discerning Christ's self-talk ("B") since we can't know for sure. Do your best to get inside the "mind" of Christ and figure out what He told Himself in the face of the things that happened to Him. Remember, as you fill in "B," whatever you put there has to be objective truth. Christ never told Himself anything that was untrue, so the entries you make for "B" must reflect that.

To help you along, let me take an event from the life of Christ and run it through the A-B-C model:

"A" (Event)	"B" (Self-Talk)	"C" (Response)
Christ asked three of His disciples to watch and pray while He prayed in the Garden of Gethsemane.	*I needed their support, and they fell asleep in My hour of need. It hurts that they were unwilling to do what I asked. I love them, but they have let Me down.*	Felt hurt and disappointed; told them what He felt; went and prayed.

Now, it's your turn. I have provided space for nine A-B-Cs from the life of Christ for you to enter. Make any additional entries on separate pieces of paper.

"A" (Event) What Happened to Christ	"B" (Self-Talk) What Christ Thought	"C" (Response) How Christ Responded

Passage:_____

_____ _____ _____
_____ _____ _____
_____ _____ _____
_____ _____ _____

Passage:_____

_____ _____ _____
_____ _____ _____
_____ _____ _____

Passage:_____

_____ _____ _____
_____ _____ _____
_____ _____ _____
_____ _____ _____

Passage:_____

_____ _____ _____
_____ _____ _____
_____ _____ _____
_____ _____ _____

Passage:_____

_____ _____ _____
_____ _____ _____
_____ _____ _____
_____ _____ _____

Passage:_____

_____ _____ _____
_____ _____ _____
_____ _____ _____
_____ _____ _____

Passage:_____

_____ _____ _____
_____ _____ _____
_____ _____ _____
_____ _____ _____

Passage:_____

_____ _____ _____
_____ _____ _____
_____ _____ _____
_____ _____ _____

Passage:_____

_____ _____ _____
_____ _____ _____

_____   _____   _____
_____   _____   _____

When you finish, I want you to take a minute and review your entries. What main thing did you learn about the mind of Christ from doing this assignment?

_____
_____
_____
_____
_____

In what ways would you say that Christ's self-talk (His thoughts) is different from your own? _____

_____
_____
_____
_____

One of the more interesting statements about the mind of Christ is found in Philippians 2:5–7. Read that passage and summarize what it says in your own words in the space provided: _____

_____
_____
_____
_____

Do you have this same attitude in you? Explain. _____

_____
_____
_____
_____

A final assignment. I want you to put into action what you have learned about the mind of Christ. What attitude did Christ have that you can translate into action? For example, Christ had the attitude of "servant." In what way could you translate that attitude into serving somebody this week? Think about the various attitudes of Christ and how you could put them into action if you thought that way too.

Congratulations! You have completed twelve weeks of growing stronger in the truth. I hope you can see positive results in your life that are encouraging to you. May God continue to richly bless all the effort you have put into reading this book and doing the assignments. May I encourage you to keep working on defeating your lies with the truth and becoming the person God wants you to be. Keep fighting the good fight!

In order to help you maintain the gains you have made and progress even further, I want to give you your final assignment. It is aimed at helping you stay "fit" the rest of your life as far as dedicating yourself to the truth and enjoying all the benefits of doing so. The workout I want you to do the rest of your life is this:

1. Begin every day with thirty minutes of reading the Bible and praying to God. Ask God not only for help to believe what the Bible says but the courage to apply it to your life.

2. Memorize key passages of the Bible that speak to the issues you struggle with.

3. Meditate on key passages of the Bible that speak to the issues you struggle with.

4. Fellowship on a regular basis with other Christians. Share your life openly with them, allow them to support and challenge you to live your life according to the Bible.

5. Read biblically-solid books on topics that you need to help with (see Appendix E for a short list of the ones I recommend).

6. Seek biblical counseling for help with chronic problems.

7. Never quit!

I pray that God will continue to richly bless your efforts to know the truth and be set free by it.

Epilogue

The world is a fractured place. One sign of that is how much pain people are in. Everywhere you look, human beings are hurting and hurting deeply. Perhaps the ultimate sign that the world is fractured is that some people are in so much pain and feel so hopeless that they take their own lives.

Why is the world so broken? Why are so many people miserable? Why are so many relationships troubled? Why does God seem so far away, and why do things seem so meaningless and hopeless? While there are numerous reasons, the focus of this book has been on what I believe to be the main one—the lies we tell ourselves. Lies destroy those of us who believe them and make the world the troubled place it is.

Lies killed Admiral Boorda. Which lies? None of us can know for sure, but we have covered some in this book that allow us to make an educated guess. Of the many lies he might have told himself, one might have been, "It is unforgivable to make a serious error." Yes, he may have made a serious error in judgment (some in the navy apparently believe he was entitled to wear the ribbons). The *lie* is that what he did was unforgivable. Other than not believing in God, no mistake we make is unforgivable.

Perhaps another lie Admiral Boorda told himself was, "The mistakes we make should be severely punished, and some mistakes are so horrible that they should cost you your life." The truth is that mistakes, however large or small, have their own built-in punishment. Admiral Boorda's was personal embarrassment and the possible disciplinary action the navy might have taken. That was more than enough. We do not need to add any further punishment on top of what our mistakes cause on their own. Admiral Boorda might also have believed the lie "I must have everyone's approval." The medal he wore indicated combat experience. According to the reports Admiral Boorda had never been in combat. Maybe he felt bad about that. Maybe Admiral Boorda thought that left him with less approval and respect from the men who served under him who had been in combat. Quite possibly, Admiral Boorda's need for their approval led him to wear a medal he may not have earned the right to wear.

A final lie Admiral Boorda might have told himself was, "My life is mine to take." The truth of the matter is that God is the Giver of life. He is the reason we exist. We do not give ourselves life, and God does not want any of us presuming to end our lives as if they are ours to take.

If Admiral Boorda had told himself to the truth, I believe he would still be alive today. If he shouldn't have worn certain medals, the truth he could have told himself would have been, "God, I made a mistake, a serious mistake. What I did was wrong. Forgive me for misrepresenting myself to others and for needing their approval so badly that I would violate Your moral law. Help me to be courageous enough to face the consequences for what I did, however severe they may be. Thank You for giving me life and all the blessings of my life. I know that Your ways are best and that You will bring good out of this bad situation. My life is in Your hands." The truth would have set Admiral Boorda free.

Is the truth setting you free? Are you dedicating yourself to believing and living the truth each day whatever your circumstances may be? Are you allowing the truth to give you life and life in full? I pray that you are.

APPENDICES

Appendix A

■

SECULAR AND BIBLICAL TEACHINGS ON THE IMPORTANCE OF "RIGHT" THINKING FOR EMOTIONAL AND SPIRITUAL HEALTH

Secular Teachings

Epictetus: "Man is disturbed not by things but by the view he takes of them."

William Shakespeare: "There is nothing either good or bad, but thinking makes it so."

Benedict (Baruch) Spinoza: "I saw that all the things I feared, and which feared me, had nothing good or bad in them insofar as the mind was affected by them."

Marcus Aurelius: "If you are pained by an external thing, it is not the thing that disturbs you, but your own judgment about it. And it is in your power to wipe out this judgment now."

Immanuel Kant: "The only feature common to all mental disorders is the loss of common sense and the compensatory development of a unique private sense of reasoning."

W. E. B. DuBois: "If we wish to change the sentiments it is necessary before all to modify the idea which produced them, and to recognize either that it is not correct itself, or that it does not touch our interests."

Alfred Adler: "It is very obvious that we are influenced not by 'facts' but by our interpretation of facts."

John Milton: "The mind as its own place, and in itself / Can make a heaven of Hell, a hell of Heaven."

I. E. Farber: "The one thing psychologists can count on is that their subjects will talk if only to themselves; and not infrequently, whether relevant or irrelevant, the things people say to themselves determine the rest of the things they do."

Biblical Teachings

Philippians 2:5 (NIV): "Your attitude should be the same as that of Christ Jesus."

Romans 12:2 (NIV): "Do not conform any longer to the pattern of this world, but be transformed by the renewing of your mind. Then you will be able to test and approve what God's will is—his good, pleasing and perfect will."

Philippians 4:8 (NIV): "Finally, brothers, whatever is true, whatever is noble, whatever is right, whatever is pure, whatever is lovely, whatever is admirable—if anything is excellent or praiseworthy—think about such things."

Romans 1:28 (NIV): "Furthermore, since they did not think it worthwhile to retain the knowledge of God, he gave them over to a depraved mind, to do what ought not to be done."

Romans 8:6–7 (NIV): "The mind of sinful man is death, but the mind controlled by the Spirit is life and peace; the sinful mind is hostile to God. It does not submit to God's law, nor can it do so."

Ephesians 4:22–24 (NIV): "You were taught, with regard to your former way of life, to put off the old self, which is being corrupted by its deceitful desires; to be made new in the attitude of your minds; and to put on the new self, created to be like God in true righteousness and holiness."

Colossians 3:2 (NIV): "Set your minds on things above, not on earthly things."

2 Corinthians 10:5 (NIV): "We demolish arguments and every pretension that sets itself up against the knowledge of God, and we take captive every thought to make it obedient to Christ."

Isaiah 26:3 (NIV): "You will keep in perfect peace him whose mind is steadfast, because he trusts in you."

Proverbs 14:15 (NIV): "A simple man believes anything, but a prudent man gives thought to his steps."

Appendix B

■

SECULAR AND BIBLICAL TRUTHS FOR DEFEATING THE LIES WE TELL OURSELVES

In this appendix, I list all the lies discussed in Chapters 2 through 6 and the truths, both secular and biblical, that can be used to challenge and replace them. The truths listed are good memory and meditation verses in your war against the lies you tell yourself.

Self-Lies

Lie #1: "I Must Be Perfect."
Secular Truth: To err is human.
Theological Truth: "This righteousness from God comes through faith in Jesus Christ to all who believe. There is no difference, for all have sinned and fall short of the glory of God" (Rom 3:22–23 NIV); "If we claim to be without sin, we deceive ourselves and the truth is not in us" (1 John 1:8 NIV).

Lie #2: "I Must Have Everyone's Love and Approval."
Secular Truth: You can't please all of the people all of the time.
Theological Truth: "Whatever you do, work at it with all your heart, as working for the Lord, not for men, since you know that you will receive an inheritance from the Lord as a reward" (Col. 3:23–24 NIV); "Am I now trying to win the approval of men, or of God? Or am I trying to please men? If I were still trying to please men, I would not be a servant of Christ" (Gal. 1:10 NIV).

Lie #3: "It Is Easier to Avoid Problems Than to Face Them."
Secular Truth: Problems usually get worse when avoided.
Theological Truth: "Brothers, I do not consider myself yet to have taken hold of it. But one thing I do: Forgetting what is behind and straining toward what is ahead, I press on toward the goal to win the prize for which God has called me heavenward in Christ Jesus" (Phil. 3:13–14 NIV).

Lie #4: "I Can't Be Happy Unless Things Go My Way."
Secular Truth: It isn't what happens to you that makes you unhappy; it's

how you view it. So even when things don't go your way, you can still be "happy" with the proper attitude.

Theological Truth: "And now, compelled by the Spirit, I am going to Jerusalem, not knowing what will happen to me there. I only know that in every city the Holy Spirit warns me that prison and hardships are facing me. However, I consider my life worth nothing to me, if only I may finish the race and complete the task the Lord Jesus has given me—the task of testifying to the gospel of God's grace" (Acts 20:22–24 NIV); "I am not saying this because I am in need, for I have learned to be content whatever the circumstances. I know what it is to be in need, and I know what it is to have plenty. I have learned the secret of being content in any and every situation, whether well fed or hungry, whether living in plenty or in want. I can do everything through him who gives me strength" (Phil. 4:11–13 NIV); "Consider it pure joy, my brothers, whenever you face trials of many kinds, because you know that the testing of your faith develops perseverance" (James 1:2–3 NIV).

Lie #5: "My Unhappiness Is Somebody Else's Fault."
Secular Truth: Our feelings, whether pleasant or unpleasant, are caused by how we think. Since no one forces us to think the way we choose to think, we are responsible for the feelings that our thoughts create. Our unhappiness (or happiness) is our "fault."

Theological Truth: "As [a man] thinks in his heart, so is he" (Prov. 23:7 NKJV).

Worldly Lies

Lie #1: "You Can Have It All."
Secular Truth: No one really has it all. Everyone has gaps in his life.

Theological Truth: "Do not love the world or anything in the world. If anyone loves the world, the love of the Father is not in him. For everything in the world—the cravings of sinful man, the lust of his eyes and the boasting of what he has and does—comes not from the Father but from the world. The world and its desires pass away, but the man who does the will of God lives forever" (1 John 2:15–17 NIV); "We brought nothing into the world, and we can take nothing out of it. But if we have food and clothing, we will be content with that. People who want to get rich fall into temptation and a trap and into many foolish and harmful desires that plunge men into ruin and destruction. For the love of money is a root of all kinds of evil. Some people, eager for money, have wandered from the faith and pierced themselves with many griefs" (1 Tim. 6:7–10 NIV).

Lie #2: "My Worth Is Determined by My Performance."

Secular Truth: Your worth is tied to who you are, not what you do.

Theological Truth: "For you created my inmost being; You knit me together in my mother's womb. I praise you because I am fearfully and wonderfully made; Your works are wonderful, I know that full well."(Psalm 139:13–14 NIV).

Lie #3: "Life Should Be Easy."

Secular Truth: Life is difficult. A great deal of hardship and frustration is built into it.

Theological Truth: "I have told you these things, so that in me you may have peace. In this world you will have trouble. But take heart! I have overcome the world" (John 16:33 NIV).

Lie #4: "Life Should Be Fair."

Secular Truth: Life is sometimes fair and sometimes unfair.

Theological Truth: "There is something else meaningless that occurs on earth: righteous men who get what the wicked deserve, and wicked men who get what the righteous deserve. This too, I say, is meaningless" (Eccl. 8:1\ NIV).

Lie #5: "You Shouldn't Have to Wait for What You Want."

Secular Truth: Patience is a virtue. It is often healthier to delay gratification rather than seek immediate gratification.

Theological Truth: "Do not be deceived: God cannot be mocked. A man reaps what he sows. The one who sows to please his sinful nature, from that nature will reap destruction; the one who sows to please the Spirit, from the Spirit will reap eternal life" (Gal. 6:7–8 NIV); "A patient man has great understanding, but a quick-tempered man displays folly" (Prov. 14:29 NIV).

Lie #6: "People Are Basically Good."

Secular Truth: People have both good and evil inside them, and they seem as bent on self-destruction as they do on growth.

Theological Truth: "The heart is deceitful above all things and beyond cure. Who can understand it?" (Jer. 17:9 NIV); "For out of the heart come evil thoughts, murder, adultery, sexual immorality, theft, false testimony, slander" (Matt. 15:19 NIV); "As it is written: 'There is no one righteous, not even one; there is none who understands, no one who seeks God. All have turned away, they have together become worthless; there is no one who does good, not even one'" (Rom. 3:10–12 NIV); "The acts of the sinful nature are obvious: sexual immorality, impurity and debauchery; idolatry and witchcraft; hatred, discord, jealousy, fits of rage, selfish ambition, dissensions, factions and envy; drunkenness, orgies, and the like" (Gal. 5:19–21 NIV).

Marital Lies

Lie #1: "All Our Marital Problems Are Your Fault."

Secular Truth: It takes two to tango. Marriage problems are rarely one person's fault.

Theological Truth: "You, therefore, have no excuse, you who pass judgment on someone else, for at whatever point you judge the other, you are condemning yourself, because you who pass judgment do the same things" (Rom. 2:1 NIV).

Lie #2: "If Our Marriage Takes Hard Work, We Must Not Be Right for Each Other."

Secular Truth: Hard work in marriage is the norm, not the exception. It means you and your partner need each other's help to work out personality flaws and weaknesses.

Theological Truth: "Those who marry will face many troubles in this life" (1 Cor. 7:28 NIV).

Lie #3: "You Can and Should Meet All of My Emotional Needs."

Secular Truth: No one person can meet all your needs. Your needs can best be met through a variety of sources.

Theological Truth: "My God will meet all your needs according to his glorious riches in Christ Jesus" (Phil. 4:19 NIV).

Lie #4: "You Owe Me (for All I Do for You)."

Secular Truth: Your spouse doesn't really "owe" you anything for what you do. You do what you do because, at some level, you choose to do it. You aren't owed anything for what you choose to do.

Theological Truth: "Clothe yourselves with humility toward one another, because, 'God opposes the proud but gives grace to the humble'" (1 Peter 5:5 NIV).

Lie #5: "I Shouldn't Have to Change to Make Our Marriage Better."

Secular Truth: Marriage requires change. People who refuse to change stagnate themselves and their marriages. The important issue is deciding what we need to change about ourselves and what we don't.

Theological Truth: "Make every effort to live in peace with all men and to be holy" (Heb. 12:14 NIV).

Lie #6: "You Should Be Like Me."

Secular Truth: Every person is unique and can't be a carbon copy of anyone else. Life would be boring if it weren't that way.

Theological Truth: "But in fact God has arranged the parts in the body, every one of them, just as he wanted them to be. If they were all one part, where would the body be?" (1 Cor. 12:18–19 NIV).

Distortion Lies

Lie #1: "Magnification"

Secular Truth: Molehills are not mountains. Five-dollar events are five-dollar events, not fifty-dollar events.

Lie #2: "Personalization"

Secular Truth: We are not the target or cause of everything that happens to us. Many life events that happen directly to us are not meant personally and are more a statement about the person who did them than about us.

Lie #3: "Polarization"

Secular Truth: Although some issues in life are black/white, many issues are a shade of gray. Black/white issues need to be seen as black or white, but issues that are gray need to be seen that way.

Lie #4: "Selective Abstraction"

Secular Truth: While we often have to focus on a specific "tree" in life, we need to keep the whole "forest" in mind. No matter what parts there are to focus on, we need to see the whole.

Lie #5: "Overgeneralization"

Secular Truth: What happens to us in the here and now is not necessarily what has to happen again to us in the future. How things are going in our lives right now is not necessarily how they are going to be in the future. History doesn't have to repeat itself.

Lie #6: "Emotional Reasoning"

Secular Truth: Feelings aren't facts; feelings are feelings.

Religious Lies

Lie #1: "God's Love Must Be Earned."
Theological Truth: "God demonstrates his own love for us in this: While we were still sinners, Christ died for us" (Rom. 5:8 NIV); "For by grace you have been saved through faith, and that not of yourselves; it is the gift of God, not of works, lest anyone should boast" (Eph. 2:8–9 NKJV).

Lie #2: "God Hates the Sin and the Sinner."
Theological Truth: The story of the woman caught in adultery (John 8:1–11); "God demonstrates his own love for us in this: While we were still sinners, Christ died for us" (Rom. 5:8 NIV).

Lie #3: "Because I'm a Christian, God Will Protect Me from Pain and Suffering."
Theological Truth: "Dear friends, do not be surprised at the painful trial you are suffering, as though something strange were happening to you. But rejoice that you participate in the sufferings of Christ, so that you may be over-joyed when his glory is revealed" (1 Peter 4:12–13 NIV); "I have told you these things, so that in me you may have peace. In this world you will have trouble. But take heart! I have overcome the world" (John 16:33 NIV); "It has been granted to you on behalf of Christ not only to believe on him, but also to suf-fer for him" (Phil. 1:29 NIV).

Lie #4: "All My Problems Are Caused by My Sins."
Theological Truth: "As he went along, he saw a man blind from birth. His disciples asked him, 'Rabbi, who sinned, this man or his parents, that he was born blind?' 'Neither this man nor his parents sinned,' said Jesus, 'but this hap-pened so that the work of God might be displayed in his life'" (John 9:1–3 NIV).

Lie #5: "It Is My Christian Duty to Meet All the Needs of Others."
Theological Truth: "Now you are the body of Christ, and each one of you is a part of it. And in the church God has appointed first of all apostles, second prophets, third teachers, then workers of miracles, also those having gifts of healing, those able to help others, those with gifts of administration, and those speaking in different kinds of tongues. Are all apostles? Are all prophets? Are all teachers? Do all work miracles? Do all have gifts of healing? Do all speak in tongues? Do all interpret? But eagerly desire the greater gifts" (1 Cor. 12:27–31

NIV); "We have different gifts, according to the grace given us. If a man's gift is prophesying, let him use it in proportion to his faith. If it is serving, let him serve; if it is teaching, let him teach; if it is encouraging, let him encourage; if it is contributing to the needs of others, let him give generously; if it is leadership, let him govern diligently; if it is showing mercy, let him do it cheerfully" (Rom. 12:6–7 NIV).

Lie #6: "A Good Christian Doesn't Feel Angry, Anxious, or Depressed."

Theological Truth: "When Jesus saw her weeping, and the Jews who had come along with her also weeping, he was deeply moved in Spirit and troubled. 'Where have you laid him?' he asked. 'Come and see, Lord,' they replied. Jesus wept" (John 11:33–35 NIV); "They went to a place called Gethsemane, and Jesus said to his disciples, 'Sit here while I pray.' He took Peter, James and John along with him, and he began to be deeply distressed and troubled. 'My soul is overwhelmed with sorrow to the point of death,' he said to them. 'Stay here and keep watch'" (Mark 14:32–34 NIV); "On reaching Jerusalem, Jesus entered the temple area and began driving out those who were buying and selling there. He overturned the tables of the money changers and the benches of those selling doves, and would not allow anyone to carry merchandise through the temple courts" (Mark 11:15–16 NIV); "In your anger do not sin" (Eph. 4:26 NIV).

Lie #7: "God Can't Use Me Unless I'm Spiritually Strong."

Theological Truth: "To be sure, he was crucified in weakness, yet he lives by God's power. Likewise, we are weak in him, yet by God's power we will live with him to serve you" (2 Cor. 13:4 NIV); "He said to me, 'My grace is sufficient for you, for my power is made perfect in weakness.' Therefore I will boast all the more gladly about my weaknesses, so that Christ's power may rest on me. That is why, for Christ's sake, I delight in weaknesses, in insults, in hardships, in persecutions, in difficulties. For when I am weak, then I am strong" (2 Cor. 12:9–10 NIV); "God chose the foolish things of the world to shame the wise; God chose the weak things of the world to shame the strong" (1 Cor. 1:27 NIV); "To the weak I became weak, to win the weak" (1 Cor. 9:22 NIV).

Appendix C

■

BIBLICAL SUPPORT FOR THE TEN TRUTHS NECESSARY FOR EMOTIONAL AND SPIRITUAL HEALTH

In this appendix, I provide biblical support for the truths covered in Chapters 8 through 17.

Truth #1: To Err Is Human

To morally err is very much a part of being human. The Bible teaches that we have a sin nature. It is our natural "bent" to sin (miss the moral mark). Contrast this with humanistic psychology's assumption that man is basically good, and you can see that the two views of man's nature are worlds apart.

For biblical support for the reality of the sin nature of all people, see the following passages:

> Behold, I was brought forth in iniquity,
> And in sin my mother conceived me. (Ps. 51:5 NKJV)

> As it is written:
> "There is none righteous, no, not one;
> There is none who understands;
> There is none who seeks after God." (Rom. 3:10–11 NKJV)

> There is no difference; for all have sinned and fall short of the glory of God. (Rom. 3:22–23 NKJV)

> I know that nothing good lives in me, that is, in my sinful nature. For I have the desire to do what is good, but I cannot carry it out. (Rom. 7:18 NIV)

> Therefore, brethren, we are debtors—not to the flesh, to live according to the flesh. For if you live according to the flesh you will die. (Rom. 8:12–13 NKJV)

Now the works of the flesh are evident, which are: adultery, fornication, uncleanness, lewdness, idolatry, sorcery, hatred, contentions, jealousies, outbursts of wrath, selfish ambitions, dissensions, heresies, envy, murders, drunkenness, revelries, and the like. (Gal. 5:19–21 NKJV)

Truth #2: You Can't Please Everyone

The clearest biblical basis for this truth is the life of Christ. He was morally perfect, yet many people hated Him.

He is despised and rejected by men,
A Man of sorrows
and acquainted with grief.
And we hid, as it were, our faces from Him;
He was despised, and we did not esteem Him. (Isa. 53:3 NKJV)

You would think that if anyone would be pleasing to everyone, he would be a morally perfect person. The life of Christ proves otherwise.

The Bible teaches that we can't have everyone's approval, and that seeking it is not even desirable. Seeking man's approval puts us at odds with God's desire that we glorify Him and that we mature as human beings. Here are supporting verses:

For do I now persuade men, or God? Or do I seek to please men? For if I still pleased men, I would not be a bondservant of Christ. (Gal. 1:10 NKJV)

But as we have been approved by God to be entrusted with the gospel, even so we speak, not as pleasing men, but God who tests our hearts. (1 Thess. 2:4 NKJV)

Adulterers and adulteresses! Do you not know that friendship with the world is enmity with God? Whoever therefore wants to be a friend of the world makes himself an enemy of God. (James 4:4 NKJV)

God's approval, not the approval of man, is to be our focus. I would be more concerned about someone who seemingly had everyone's approval than someone who didn't. After all, what kind of person would be pleasing to *everyone*? That would be one "chameleon" of a person with little firmness of beliefs and values. I'd rather stand for something and be despised or disliked than stand for nothing and be accepted by most.

Truth #3: There Is No Gain without Pain

The idea that suffering is required to produce maturity runs throughout the Bible. The Bible clearly teaches that suffering for righteousness' sake is "good" suffering and not to be avoided. James told us, "Consider it pure joy, my brothers, whenever you face trials of many kinds, because you know that the testing of your faith develops perseverance. Perseverance must finish its work so that you may be mature and complete, not lacking anything" (James 1:2–4 NIV).

While we often complain about problems and the suffering they can bring, we can achieve maturity through having problems. Paying the price of personal suffering in order to mature is difficult but yields great reward. As Paul put it in Philippians 3:8 (NKJV), "Indeed I also count all things loss for the excellence of the knowledge of Christ Jesus my Lord, for whom I have suffered the loss of all things, and count them rubbish, that I may gain Christ."

Just as we put difficult math problems in front of our children so that they might learn important mathematical skills, life throws us difficult problems that when endured produce important life skills. Don't let anyone sell you a pain-free approach to gain. He is leading you down a deadly garden path you don't want to be on.

Truth #4: You Don't "Have to" Do Anything

The Bible teaches that we have free will (see the following verses), which means we are free to do whatever we want. In light of this, there are no pure *have to*'s in life. We are free to go our own way, but there are consequences of our choices.

One of the important aspects of Christ's death on the cross was to set us free from the impossible burden of the "law" as the means by which to gain God's favor (Matt. 10:8). The law was "you have to do _____ to please God," something that sinful man couldn't, on his own, ever do well enough. Christ's death has set us free from having to do things to merit God's favor. In response, we believers are to pursue righteousness as a way to show gratefulness and appreciation for what Christ did on the cross.

Here are some verses supporting the truth "you don't 'have to' to do anything":

I call heaven and earth as witnesses today against you, that I have set before you life and death, blessing and cursing; therefore choose life, that both you and your descendants may live; that you may love the LORD your God, that you may obey His voice, and that you may cling to Him. (Deut. 30:19–20 NKJV)

Receive my instruction, and not silver,
And knowledge rather than choice gold;
For wisdom is better than rubies,
And all the things one may desire cannot be compared with her. (Prov. 8:10–11 NKJV)

How much better to get wisdom than gold!
And to get understanding is to be chosen rather than silver. (Prov. 16:16 NKJV)

Freely you have received, freely give. (Matt. 10:8 NKJV)

If anyone wills to do His will, he shall know concerning the doctrine, whether it is from God or whether I speak on My own authority. (John 7:17 NKJV)

It is for freedom that Christ has set us free. Stand firm, then, and do not let yourselves be burdened again by a yoke of slavery. (Gal. 5:1 NIV)

Truth #5: The Virtue Lies in the Struggle, Not the Prize

The Bible teaches that we will never be perfectly moral or mature during our lives, no matter how hard we try (see verses supporting the truth "to err is human"). With that in mind, I would argue that *the effort* to grow in righteousness and maturity is the virtue since the prize of perfect righteousness and maturity is unattainable.

The "good news" is that Christ's death on the cross took care of the problem that we can never be morally perfect. The fact that we can never live perfect moral lives has been solved through Christ's willingness to die for our sins. Those who believe in Christ and accept Him as their Savior are made righteous in God's eyes through the atoning death of Christ on the cross.

The key verses that I believe support the truth "the virtue lies in the struggle, not the prize" are these:

Not that I have already attained, or am already perfected; but I press on, that I may lay hold of that for which Christ Jesus has also laid hold of me. Brethren, I do not count myself to have apprehended; but one thing I do, forgetting those things which are behind and reaching forward to those things which are ahead, I press toward the goal for the prize of the upward call of God in Christ Jesus. Therefore let us, as many as are mature, have this mind; and if in anything you think otherwise, God will reveal even this to you. (Phil. 3:12–15 NKJV)

Therefore we also, since we are surrounded by so great a cloud of witnesses, let us lay aside every weight, and the sin which so easily ensnares us, and let us run with endurance the race that is set before us, looking unto Jesus, the author and finisher of our faith, who for the joy that was set before Him endured the cross, despising the shame, and has sat down at the right hand of the throne of God. (Heb. 12:1–2 NKJV)

Truth #6: Life Is Difficult

The Bible teaches that since the Fall, life has been difficult for all (Gen. 3:17–19). Sin entered the world, and things have been rough ever since. Perhaps the most staggering proof that life is difficult for everyone is the life of Christ. He, as cocreator of the universe with God the Father and God the Holy Spirit, found life to be difficult. You would think that if life would ease off for anyone, it would ease off for the very Being who helped to create it. Birth in a smelly manger, attempts on His life, unfair attacks on His character, disloyalty by friends, beatings, and death on a cross suggest otherwise.

These biblical verses support the truth "life is difficult":

Then to Adam He said, "Because you have heeded the voice of your wife, and have eaten from the tree of which I commanded you, saying, 'You shall not eat of it':
Cursed is the ground for your sake;
In toil you shall eat of it
All the days of your life.
Both thorns and thistles it shall bring forth for you,
And you shall eat the herb of the field.
In the sweat of your face you shall eat bread
Till you return to the ground,

For out of it you were taken;
For dust you are,
And to dust you shall return." (Gen. 3:17–19 NKJV)

All things are wearisome, more than one can say. (Eccl. 1:8 NIV)

For what has man for all his labor, and for the striving of his heart with
which he has toiled under the sun? For all his days are sorrowful, and his
work burdensome; even in the night his heart takes no rest. This also is
vanity. (Eccl. 2:22–23 NKJV)

Do not worry about tomorrow, for tomorrow will worry about its own
things. Sufficient for the day is its own trouble. (Matt. 6:34 NKJV)

Truth #7: You Reap What You Sow

The truth "you reap what you sow" shows up frequently in the Bible.
According to Scripture, this principle applies both negatively and positively to
our lives (Prov. 11:18). Applied to the basic focus of this book, the thoughts we
sow create the life we reap. Or as Proverbs 23:7 (NKJV) puts it, "As [a man]
thinks in his heart, so is he."

Here are some verses that support the truth "you reap what you sow":

Even as I have seen,
Those who plow iniquity
And sow trouble reap the same. (Job 4:8 NKJV)

The wicked man does deceptive work,
But he who sows righteousness will have a sure reward. (Prov. 11:18 NKJV)

He who sows iniquity will reap sorrow,
And the rod of his anger will fail. (Prov. 22:8 NKJV)

But this I say: He who sows sparingly will also reap sparingly, and he who
sows bountifully will also reap bountifully. (2 Cor. 9:6 NKJV)

Do not be deceived, God is not mocked; for whatever a man sows, that he
will also reap. For he who sows to his flesh will of the flesh reap corruption,

but he who sows to the Spirit will of the Spirit reap everlasting life. (Gal. 6:7–8 NKJV)

Truth #8: You Are Not Entitled to Anything

If the Bible teaches we were entitled to anything, it teaches we were entitled to eternity in hell for our sinfulness ("But God, who is rich in mercy, because of His great love with which He loved us, even when we were dead in trespasses, made us alive together with Christ (by grace you have been saved)" [Eph. 2:4–5 NKJV]). Walking around feeling entitled to things is quite prideful, and Scripture says that God detests pride: "God resists the proud, / But gives grace to the humble" (James 4:6 NKJV). Salvation itself is the result of God's grace, not something we earned through good behavior.

I would make the same point about human relationships. Just as we were not entitled to God's love or forgiveness (or anything else He offers), we are not entitled to love or forgiveness from people, either. It is not our birthright to get our needs met by others, and to feel entitled to getting our needs met is to invite great anger and bitterness. Desiring to get our needs met—and humbly trying to get them met—is the more appropriate stance.

> And you He made alive, who were dead in trespasses and sins, in which you once walked according to the course of this world, according to the prince of the power of the air, the spirit who now works in the sons of disobedience, among whom also we all once conducted ourselves in the lusts of our flesh, fulfilling the desires of the flesh and of the mind, and were by nature children of wrath, just as the others. But God, who is rich in mercy, because of His great love with which He loved us, even when we were dead in trespasses, made us alive together with Christ (by grace you have been saved), and raised us up together, and made us sit together in the heavenly places in Christ Jesus, that in the ages to come He might show the exceeding riches of His grace in His kindness toward us in Christ Jesus. For by grace you have been saved through faith, and that not of yourselves; it is the gift of God, not of works, lest anyone should boast. (Eph. 2:1–9 NKJV)

Truth #9: Emotional Pain Is Good

No one wants to be emotionally troubled, and the ideal would be that we never experience clinically significant emotional problems. But given our sinful nature (and everyone else's), significant emotional problems are going to occur. While we may bemoan our emotional problems, they are an important signal to us that something inside our thoughts needs correction. Thus, emotional suffering can be a springboard to growth and maturity. Emotional suffering can be "good" in that it alerts us and motivates us to change when we have gotten off course.

Another "good" aspect of emotional problems is that they enable us to empathize with others who suffer. When we go through emotional suffering, we know what it is like when others do. Then we can offer comfort to them.

I, like you, would like to stay mentally healthy enough that I never suffer emotional problems. But given my tendency to not listen to or practice truth, painful emotional problems will come my way. Because they signal me that I need to correct something, I can actually thank God for their important role in my life.

Some biblical verses supporting the truth that "emotional pain is good" include the following:

> Blessed are those who mourn,
> For they shall be comforted. (Matt. 5:4 NKJV)

> Blessed be the God and Father of our Lord Jesus Christ, the Father of mercies and God of all comfort, who comforts us in all our tribulation, that we may be able to comfort those who are in any trouble, with the comfort with which we ourselves are comforted by God. (2 Cor. 1:3–4 NKJV)

> And not only that, but we also glory in tribulations, knowing that tribulation produces perseverance; and perseverance, character; and character, hope. (Rom. 5:3–4 NKJV)

> We know that all things work together for good to those who love God, to those who are the called according to His purpose. (Rom. 8:28 NKJV)

> Consider it pure joy, my brothers, whenever you face trials of many kinds, because you know that the testing of your faith develops perseverance. Perseverance must finish its work so that you may be mature and complete, not lacking anything. (James 1:2–4 NIV)

Truth #10: You Are Going to Die

The Bible is pretty straightforward about this truth. We are given life by God, and that life will come to an end someday. The Bible also teaches that we die once, which makes reincarnation untenable. We truly "only go around once in life," according to the Bible, which is to be used as a motivation to make sure our journey through life is dedicated to important things that last rather than temporary things that please only us. We are to base our lives on God's plan, not our own.

Some biblical passages that teach the truth "you are going to die" are these:

> What man can live and not see death?
> Can he deliver his life from the power of the grave? (Ps. 89:48 NKJV)

> A time to be born,
> And a time to die. (Eccl. 3:2 NKJV)

> It is better to go to a house of mourning
> than to go to a house of feasting,
> for death is the destiny of every man. (Eccl. 7:2 NIV)

> It is appointed for men to die once. (Heb. 9:27 NKJV)

Appendix D

■

BIBLICAL TEACHINGS ON TRUTH

Truth as Protection

Do not withhold Your tender mercies from me, O LORD;
Let Your lovingkindness and Your truth continually preserve me.
(Ps. 40:11 NKJV)

Dedication to Truth

I have walked in Your truth. (Ps. 26:3 NKJV)

Teach me Your way, O LORD;
I will walk in Your truth. (Ps. 86:11 NKJV)

Buy the truth, and do not sell it. (Prov. 23:23 NKJV)

But be doers of the word, and not hearers only, deceiving yourselves. For if anyone is a hearer of the word and not a doer, he is like a man observing his natural face in a mirror; for he observes himself, goes away, and immediately forgets what kind of man he was. But he who looks into the perfect law of liberty and continues in it, and is not a forgetful hearer but a doer of the work, this one will be blessed in what he does. (James 1:22–25 NKJV)

The Absence of Truth in the World

Justice is turned back,
And righteousness stands afar off;
For truth is fallen in the street,
And equity cannot enter.

So truth fails,
And he who departs from evil makes himself a prey. (Isa. 59:14–15 NKJV)

You shall say to them, "This is a nation that does not obey the voice of the
LORD their God nor receive correction. Truth has perished and has been cut
off from their mouth." (Jer. 7:28 NKJV)

Everyone will deceive his neighbor,
And will not speak the truth. (Jer. 9:5 NKJV)

[They] exchanged the truth of God for the lie, and worshiped and served the
creature rather than the Creator, who is blessed forever. (Rom. 1:25 NKJV)

For the time will come when they will not endure sound doctrine, but
according to their own desires, because they have itching ears, they will
heap up for themselves teachers; and they will turn their ears away from the
truth, and be turned aside to fables. (2 Tim. 4:3–4 NKJV)

Christ's Claim to Be Truth

Jesus said to him, "I am the way, the truth, and the life. No one comes to
the Father except through Me." (John 14:6 NKJV)

Pilate therefore said to Him, "Are You a king then?" Jesus answered, "You
say rightly that I am a king. For this cause I was born, and for this cause I
have come into the world, that I should bear witness to the truth. Everyone
who is of the truth hears My voice." (John 18:37 NKJV)

Consequences of Rejecting Truth

For the wrath of God is revealed from heaven against all ungodliness and
unrighteousness of men, who suppress the truth in unrighteousness. (Rom.
1:18 NKJV)

But for those who are self-seeking and who reject the truth and follow evil,
there will be wrath and anger. (Rom. 2:8 NIV)

They perish because they refused to love the truth and so be saved. (2 Thess. 2:10 NIV)

All may be condemned who did not believe the truth but had pleasure in unrighteousness. (2 Thess. 2:12 NKJV)

Consequences of Accepting Truth

Paul, a bondservant of God and an apostle of Jesus Christ, according to the faith of God's elect and the acknowledgment of the truth which accords with godliness. (Titus 1:1 NKJV)

Of His own will He brought us forth by the word of truth, that we might be a kind of firstfruits of His creatures. (James 1:18 NKJV)

Since you have purified your souls in obeying the truth through the Spirit in sincere love of the brethren, love one another fervently with a pure heart. (1 Peter 1:22 NKJV)

God the Holy Spirit Guiding Us in Truth

When the Helper comes, whom I shall send to you from the Father, the Spirit of truth who proceeds from the Father, He will testify of Me. (John 15:26 NKJV)

However, when He, the Spirit of truth, has come, He will guide you into all truth; for He will not speak on His own authority, but whatever He hears He will speak; and He will tell you things to come. He will glorify Me, for He will take of what is Mine and declare it to you. All things that the Father has are Mine. Therefore I said that He will take of Mine and declare it to you. (John 16:13–15 NKJV)

But the fruit of the Spirit is love, joy, peace, longsuffering, kindness, goodness, faithfulness, gentleness, self-control. Against such there is no law. (Gal. 5:22–23 NKJV)

The Role of the Bible in Our Lives

Your word is a lamp to my feet
And a light to my path. (Ps. 119:105 NKJV)

All Scripture is given by inspiration of God, and is profitable for doctrine, for reproof, for correction, for instruction in righteousness, that the man of God may be complete, thoroughly equipped for every good work. (2 Tim. 3:16–17 NKJV)

For the word of God is living and powerful, and sharper than any two-edged sword, piercing even to the division of soul and spirit, and of joints and marrow, and is a discerner of the thoughts and intents of the heart. (Heb. 4:12 NKJV)

Appendix E

∎

RECOMMENDED READINGS

Allen, Charles. *God's Psychiatry*. Grand Rapids: Fleming H. Revell, 1953.

Allen, James. *As a Man Thinketh*. Fort Worth, Tex.: Brownlow, 1985.

Backus, William, and Marie Chapian. *Telling Yourself the Truth*. Minneapolis: Bethany House, 1980.

Blackaby, Henry, and Claude King. *Experiencing God*. Nashville: Broadman and Holman, 1994.

Burns, David D. *Feeling Good: The New Mood Therapy*. New York: Signet, 1981.

Crabb, Larry. *Inside Out*. Colorado Springs: NavPress, 1988.

Ellis, Albert, and Robert Harper. *A New Guide to Rational Living*. North Hollywood, Calif.: Wilshire, 1975.

May, Gerald. *Addiction and Grace*. San Francisco: Harper Collins, 1988.

Packer, J. I. *Knowing God*. Downers Grove, Ill.: InterVarsity Press, 1973.

Sproul, R. C. *Essential Truths of the Christian Faith*. Wheaton, Ill.: Tyndale, 1992.

Stoop, David. *Self Talk: Key to Personal Growth*. Old Tappan, N.J.: Revell, 1981.

———. *Hope for the Perfectionist*. Nashville: Thomas Nelson, 1991.

Tozer, A. W. *The Pursuit of God*. Camp Hill, Penn.: Christian Publications, 1982.

Woodbridge, John D., ed. *Renewing Your Mind in a Secular World*. Chicago: Moody, 1985.

■

Notes

Chapter 1

1. James Allen, *As a Man Thinketh* (Fort Worth, Tex.: Brownlow, 1985), 11.

Chapter 2

1. David D. Burns, "The Perfectionist's Script for Self-Defeat," *Psychology Today*, November 1980, 34.

2. M. Scott Peck, *The Road Less Traveled: A New Psychology of Love, Traditional Values and Spiritual Growth* (New York: Simon and Schuster, 1978), 16–17.

3. Albert Ellis and Robert Harper, *A New Guide to Rational Living* (North Hollywood, Calif.: Wilshire, 1975).

Chapter 3

1. Ecclesiastes 2:4–10 (NKJV).

2. Ecclesiastes 5:12 (NKJV).

3. Ecclesiastes 5:10 (NKJV).

4. Ecclesiastes 1:14 (NKJV).

5. 1 Timothy 6:7–8 (NKJV).

6. Peck, *Road*, 15.

7. Ecclesiastes 8:14 (NKJV).

8. Abraham Maslow, *Toward a Psychology of Being*, 2nd ed. (New York: Van Nostrand, 1968), 3–4.

Chapter 4

1. William J. Lederer and Don Jackson, *The Mirages of Marriage* (New York: Norton, 1968), 40.

2. Matthew 7:3–5 (NKJV).

3. 1 Corinthians 7:28 (NIV).

4. Genesis 2:24 (NKJV).

Chapter 5

1. Peck, *Road*, 44.

2. David D. Burns, *Feeling Good: The New Mood Therapy* (New York: Signet, 1981).

Chapter 6

1. Doug Moo, "Putting the Renewed Mind to Work," in *Renewing Your Mind in a Secular World*, ed. John D. Woodbridge (Chicago: Moody, 1985), 145.

2. Ephesians 2:8–9 (NKJV).

3. 2 Timothy 1:9 (NKJV).

4. Romans 5:8 (NKJV).

5. John 8:7 (NKJV).

6. John 8:11 (NKJV).

7. John 16:33 (NIV).

8. John 9:1–3 (NKJV).

9. Romans 8:28 (NIV).

10. Matthew 5:45 (NKJV).

11. Matthew 11:28–30 (NKJV).

12. Luke 10:41–42 (NKJV).

13. Matthew 26:38 (NIV).

14. 2 Corinthians 12:10 (NKJV).

15. Matthew 9:12 (NKJV).

Chapter 7

1. 2 Timothy 3:16–17 (NKJV).

2. John 8:32 (NKJV).

Chapter 12

1. Lord Houghton as quoted in *Stress, Sanity, and Survival* by Robert Woolfolk and Frank Richardson (New York: Simon and Schuster, 1978), 65.

2. Donald Trump, *Survival at the Top* (New York: Random House, 1990), 118.

Chapter 17

1. Dr. Irvin Yalom, *Existential Psychotherapy* (New York: Basic Books, 1980), 8.

2. Dr. Dennis E. Hensley, *How to Manage Your Time* (Anderson, Ind.: Warner Press, 1989), vii.

3. Russel Noyes, "Attitude Changes Following Near Death Experiences," *Psychiatry* as quoted by Dr. Irvin Yalom in *Existential Psychotherapy*, 34.

4. Yalom, *Existential Psychotherapy*, 35.

Chapter 19

1. J. I. Packer, *Knowing God* (Downers Grove, Ill.: InterVarsity Press, 1973), 14–15.

2. Psalm 90:2 NIV.

3. John 1:1–5 NKJV.

4. Job 42:2 NKJV.

5. Psalm 139:7–10 NKJV.

6. Romans 11:33–36 NKJV.

7. 1 Samuel 2:2 NKJV.

8. Psalm 25:8 NKJV.

9. Genesis 18:25 NKJV.

10. Romans 9:15 NIV.

11. 1 Peter 1:3 NKJV.

12. Psalm 135:6 NKJV.

13. Malachi 3:6 NKJV.

14. James 1:17 NIV.

15. 1 John 4:8 NIV.

16. Ephesians 2:4–6, 8–9 NKJV.

17. Psalm 139:13–16 NIV.

18. Psalm 51:5 NIV.

19. Westminster Confession of Faith (Committee for Christian Education & Publication, Presbyterian Church in America, 1990), Chapter 5.

20 1 Timothy 2:5–6 NIV.

21 Ephesians 1:4–6 NIV.

22 1 John 3:1 NIV.

23. Hebrews 2:11–12 NIV.

24. Galatians 4·6–7 NIV.

25. Ephesians 1:13–14 NIV.

26. Colossians 3:2–4 NIV.

27. 2 Corinthians 5:21 NIV.

28. Romans 8:1–2 NIV.

29. 1 Peter 2:11 NIV.

30. Romans 12:4–6 NIV.

31. 2 Corinthians 5:20 NIV.

32. Hebrews 4:16 NIV.

Chapter 20

1. Alice Miller, *The Drama of the Gifted Child* (New York: Basic Books, 1981), 3.

2. David and Teresa Ferguson, *The Pursuit of Intimacy* (Nashville: Thomas Nelson, 1993).

About the Author

Dr. Chris Thurman is a psychologist who maintains a private counseling practice in Austin, Texas. He earned a Ph.D. in counseling psychology from the University of Texas. Dr. Thurman is a best-selling author and a popular speaker who has conducted hundreds of seminars for churches and corporations around the country. He and his wife, Holly, have three children, Matthew, Ashley, and Kelly.

For more information concerning Dr. Thurman's seminars, please contact him at 800-881 8000.